THE MAQUILADORA READER:
CROSS-BORDER ORGANIZING SINCE NAFTA

Edited by Rachael Kamel and Anya Hoffman

American Friends Service Committee
1999

Cover photos: CFO activists in Piedras Negras, Coahuila,
April 1998. Photos by Terry Foss.

Design: John D. Gummere

The Maquiladora Reader is published by
Mexico-U.S. Border Program
American Friends Service Committee
1501 Cherry Street
Philadelphia, PA 19102

ISBN 0-910082-35-9

Acknowledgments for permission to reprint
previously published material appear on page 131.

Printed in the United States of America
by union labor at Smith Edwards Dunlap.

CONTENTS

FOREWORD

In the early 1990s, the debate over the North American Free Trade Agreement (NAFTA) prompted an unprecedented discussion of the global economy by vast numbers of people in the United States. By the same token, the movement against the adoption of NAFTA, although ultimately unsuccessful in preventing passage of the agreement, sparked a notable increase in communication and cooperation among labor unions, other workers' organizations, environmental groups, and community-based organizations in the three NAFTA countries: Mexico, Canada, and the United States.

A major strand of such cross-border activism has focused on the Mexico-U.S. border and, especially, the maquiladora industry, which is composed of the foreign (mainly U.S.-owned) assembly plants that have moved to the Mexican side of the border to take advantage of the low cost of Mexican labor, proximity to U.S. markets, and a series of tax breaks and incentives offered by both the U.S. and Mexican governments.

In recent years not only activists but also journalists, policy makers, researchers, students, faith communities, and many others have turned their eyes to the border. If "maquiladora" has not yet become a household word in the United States, the maquiladora industry and the particular kinds of challenges it poses have become far more widely known. In Mexico, meanwhile, the "maquilization" of that country's economy has provoked widespread concern about the human impact of the economic policies promoted in recent decades by local and international elites.

Since NAFTA went into effect in 1994, the maquila industry has continued to grow and maquiladora activism has continued to mature. Little information is available, however, to those who are not directly involved. The *Maquiladora Reader* seeks to fill that gap by offering an accessible compilation of articles on maquiladora issues that have been published in the post-NAFTA era.

The American Friends Service Committee's involvement in maquiladora activism stems from our long-term engagement with Mexico-U.S. border issues. Staff members working at the border in the late 1970s became aware of the effects of the expanding maquiladora industry on border communities, the border environment, and, particularly, living and working conditions for women workers. This led the Service Committee to begin supporting maquiladora workers in their efforts to protect their health and safety on the job and to exercise other rights guaranteed by Mexico's labor code, work that has been continuous since 1979.

For nearly two decades we have worked in close partnership with the Comité Fronterizo de Obreras (Border Committee of Women Workers), an autonomous Mexican grassroots organization that emerged from these initiatives. Our ongoing work on border issues is multifaceted, comprising efforts in support of maquiladora organizing, support for the rights and dignity of border crossers and all immigrants, and participation in national and international coalition efforts focused on the global economy. All of this work is based in our commitment to the Quaker belief in the infinite worth of every human life, as well as our commitment to countering the root causes of violence, including economic injustice.

At this writing, in 1998, the types of economic arrangements represented by NAFTA and the maquiladora industry are on the upswing. In the Western Hemisphere, governments are negotiating the Free Trade Area of the Americas, planned to include every country in the region (with the exception of Cuba). Other regional agreements, like the European Community or the Asia Pacific Agreement on Economic Cooperation, are growing in importance. In the international arena, the World Trade Organization is rewriting the legal framework for international economic relations, with relatively little scrutiny from the public and its elected representatives, in the United States or other nations. Likewise, if the proposed Multilateral Agreement on Investments comes to fruition, it is likely to have a similar effect.

While "free-trade" agreements may frame the issues in public perception, AFSC's experience at the border has led us to understand that the problems inherent in the maquiladora industry began long before NAFTA. They stem, not from any single policy decision, but from an entire approach to economic development. At the same time, NAFTA has sparked a notable intensification of many of the underlying trends in the maquiladora economy. This volume focuses on how activists, especially maquiladora workers themselves, have responded to this situation.

Like the maquiladoras, global economic integration is here to stay. We do not believe that it is viable, or even desirable, to simply reject these developments as if we could wish them away. What we can and must contest, however, are the terms under which such trends will progress. Who will have a seat at the table when decisions are made that affect living and working conditions for the world's peoples,

or the health and sustainability of our natural environment? Whose needs and interests will be enshrined in international treaties, and whose will be dismissed as irrelevant?

Some analysts of the global economy have posed the choice as one between the "upward harmonization" of wages and working conditions around the world, or the cut-throat "race to the bottom" in which we are now immersed. This framework suggests that "globalization" could potentially offer benefits, as well as threats, to the world's peoples, thereby challenging us to articulate and work toward a positive vision of international cooperation, rather than simply reacting from a defensive posture.

This formulation also allows us to appreciate that across national borders, as well as across boundaries of language, gender, class, race, or ethnic group, our futures are inextricably linked. When U.S. groups support maquiladora workers in their fight for a living wage and a healthy workplace, we are defending our own interests as well.

It is our hope that this volume will help to strengthen that understanding, by offering a window onto the world of the maquiladoras. For us, knowing and working with some of the maquiladora activists who speak their truth in these pages has deepened our resolve to challenge economic injustice wherever it exists. Entering into their world has served us as an unfailing source of admiration, indignation, hope, irony, outrage, and renewal.

— *Rachael Kamel*

ACKNOWLEDGMENTS

The Maquiladora Reader seeks to chronicle the growth of a social movement, and to fulfill that purpose we have drawn on the experiences, insights, and connections of many people.

This book grew out of an initiative originally conceived by Phoebe McKinney when she was director of AFSC's Maquiladora Project. Fernando García and Melissa Forbis contributed to the project in its early stages.

Since joining the AFSC in 1997 as director of the Mexico-U.S. Border Program, Ricardo Hernández has contributed greatly to the breadth and depth of the analysis reflected in these pages, offering thoughtful feedback on several successive versions of the manuscript.

Many members of the Comité Fronterizo de Obreras, AFSC's partner organization at the border, shared their perspectives with us, including Margarita del Angel, Guadalupe del Río, Teresa Hernández, Julia Quiñonez, and María Guadalupe Torres. Additional CFO members, more vulnerable to management reprisals, have offered their testimony using fictitious names. Other people who gave freely of their energy and expertise include Robin Alexander, Saralee Hamilton, Pharis Harvey, Rachel Hays, Jorge Hinojosa, Robert Huesca, Ed Krueger, Cesar Luna, Eric Meyers, Susan Mika, Marta Ojeda, David Schilling, and Gregoria Rodriguez.

The completed manuscript has benefited greatly from the suggestions of Frank Bonilla, Garrett Brown, Karen Cromley, Dick Erstad, Mary McCann Sánchez, Joyce Miller, Debbie Nathan, and Don Reeves. Bertha Mwantembe and Luis Perez offered administrative and editorial support.

Grateful acknowledgment is made for the assistance of all of those named here. The deepest recognition, of course, is due to the countless workers and activists whose courage and persistence have made possible the enormous growth of maquiladora activism, and who are too many to name.

ONE

THE MAQUILADORA INDUSTRY: AN OVERVIEW

We are the real experts on maquiladora issues, on the impact of transnational corporations on our lives. For the corporations, workers are simply one more input in the production process. That's why we encourage women workers to search for strategies and alternatives to solve their problems, stating always that their dignity and their rights are the most important things.

As I recently said in Flint, Michigan, to an audience of auto workers, "we are not here for people to say, 'look at these poor Mexican workers, their wages are so low.' Or, 'look at those poor U.S. workers, all their jobs are going to Mexico.' We are here to develop effective international strategies so we can overcome these problems."[1]

—*Julia Quiñonez*
Comité Fronterizo de Obreras

The maquiladoras—foreign-owned assembly plants clustered along the Mexico-U.S. border—are one manifestation of a worldwide trend in which industrial production is concentrated in areas of the world with an abundant supply of low-wage labor. Also known as "export-processing" plants, such factories operate in economic enclaves or "free-trade zones" with relatively little interrelationship with the economies of their host countries. Capital investment, upper management, and even supplies and components are brought in from outside, and products are likewise destined for foreign markets.

This type of arrangement corresponds to a model that has been increasingly promoted over the past twenty-five years, in which developing countries are encouraged (and, sometimes, pressured) to reorient their economies to emphasize production for export, rather than increasing their capacity to meet local needs, even in such basic areas as the production of foodstuffs, clothing, and the like. The

wisdom of such policies, and the negative costs of their human and environmental impact, are a major theme of contention for nongovernmental organizations and popular movements worldwide.

In Mexico, as around the world, the maquiladoras have preferentially hired women. Most maquiladora workers are migrants from Mexico's rural interior, where declining government support for small-scale agriculture has provoked widespread unemployment, the loss of communal land holdings, and drastic impoverishment. (Such policies, which have been aggressively promoted by the international financial community throughout the 1980s and 1990s, have been actively embraced by the Mexican government since 1988.)

Working in the Maquiladoras

While the maquiladoras mean new jobs for desperate people, they have also brought substandard (and, sometimes, inhuman) working and living conditions. Although Mexico has one of the strongest labor codes in the world, inside the maquiladoras enforcement of labor laws is lax. Workers new to industrial labor may be unaware of their rights and are thus easily abused. Illegal payroll deductions, harsh and arbitrary discipline, sexual harassment, obligatory double shifts, nighttime industrial work for persons under eighteen years of age, and preventing workers from going to clinics when ill or injured on the job are examples of frequent abuses, all of them illegal in Mexico.

Workers must also contend with below-subsistence wages. "Our biggest problem is the salary," says Aleja,* a

---

* Where only first names are given, names have been changed to protect workers from reprisals.

worker from General Motors who lives in Rio Bravo, in the Mexican state of Tamaulipas. "Look, a newspaper from the U.S. costs 50 cents. Here it costs 3 pesos, but we have to work nearly an hour for that."[2] Aleja makes about 350 pesos a week (about $45 in 1997) for 45 hours of work. Her husband, José, makes a comparable amount at the Invamex plant in the area. The family of six is surviving on a diet of eggs and potatoes. Meat, at 48 pesos (about $6.15) a kilo, is out of the question.

Management representatives defend workers' low wages by arguing that the cost of living is lower in Mexico. "Remember, it's a different country, different wages, [a] different approach," says Michael Hissam, a spokesman for the Delco Electronics division of General Motors.[3] Yet the cost of living in Mexican border towns is comparable to that in the United States. Further, maquiladora wages, which have traditionally been below-average for Mexican industry, lost 50 percent of their value in real terms following the peso crisis of December 1994. Most maquila workers are earning the equivalent of $25 to $50 a week* in an area where a pair of pants cost $15 to $20. According to a 1994 Market Basket Survey compiled by Dr. Ruth Rosenbaum, it took an average maquiladora worker nearly 2 + hours worth of wages to buy a gallon of milk—before the peso crash.[4]

The lax enforcement of health and safety standards in the maquiladora industry, which has made the border an attractive location for businesses looking to cut costs, has made it a dangerous place for workers and nearby communities. Inside the plants, worker safety is often overlooked in the interest of maximizing profits. Workers are exposed to a variety of hazardous substances that have been linked to cancer, reproductive problems, skin diseases, and other disorders. Warning labels, if available, are almost always in English.

A Strategy for Development?

The rapid surge in population in maquiladora towns has brought about a particularly lopsided form of urban development. The maquiladoras themselves operate in clean, modern industrial parks, often with state-of-the-art facilities. Countless thousands of maquiladora workers, meanwhile, live in cardboard shacks in shantytowns, or colonias, without plumbing, electricity, running water, or garbage collection. In some cases, colonia residents are also exposed to hazardous industrial wastes, even though Mexican law nominally requires that toxic wastes from the maquiladoras must be returned to the United States for disposal. The lack of sewage systems, severe air and water pollution, and a critical shortage of adequate housing all have profound effects on the workers' lives.

While outsiders may interpret such phenomena as evidence of Mexico's poverty or "underdevelopment," in fact they are a consequence of the tax incentives that underlie the maquiladora system. In the name of job creation, Mexico's government has exempted maquiladora firms from paying local taxes. Border towns are thus left without a tax base to accommodate the needs of their burgeoning populations. The existing infrastructure in border cities like Matamoros, Nuevo Laredo, or Reynosa is strained beyond capacity. The maquiladoras also contribute little or nothing to the cost of environmental protection and clean-up. In Ciudad Juárez, maquiladora firms have agreed pay a voluntary "contribution" to the municipality; a 1996 attempt by the city's mayor to make these contributions obligatory was unsuccessful.[§]

While supporters of the maquiladoras argue that the industry has transformed border towns from entertainment centers catering to visitors from the United States into booming industrial cities, critics counter that detailed analyses prove that the export sector drains and destabilizes the rest of Mexico's economy. According to the Red Mexicana de Acción Frente al Libre Comercio (RMALC—Mexican Free Trade Action Network), the maquiladora industry operates as an export enclave, with few purchases of raw materials or components from Mexican suppliers and little technological transfer.[5] Profits from maquiladora operations are typically repatriated to the United States or other countries where investors are based (such as South Korea). As a result, the maquiladoras do not promote true development of the Mexican economy.

Origins: The Border Industrialization Program

The maquiladoras first came to the Mexico-U.S. border region in 1965, when the Mexican government initiated the Border Industrialization Program (BIP) as a means of attracting foreign investment to the area. The BIP was introduced as a response to the termination of the Bracero Program, which had been created by the U.S. government

---

* According to 1998 estimates by the CFO.

§ As of 1998, this "contribution" was set at $10 per worker per year. Local activists report that many firms do not make these contributions, and that a portion of the funds that are raised are used for improvements to the industrial parks where the maquila plants are located.

during World War II to supply Mexican agricultural workers as contract laborers to meet labor shortages in the United States. The U.S. decision to end the Bracero Program in 1964 caused a vast increase in the number of unemployed workers who returned to border towns and cities. The BIP was intended to curb Mexican unemployment by shifting U.S. production operations to locations of low-cost labor in Mexico.

Under the BIP, Mexico has granted licenses to foreign companies, mostly U.S.-owned, for the duty-free importation of machinery, raw materials, parts, and components. After being assembled in plants in Mexico, the semi-final or final products are then re-exported, primarily to the U.S. market. Import duties levied by the United States are based solely on the "value added," that is, the actual cost of wages and related costs in Mexico, rather than the full value of the products.

Since its inception the maquiladora industry has confounded the predictions of its promoters in government and industry. Far from providing an alternative source of employment to displaced *braceros,* nearly all of whom were male, the industry has exhibited a marked preference for women workers—who can be hired more cheaply and would presumably offer a more pliable and docile labor force.

Likewise, the North American Free Trade Agreement (NAFTA), which went into effect in 1994, was touted as a way of counterbalancing the impact of the maquiladora industry. Under NAFTA, the tax breaks enjoyed by the maquiladora industry are no longer confined to the border area, but are available throughout Mexico. In response, the U.S. and Mexican governments expected the industry to leave the overstressed border area and expand into Mexico's interior. Instead of decreasing, however, the number of Mexicans employed in the maquiladoras has risen from 689,420 in October 1995 to more than a million by July 1998.[6] More than 85 percent of these workers continue to be employed at the border, stretching the area's weak infrastructure even further.[7]

Grappling with the Maquiladoras

The maquiladora industry, like the border as a whole, is a scene of dynamic, turbulent change. Workers seek to better their situation, in a thousand small and large ways: through individual and group shopfloor actions, in organized campaigns to assert their legal rights, through union organizing drives and attempts to make established unions

more responsive to their concerns, and, increasingly, through cross-border initiatives that engage the support of U.S. and Canadian unions, social movements, religious groups, corporate shareholders, journalists, and others.

As the 1990s draw to a close, Mexico as a whole is undergoing profound social and political changes, whose ultimate outcome is yet to emerge. The Zapatista insurrection, based among impoverished and marginalized Mayan Indians in the country's southernmost state of Chiapas, burst onto the world scene the same day that NAFTA went into effect, on January 1, 1994. In the national elections of 1997, for the first time in more than seven decades, Mexico's entrenched ruling party, the Partido de la Revolución Institucional (PRI—Institutional Revolutionary Party), lost its majority in the lower chamber of Mexico's legislature, and the mayoralty of Mexico City was won by the center-left Partido de Revolución Democrática (Democratic Revolutionary Party). That same year, the death of Fidel Velázquez, for nearly six decades the leader of the Confederación de Trabajadores Mexicanos (Federation of Mexican Workers), eased the way for a historic realignment of forces in the country's labor movement, further weakening the PRI's monopoly on political power.

All of these changes have both resulted from and contributed to a dramatic upswelling of popular mobilization by hundreds and thousands of "civil society" organizations—which has in turn come about as a deep-seated response to the wrenching impoverishment and economic dislocation caused by the full range of "neoliberal"* economic policies, of which NAFTA is only the most visible example. While these larger phenomena fall beyond the scope of this book, they form an integral part of the background against which maquiladora activism is traced.

This *Maquiladora Reader* explores the issues that have been raised, the strategies that have been crafted, and the networks that have been formed through more than two decades of maquiladora activism. Starting as a mere trickle in the late 1970s, such activist initiatives began to grow substantially in their scope and visibility in the 1980s, in response to the growing impact, in both Mexico and the

---

* The term "neoliberal" is widely used in Mexico and throughout Latin America to refer to an overall framework for economic policy that emphasizes privatization, production for export, reduced public investment in health, education, and social services, reduction or elimination of barriers to foreign investment, weakening of labor and environmental regulations, and fiscal and monetary policies that favor the needs of transnational capital.

United States, of corporate flight across the border.[8] The emergence of NAFTA in the early 1990s gave a further impetus to cross-border contacts, and as the decade has advanced both labor-oriented and environmental initiatives have proliferated.

This volume offers a portrait of the diversity and the dynamism of maquiladora activism in the years since NAFTA. Following this initial overview, subsequent chapters provide more detail on critical themes, including women's issues; environment and health; cross-border organizing; the efforts of the American Friends Service Committee and its grassroots partner organization, the Comité Fronterizo de Obreras (CFO—Border Committee of Women Workers); and the impact of NAFTA. Each of these chapters includes an introductory discussion, followed by readings culled from a variety of sources. Two final sections offer a directory of organizations on both sides of the border working on maquiladora issues and a bibliography of additional readings.

The maquiladora industry offers a vivid example of the costs of economic policies that privilege corporate profits above all other considerations, rather than bringing them into balance with the needs of workers, communities, and the environment. By the same token, maquiladora activism offers a model for a people-oriented response, based on an array of demands including a living wage, respect for basic labor rights, and enforcement of health-and-safety regulations and environmental codes. In the coming years, as governments and global economic institutions continue their push for the "maquilization" of the world, the example of maquiladora activists will only grow in importance.

Notes

1 The quoted comment in the second paragraph is from *Labor Notes,* Jan. 1999, p. 8.

2 Interview with Anya Hoffman, Rio Bravo, Tamaulipas, June 1997.

3 Jeanne Russell, "Maquila laborer talks issues with GM brass," *The Monitor,* McAllen, Texas, June 23, 1997, p.8.

4 Ruth Rosenbaum, "Market Basket Survey: A Comparison of the Buying Power of Maquiladora Workers in Mexico and UAW Assembly Workers in GM Plants in the U.S.," F. L. Putnam Securities and the Coalition for Justice in the Maquiladoras, San Antonio, Sept. 1994.

5 Red Mexicana de Acción Frente al Libre Comercio, *Espejismo y Realidad: El TLCAN Tres Años Después: Análisis y Propuestas Desde La Sociedad Civil* [Myth and Reality: NAFTA After Three Years; Analysis and Proposals from Civil Society], Mexico City, April 1997, p.30.

6 Global Trade Watch, "The Border Betrayed 1996," executive summary, Public Citizen, Washington, DC, 1996, p.1; 1998 statistics are from INEGI (see reading at end of this chapter).

7 Sarah Anderson et al., "NAFTA's First Two Years: The Myths and the Realities," March 26, 1996.

8 For an in-depth exploration of maquiladora activism in the 1980s, see AFSC's 1990 publication, *The Global Factory: Analysis and Action for a New Economic Era.*

READINGS

U.S. audiences have had little access to Mexican viewpoints on the maquiladoras. We reprint here two articles by Mexican journalist Arturo Cano, published as part of a series entitled "Border Stories" in the Mexican daily Reforma. *Cano offers a richly textured look at the social and cultural, as well as the economic, dimensions of the maquiladora phenomenon, a welcome contrast to the unfortunate tendency of many U.S. observers to paint one-dimensional portraits of the victims (and perpetrators) of economic injustice.*

In a third article, Rick Ufford-Chase, director of BorderLinks, an experiential education program based in Tucson, explores how the global economy comes to rest on Nogales, Sonora, and the bordering town of Nogales, Arizona. While his comments are directed to the Christian activist readership of The Other Side *magazine, where this piece was originally published, they ring true for anyone who believes that our economic institutions should reflect our most deeply held values.*

Finally, readers will note a great deal of variability in the statistics about the maquiladora industry and the Mexican economy that are cited in this collection. This is due in part to the fact that the original publication of these materials spans the years from 1992 to 1998; in part to differences in sources or techniques for data collection. As a partial corrective, the fourth reading in this chapter presents the latest available statistics from Mexico's Instituto Nacional de Estadística, Geografía e Informática (INEGI—National Institute of Statistics), the most authoritative source for statistical data on the maquiladora industry.

In the Maquila Kingdom

By Arturo Cano

As soon as the bell rings, they rush off in a clump, almost running. They have fifteen precious minutes for lunch: the second of their three breaks during the day. We are with thirty young women who work at Duro, the biggest maquiladora in Rio Bravo in the state of Tamaulipas. A thousand employees, nine hundred women. Every month they put out a million paper bags for stores all over the United States.

"Women have more patience for this kind of work," says Alejandro de la Rosa, the personnel manager, repeating an argument made over and over again.

Most of the workers are between eighteen and twenty-two years old. They do indeed have great patience, standing for hour after hour in a single large workroom. Ten hours, with a total of an hour's rest sprinkled throughout the day. For many their sole task is to glue the handles to the bags. Others make a fold. All day long.

Duro has seven other plants in the United States, but the others all make plastic bags. None of them has as many employees as the Mexican plant. The bags that require manual labor—"detail work"—are made here. It's a case of comparative advantage: the workers in Rio Bravo cost $3.50 a day, less than their U.S. counterparts earn in an hour.

And that's with Duro paying seven pesos over the minimum wage.

"In any event, we give more in benefits than the law requires. And in all the history of the plant, we have only had two serious accidents."

"Which were?"

"Amputations of fingers."

The maquiladoras are already more than thirty years old. Today, even though some have begun to move to other parts of the country, 85 percent are still in the border states, especially in cities that are close to U.S. highways.

For thirty years, the Maquila Kingdom has been growing, and the harvest of benedictions never comes to an end. "At a moment when salaries are rising in South Korea and Taiwan, Mexican workers are still a bargain, especially following the devaluation in which the Mexican peso lost almost half its value." (*The Wall Street Journal*, Sept. 1996.)

Originally published in *Reforma*, a Mexican daily, in the *Enfoque* (Focus) section, Dec. 1, 1996, pp. 11–14. Reprinted by permission. Translation by Rachael Kamel.

A bargain. Along the border, there are many protestations. "If it was only the low wages, they'd go to Haiti." The point is well taken.

The specialists talk about the competitivity and productivity of the Mexican worker. You bet.

But does anyone really believe that Matsushita, Mitsubishi, Daewoo, and Sony *weren't* thinking about the low wages when they decided to make no less than ten million televisions along the border in 1996?

Gustavo Elizondo, a spokesman for the state government of Chihuahua in Ciudad Juárez, gives an irrefutable response: "The maquiladora industry may not pay the best, but it does bring an important benefit. In the rest of the country, there are no jobs, and here there are. They may not be well paid, but you can't underestimate that."

• • •

After thirty years of maquiladoras, Mexican firms only provide 1.5 percent of the inputs that the industry requires. In Ciudad Juárez, the Maquiladora Association maintains that if Mexico succeeded in providing 50 percent of the inputs for maquiladora exports, then national exports would automatically increase by $20 to $25 billion. As things are, the figure doesn't even reach $1 billion.

That doesn't mean that Mexicans aren't making any money off the maquiladoras. "In Juárez, the businessmen have turned to real estate development. They speculate in land, build the factories, and provide legal and financial services, but they are not involved in production," says Victor Orozco, director of the Center for Regional Studies at the Autonomous University of Ciudad Juárez.

Predatory Industries

Nothing more could possibly fit in the Duro plant. The Christmas season is coming, and the demand for paper bags is at a peak. The factory is crammed with rolls of paper and plastic, with handles by the truckload, working to 100 percent of capacity.

Duro has been in Rio Bravo for seven years. Its managers count on labor stability, even though only 10 percent of the workforce has been there since the beginning.

The capital investment and the raw materials come from the United States. The bags will end up there, and the designs for them came from there. Duro's manager, of course, does not live in Rio Bravo, but in McAllen, Texas.

Something else goes back to the other side of the border: the left-over dyes. "The only thing we dispose of here is water in the drains, because of local environmental regulations and NAFTA," says the personnel manager.

("Economic and population growth, resulting from the influx of people drawn by the establishment of maquiladoras, are key to understanding environmental deterioration in the border region," according to a report by the General Accounting Office, an arm of the U.S. Congress.)

Of course, gluing handles to paper bags is not all there is to the maquiladoras. Nonetheless, Duro fits the description of "industries that prey on the labor force and never permit us to create our own healthy, workable industrial base," as outlined by Victor Orozco.

The Statue of Agapito

They haven't said yet if they'll put it in El Chamizal,* but the business owners of Ciudad Juárez are convinced that Agapito González deserves a statue. It's to his credit, they say, that the transnational maquila firms have looked to Juárez.

Agapito González is the leader in perpetuity of the Union of Industrial Workers and Laborers of Matamoros. With 50,000 members, it belongs to the Confederation of Mexican Workers (CTM). Agapito is the one who frightened away the investors with his demands and sent them running to Juárez. At least, that's what they say out there.

Arturo Zarate of Matamoros, a scholar and researcher at the Colegio de la Frontera Norte,§ furrows his brow. "Which are these maquiladoras that have left? The only shops that go to Juárez are fly-by-night operations that make toys and knicknacks. Here in Matamoros the average is 420 to 450 workers per plant. Tijuana is in second place, with 120."

Back east, in Tamaulipas,⁋ they'll tell you that, far from scaring off investors, the union should receive credit for keeping the big firms in town and attracting more all the time. "They appreciate the stability. Here turnover and absenteeism are lower—which is undoubtedly due to union discipline," rejoins Zarate.

Agapito Laughs Last

You can find him any morning in his office. In shirtsleeves and sandals, with his cane on his desk, Agapito González is watching TV, while a few steps away young

people who hope for work in the maquiladoras are waiting in line.

The doorkeeper brings in a child, holding his hand, and Agapito González—with gaps in his teeth and sunglasses that cover at least a third of his face—hands him a toffee stick. The leader as grandfather.

Agapito, who was born in the state of Nuevo Leon, laughs out loud. "A statue?"

"That's what they say in Juárez."

"How many workers did they ask us for today?" calls out Agapito.

From the other end of the office, a secretary answers: "A hundred and sixty-one."

"You see? They keep asking us for more."

Tuesdays and Thursdays for the men, Mondays and Fridays for the women. By the truckload. Every day Agapito sends the maquiladoras between 150 and 250 union workers. And that's without counting special requests.

Another assistant enters with a pile of papers and Agapito González scribbles his signature on one after another. "Letters of reference." The youths go right to the plants with their papers in their hands.

"So, Agapito, how's it going with the owners?"

"They're happy with us. There's a reason why Matamoros has the best salaries and benefits in the country. And Mr. Fidel Velázquez‡ has said so himself.

"What about in other places—how are things going for maquiladora workers?"

"Badly."

"Why so?"

"Because they've had bad leaders."

"Are you a good leader?"

"Not really. I guess I'm not so bad."

"What does it take to be a good leader?"

"You have to be serious about what you're doing, and you have to want to get something for the workers. Union leaders today don't have teeth and they don't have guts. Unions have pretty much stopped fighting."

Agapito nearly became history a few years back, when the Salinas Administration** fired five labor leaders from

---

* A Juárez neighborhood close to the Rio Grande.

§ Institute of the Northern Border.

⁋ The state in which Matamoros is located.

‡ Head of Mexico's official labor confederation, the CTM, from its origin until his death in 1997.

** Former Mexican president Carlos Salinas de Gortari was in office from 1988 to 1994.

Tamaulipas, starting with La Quina.* Agapito was the only one who got his job back, thanks to (who else?) Fidel Velázquez.

Traditional and Subordinate

Dr. Cirila Quintero of Colef§ is an undisputed expert on maquila labor issues. She runs down the list: in Matamoros, the maquiladoras pay the best salaries in the industry, they pay profit-sharing,¶ they have the lowest turnover, there are more than twenty firms that meet ISO 9000 quality standards, and the levels of technical skill are the highest in the country.

The obvious conclusion: the maquiladoras are not here just for the low salaries, and Agapito hasn't frightened anyone away.

"Whenever the companies have had problems, Agapito has found a way to be flexible," says Dr. Quintero, who categorizes maquila unions as either traditional or "subordinate."

Traditional unionism, with varying degrees of effectiveness, is present from Matamoros, where 100 percent of the workforce is unionized, out to Ciudad Acuña, "which may be one of the last bastions of the CTM. Overall, in that corridor there are an estimated 75,000 workers in CTM ranks."

"Subordinate" unions stretch from Ciudad Juárez to Tijuana. In the first of these cities, the rate of unionization is between 10 and 15 percent, while in the second it stands at about 30 percent. "We're talking about ghost unions, which in some cases may have negotiated entire contracts without the workers even knowing they exist. The union fees are paid directly by the companies."

With a smile, Dr. Cirila Quinteros says that the unions consider her to be pro-business and the businesses say she is pro-union. "I deal in facts. If there's one place where union contracts are not dead, it's in Matamoros."

• • •

The Coalition for Justice in the Maquiladoras sent out word over the Internet about 60 workers who were beaten last January after being fired from a maquiladora known as Favesa in Ciudad Juárez.

Municipal police beat up workers who were demanding their obligatory severance pay after they were fired for trying to form a union. Favesa belongs to the Lear Co. of Michigan, which manufactures seat coverings for Ford.

Nora Soto, a young woman from Durango, works in one of Favesa's three plants. She didn't see the conflict at all. She complains: "When they hire us, we have to sign a paper saying that overtime is obligatory."

Juana Medina of Zacatecas, who works in another maquiladora, sums up the situation: "There's always the threat hanging over us that we will be fired if we can't meet the quotas that the supervisors establish." Where Juana works there is a union; it's a member of the CROC‡ and the leaders are a mother and daughter.

A union outreach worker tells the story of other organizers who have failed. "They were starting from a false premise. They thought that when they came to the maquilas they would find a dark and gloomy place like a nineteenth-century factory. When they arrive they find superplants, with air-conditioning and good lighting."

A few months ago, a group from the Authentic Labor Front** asked for a recount in a subsidiary of General Electric in Juárez. They lost by a wide margin. The company had no trouble convincing a majority of the workers that unions are corrupt and their dues come out of your paycheck.

In the Maquila Kingdom, labor flexibility reigns.

• • •

Sign on a maquiladora: "Vacancies, first or second shift, for experienced operators."

More than a few maquiladora workers have been through five or more plants. Qualifications? What difference does it make, if your job is to place an electronic component or sew in a belt in a simple operation without machinery?

"Although it doesn't seem that way, the workforce is not inexhaustible. They used to ask for people between nineteen and twenty-seven years old. Now they've dropped the lower limit to sixteen and raised the upper one to thirty-five."

War and Stereotypes

Arturo Zarate runs through what he considers "the stereotype": "industry for the least skilled workers, for basic assembly, the crudest technology, inhuman working conditions, and corrupt unions."

---

* The former leader of the oil workers union and a member of the labor movement's old guard.

§ Colegio de la Frontera Norte (Institute of the Northern Border).

¶ Legally mandated under Mexican labor code, but frequently evaded through the accounting practices of foreign firms.

‡ A traditionally oriented labor confederation, the Confederación Regional de Obreros y Campesinos (Workers and Peasants Regional Federation).

** An independent labor confederation.

Like with the paper bags.

With the maquiladoras, as with everything else about the border region, Zarate is convinced that what dominates is a distorted image as seen from the capital. "Without overgeneralizing, I could cite counterexamples of companies where the rank-and-file workers are involved in decision making. Tamaulipas is first in the country in links between education and industry."

The maquilas: the salvation of the border cities, the magnet that attracts southerners by the thousands, that fills up the shantytowns all along the border, that overwhelms local governments, who are completely unable to provide water or sewers to the new arrivals.

The maquilas: the only job when there are no jobs.

The maquilas, or all the Mexicans on the other side. The value added of the maquiladora industry is equivalent to the $6 billion that is sent or brought by Mexicans who work in the United States. Nothing less.

The maquilas: *better than nothing.* "Ciudad Juárez is a refuge for desperate people. Three hundred people arrive each day, from Coahuila, Zacatecas, Durango, and even Mexico City. At least here they find a better alternative than in their places of origin." (Ramón Galindo, the mayor of Juárez.)

Mayor Galindo recognizes that the maquiladoras leave very little. It occurred to him to create a municipal tax, so that they might leave a little more. A few days ago our nation's Supreme Court of Justice issued an opinion that found the tax to be disproportionate, inequitable, and unconstitutional. The court found in favor of fifty-one firms that had disputed the tax, including Phillips, Border Television, RCA Components, Toshiba Electromex, Atlanta Scientific of Mexico, AC Nielsen Co. of Mexico, and Delmex.

Meanwhile, the shantytowns of Juárez are growing. Without water, without sewers, without municipal services.

"All of the state governments want to promote the maquiladora industry in order to solve unemployment, which has always been low here. Chihuahua sets the example. As an economic model, the maquilas don't have a future, because of all the urban problems they create, such as pollution or social problems."

"What's next?"

"In a few years," says Orozco, "the results will be cities that are played out and filthy."

Without the maquilas, though, there would be cities that wouldn't make it, like Ciudad Juárez or Acuña, according to Cirila Quintero. Other towns have commerce, tourism, bridges. Acuña and Juárez only have maquilas.

"It's unacceptable that after thirty years in Mexico all they have left are the salaries. But we also can't adopt the kind of position that you still hear in academic meetings: 'Let's get rid of those imperialistic transnationals!' Okay—then what do we do with a half a million people at the border who make their living from the maquiladoras?" asks Dr. Quintero.

The maquilas, as portrayed in propaganda from Tijuana: "The industrial district of Otay Mesa is home to the majority of maquiladoras, almost 600 . . . A plentiful and skilled labor force, with a high educational level, thanks to four local universities: all of these factors combine to offer a population that is prepared for the international economy."

The maquilas: the bidding war among border cities to attract investors. A war with battles along three thousand kilometers, from Tijuana to Matamoros. A war of prices and facilities—and endless comparisons. Here we have the biggest plant, over here the most modern one. Here the most ambitious plans for the future, here the most skilled workers. Ad infinitum.

The maquila war is fought with weapons like the claim of Ciudad Juárez that in 1995, in the depths of the economic crisis, 20,000 new jobs were created. Or that of Matamoros, where Delphi, a subsidiary of General Motors, "uses state-of-the-art technology and hired 800 Mexican engineers." What was that about unskilled labor?

"Why do they prefer Reynosa?"

"They've been offered five other locations. They stay here because of the quiet labor climate, which has endured since they began constructing their plant—even though we are not the cheapest. Some states, like Nuevo Leon, are offering cheaper deals on land and labor costs. In order to get the companies to come they tell them, 'there aren't any unions here, you can kick the workers' asses all you like'. But they still like us better," says Juan Salvador Portillo, a CTM leader from Reynosa.

In Juárez, they say there are forty companies on a waiting list to move in.

August 1995: 642,000 jobs. August 1996: 770,000. The maquilas: the sole economic activity that emerged unscathed from the December mistake.*

The Maquila Kingdom, full steam ahead.

_____

* The reference is to the devaluation of the peso in December 1994.

The Cardboard Door

Arturo Cano

Ciudad Acuña, Coahuila. The yellow school bus bears its history on its sides. Once, it carried children to the elementary schools of Belmont County. Later, Transportes Industriales Mercantiles used it for the comings and goings of Mexican maquiladora workers. As the years passed, it was no longer used for transport, but its useful life is far from over.

Three-year-old Lucía, with her musical voice and her perfectly formed sentences, knows this quite well, because she lives in the yellow bus, along with her parents and her three brothers and sisters.

"What's your favorite game, Lucía?"

She looks thoughtful but doesn't answer. She'd rather talk about other things as she stands next to a bucket of embers, the only type of heater she knows.

Next to Lucía, her two-year-old brother Pepe tries to speak while huge gobs of mucus drip from his nose. An undershirt is his only garment.

The children's mother, Isabel Vargas, has delicate features, long, straight hair, an old jacket over her dress. "Everything's a mess." She's embarrassed as she opens the door of her house-bus.

Isabel is twenty-five years old. She met her husband at a maquiladora where she worked for five years and where her brothers still work. Her husband came north from San Luis Potosí to cross the border. He didn't make it and he's still here. To provide for his family he drives a yellow bus, much like the one where his wife and four children sleep.

You could call the Vargases an average family for Ciudad Acuña, where, according to official figures, the population is just under 80,000, including 26,000 maquiladora workers.

An average family, taking advantage of the border's special opportunities for the impoverished. In the south, those without homes might be able to scrape together a few sheets of plastic and some old cardboard. The Vargases built their home (or rather, they dragged it) on top of a small hill, from where they can see the brilliant lights of the Friendship Industrial Park. They, of course, have no electricity.

Originally published in *Reforma,* a Mexican daily, in the Enfoque (Focus) section, Dec. 15, 1996, pp. 11–14. Reprinted by permission. Translation by Rachael Kamel.

The flat-nosed bus cost them 800 pesos, plus 200 for a tow truck to bring it to the Puerta de Alcalá, one of the newest neighborhoods in Acuña's Cardboard City.

Inside the bus, a six-month-old baby, Lucía's youngest brother, opens his eyes up wide. Clothes are strewn everywhere. Up front, where the steering wheel used to be, there's a propane-fired hot plate, with leftover beans and crackers sitting on a board.

The question hangs unanswered. *Lucía, what's your favorite game?*

• • •

The advantages of being broke at the border: a Texas supermarket chain, H.E.B., has opened an "International Food Bank" in Acuña, where they give away groceries to the hungry. Lately, though, they've restricted themselves to families that include disabled people.

Every Christmas, battalions of Christian youth arrive from Oklahoma. In their vans they bring sixty tons of used clothing and thirty of food, which they hand out in "Cardboard City."

The maquiladoras and the stores give away skids and cardboard boxes, useful for walls and roofs. All you have to buy are the nails. Those who can will buy plastic sheeting to drape their houses—or sheets of ridged plastic that repel the rain.

• • •

The series of squatter shantytowns, which in Acuña are known as Cardboard City, begins a few steps beyond the Model Industrial Park, property of the ex-governor, José "Devil Boy" de las Fuentes Rodríguez.

Cardboard City. It's not a metaphor. In the Puerta de Alcalá, almost all the houses are made of cardboard. There are also at least seven school buses, like the one Lucía and her family live in. In the neighborhoods that have been there longer, walls of cinder block and concrete roofs begin to appear, bit by bit.

Mayor Emilio de Hoyos Cerna, who will step down in a few days, is surprised to see that Cardboard City has grown since his last visit a few weeks ago. "We've put in a lot of services, but we're falling behind in our coverage, like with drainage, for example. It's enough to overwhelm anyone," he laments.

Zapopan's Grandchildren

One fine day, about six months ago, Zapopan Contreras and his family decided to make a fresh start. Manuel, Zapopan's son, closed his mechanic's shop in Monclova. A friend lent him a pickup, which they loaded up with their belongings, and the whole family climbed on for the trip to Acuña.

As soon as they arrived, they heard about some lots that were available in the Puerta de Alcalá, and they parked the pickup in the one that some day—if the legal hassles ever come to an end—will be theirs.

The early days were hard. "We were out here, exposed to the elements. It even rained on us," shudders Zapopan. By now the family has a one-room cardboard shack, where Zapopan, his son, his daughter-in-law, and the youngest child all sleep. The other four children—two of them orphans whose mother, Zapopan's daughter, died of cancer—sleep in the pickup and in a decrepit station wagon that Manuel is fixing up.

"Why did you come?"

"Because there's no work in Monclova. My husband kept having to sell his tools cheap so that we could get milk for the children." For Elba Guadalupe Martínez, Zapopan's daughter-in-law, it hurts to talk about it.

"And how's it going for you here?"

"We're getting by, at least as far as eating. The rest—well, we put down some money on these tubs and we're paying twenty pesos a week."

She refers to three galvanized tubs that the family fills by the bucket, carrying the water from the neighborhood's communal spigot so that they can bathe.

The Contreras family didn't come to Acuña for the maquilas. Manuel has already found work as a mechanic. He wants to save up some money for his family before venturing across the Rio Bravo.* Seven years ago he crossed illegally and he wants to try it again. The goal of so many: the maquilas as a trampoline to the American Dream.

• • •

The Puerta de Alcalá was founded by Angel Cruz Martínez, the local leader of the Workers' Party and brother to the mayor of the capital of Durango. He's lost many followers, because, according to his opponents, he was trying to charge for each of the settlement's 270 lots, even though he didn't have an agreement worked out with the owners of the land.

Today the settlement is called "Land and Hope," a name chosen by the leaders of a group known as the Independent Political Organization, former activists with the People's Torch in La Laguna. Just like the leader of the Workers' Party, they arrived in Acuña five years ago, and they already manage a small force of 500 neighbors. In the elections they threw in their lot with the successful candidate of the PRI,§ Francisco Saracho, the former coordinator of Pronasol,¶ a former legislator for the area, and, as if that weren't enough, the nephew of the governor, Rogelio Montemayor Seguy.

The PRI activists of Acuña are bursting with glee. In the November elections they won back the mayor's office after two terms during which it had been in the hands of the Democratic Union of Coahuila of Evaristo Pérez Arreola. Evaristo's party, as it's generally known, not only lost the election, it came in third behind the PAN.‡

A Little Tijuana

Among the satisfactions of Acuña one stands out: "There's no unemployment here." Quite a triumph for a city that historically, and for many people even today, is nothing but one big brothel, a town full of hookers and loose morals.

Literature teacher Manuel Cisneros arrived thirty-four years ago, when Acuña had only one high school and not a single maquiladora. "This city didn't *have* a red-light district. It *was* a red-light district," he states with precision.

"We were a two-bit town, nothing of relevance," expounds Fernando González Garza, PAN's unsuccessful mayoral candidate and the former leader of the Chamber of Commerce. In the 1950s, Acuña was a favorite spot for soldiers from the air force base in Del Rio, Texas.

Looking through his thick glasses over a huge double chin, still recuperating from an illness that cost him his kidneys, Evaristo Pérez Arreola, a former union leader at the university and advisor to Carlos Salinas de Gortari, puts some numbers to the legend. "During the Korean War, more

* The river that forms the Texas-Mexico border, known in the United States as the Rio Grande.

§ The Partido Revolucionario Institucional (Institutional Revolutionary Party), Mexico's ruling party since early in the century.

¶ The Programa Nacional de Solidaridad (National Solidarity Program), a patronage-ridden social program launched by former president Carlos Salinas de Gortari (1988–1994).

‡ The Partido de Accion Nacional (National Action Party), the conservative opposition party.

than 1,800 of Acuña's population of 6,000 were prostitutes, and that's just counting the ones that showed up for their weekly check-ups. It was a very degenerate town."

The area coordinator for the Colegio de la Frontera Norte, Rene Vidaurrazaga, sums it up in a few words: "Acuña is a little Tijuana."

Still legendary are its red-light district and the women from the maquilas who work as weekend prostitutes to make ends meet. Every week, tourists seeking sex and alcohol invade the city. Unlike Piedras Negras, where nearly all the visitors are Chicanos, here both Anglos and Blacks arrive in significant quantities. Acuña offers them its main drag, the Avenida Revolución, with its liquor stores, pharmacies, "curiosity" shops, restaurants, and bars. Farther down, the red-light district looks like a movie set.

Local authorities don't like to admit it, but everyone in Acuña knows that foreign tourists—gringos, to be precise—have the privilege of drinking in the street. Sometimes the local police get a little tough, but with a few dollars you can fix it.

One after another, the mayors of Acuña, regardless of their party, have tried to put an end to the town's legendary red-light district. Thirteen years ago, then-mayor Jesus María Ramón, the father of the maquila boom in Acuña, threw the brothels out of the city. Nonetheless, the old red-light district doesn't want to die. Right in the center of town, run-down buildings still stand that used to hold disreputable bars like the Shamrock (you can still see the sign) and the rooms of the hookers, inhabited today by poor families. The old red-light district is still a dangerous part of town, filled with fights and youths who spend hours sniffing steel wool or cotton balls impregnated with solvents discarded by the maquiladoras, which they pull out of the garbage.

Neither Jesus María Ramón nor his one-time archenemy, Pérez Arreola, could overcome the legend. "I pulled down some of the buildings in the old red-light district, because I wanted to lay that history to rest, but nearly all of the owners got a restraining order," laments this man who has served in public office representing at least three different parties.

The maquilas have given Acuña its revenge. Every day dozens of workers leave La Laguna and Monclova, which once had thriving economies, ending up in the maquilas of Ciudad Juárez, Nuevo Laredo, and, of course, the Little Tijuana of Coahuila.

Still, the stigma never dies. "For the governor, for

Saltillo, the north is Piedras Negras." Perhaps because of the stigma, the residents of Acuña, who are so proud of their city's growth, its monuments to "Mexican identity," and its unemployment rate of zero, never mention the movies that have been filmed here, such as those of Robert Rodríguez, which portray Acuña as a town of few laws and many hustlers.

José and the Parade

"We were on our way home, we were on our way home." The young man is crying, with his arms handcuffed behind him. The police aren't listening. They have another youth spread-eagled on the ground. None of the four police has another set of handcuffs. The squad car is slow to arrive—a scene that must be common, because in Acuña there are only four squad cars for 120,000 inhabitants (that's the number locals give for their population, 50 percent above the official figure).

The two youths were arrested because they were fighting with some others and didn't run away fast enough. José Reyes tries to get close but they warn him off with shouts. He says that they work, like he does, in Acuña's biggest maquiladora, Arneses y Accesorios de México.

Like many of the city's newer inhabitants, José puts on his best clothes every Friday: white pants, a bright green shirt, cowboy boots from Texas. Acuña's streets are almost deserted all week, but they fill up beginning Friday at 5:00, when hundreds of young men and women get off the old school buses from the maquiladoras with their week's pay in their pockets. From January to October, the maquiladoras pumped out 588,875,000 pesos in wages. The motor of Acuña.

Freshly bathed and with their IDs hanging from their necks, the young people fan out through the streets and head for the stores. Many of them come back out with their hands empty: they have only come to make another week's payment on merchandise they have put on layaway. Average wages in the maquilas, about 200 pesos a week, aren't enough for cash purchases.

Coahuila is the only border state where Zone C minimum wages apply—wages set for the cost of living in states like Oaxaca and Chiapas.* With the most recent hike in the minimum wage, the daily rate here went up from 19.05 to 22.50 pesos.

Even though most of the maquiladoras pay one-and-a-half or two times the minimum wage, the total salaries

---

* Mexico's poorest and most underdeveloped states, located in the extreme south of the country.

for the 1,000 middle and upper management personnel who live across the border in Del Rio, Texas, add up to the same amount as the wages of all 26,000 Mexican workers, according to Pérez Arreola.

Regardless, the young people who work in the maquilas always find ways to compensate for their ten-hour workdays and meager salaries. José, for example, looks on glumly as his handcuffed friends are taken away in a police van—and then walks into Magic, a nearby discotheque. He doesn't like it much because "too many kids come." Just the same, José drinks half his beer and then walks over to a young woman dressed in white, as if for a wedding. They start out dancing like everyone else, circling around the dance floor without touching. An hour later, nobody could pry them apart.

An Incredible Opportunity

In the cardboard shack of Griselda de la Torre there's a large picture of the Virgin of Guadalupe, right between the two beds. It's noon and her sixteen-year-old son is sleeping in one of them. He's the only one in the family who's working, because his father, who used to drive a tractor in La Laguna, has a bad leg.

Next door to Griselda three young men are hunkered down by a half-finished cardboard shack. They're nailing up strips of cardboard. They work nights in the maquilas; during the day, instead of sleeping they're building their shack, because right now they're doubled up with relatives in a single room. They came to Acuña from San Pedro de las Colonias. "We used to work in farming, but there's nothing left there now," explains Santiago Reyna, without pausing as he nails up his scraps of cardboard.

Santiago is seventeen. He was a campesino. Now he works in a factory that makes electrical cables for General Motors. Listening to him, the words of Trinidad Herrera, the local president of the Maquiladora Association, begin to make sense. "The companies offer an incredible opportunity. Half of the workers come here from outside Acuña, from La Laguna and the coal-mining region. There all they could be was campesinos. Now they have become garment workers, drivers, welders."

Santiago Reyna's job is to position a circuit board amid a tangle of cables. He's been doing it for a year and right now his major concern is to finish the shack he will share with his cousins. "The other side? No, our people used to get across easy, but now they have those big dogs."

A Good Labor Climate

Acuña's maquila boom began in 1980, and since then the industry has grown 10 percent each year. As of today there are fifty-two companies here, with sixty plants among them.

Some people in Acuña say that it all happened without anyone lifting a finger, that it's all due to geography. In other cities in Coahuila, they say in Acuña, they've invested heavily to promote themselves as maquila heaven, with scant results. "Here, on the other hand, even though you can hardly get ten people together for a cup of coffee, investors keep arriving," says Fernando González Garza.

A former candidate for the PAN, he knows what he's talking about. He owns three buildings that he rents out as maquiladora plants. He built them without having clients—a sign of the faith that those with money here have in the industry. They stood vacant for two years before he was able to rent them.

Acuña has no airport and the infrastructure is minimal. But the customs office is quick, precisely because there is little traffic. Above all, though, what Acuña sells is its "good labor climate" and its "work ethic," which in plain language mean only one thing: in Acuña there are no unions.

Not even Evaristo Pérez Arreola, who was one of the first to unionize the university in Mexico City, could break the tradition. "We've tried at least thirty times to start unions in the maquiladoras, and none of them have done well. Unionizing simply isn't allowed here. The authorities collude with the companies to make sure that no certification campaign will go anywhere."

Trinidad Herrera, the president of the Maquiladora Association, recalls only three attempts. "The workers rejected the idea of unionizing and for years there have been no grievances."

The workers may not want unions, but they also don't want to stay long at the companies. Herrera concedes that turnover is extraordinarily high. "Many leave as soon as their first month is up."

"Why do they go?"

"We don't know. It's not the pay. When we ask them, they say their girlfriends are at another plant, that they have to go to Torreón and they're not sure when they'll be back, that they just don't like soldering. In reality, we don't know why."

Fearing the Future

The maquiladora era has its paradoxes. More workers are always needed, but the city has no capacity to provide the most basic services to its new inhabitants. In just five years, from 1990 to 1995, the population of Acuña grew by 49 percent.

Rene Vidaurrazaga says that "this part of the border has always lagged far behind, and the infrastructure is the biggest tragedy." Only 15 percent of the city has paved roads. Across the border in Texas, Del Rio not only has paving, it has four sewage treatment plants, of which only three are in use. Meanwhile, Acuña can't even pave its streets.

"If more people come, the urban problems will become critical," acknowledges Trinidad Herrera.

"This town underwent a complete change in six years," says Alberto Aguirre, the head of the PRI in Acuña. "Things go on here now that never used to happen, and there's not a single person who hasn't been robbed."

Emilio de Hoyos, who became mayor with the support of Evaristo Pérez Arreola but later distanced himself, says that "compared to other towns in Coahuila, Acuña has one of the lowest crime rates, because everyone is working from 6:00 to 6:00." But even he says that "when the kids start getting older, the children of single mothers who work in the maquilas, the problems of drug addiction and delinquency are going to get much worse."

The Little Angel; Lucía's Game

Mayor Emilio de Hoyos built a monument on the international bridge: an eagle devouring a serpent, facing toward the other side of the border. The legend reads, "Mexico will endure throughout the centuries."

Acuña, the "gateway to Mexico," and its Cardboard City keep growing uncontrollably. "Here at least we eat," says Ramón Dávila, as he strains to push up a hill the car his son-in-law just bought for 800 pesos. Ramón worked for Altos Hornos de Mexico in Monclova for ten years. Today, he drives a bus for the maquilas. He came to Acuña a year ago, with his wife, Clara Berlanga, and their entire family.

He's already sinking roots: two days ago, he buried a grandson who was barely a month old. "My little girl's only sixteen, but she took very good care of him," says Clara. Nobody knows why the little angel died. They don't think it could be the cold, because even though they live in a cardboard shack, "we always kept him well covered."

January is coming: the coldest month in the "gateway to Mexico." In spite of everything, Isabel Vargas, Lucía's mother, is content. This winter, she smiles, will be easier than the last, when they didn't even have the hot plate. "We're keeping things kind of warm now." She jumps down from her bus and shows that they now have four chickens underneath.

There's a wail. "Lucía," Isabel scolds, "the baby is crying." Lucía, the little girl with the cardboard door, hikes her three-year-old body into the school bus to take care of her brother. Obviously it made no sense to ask her about her favorite game.

Glimpsing the Future
By Rick Ufford-Chase

Welcome to Ambos Nogales, two cities balancing precariously on the line between North America and Latin America.

If you're a Christian seeking to be true to the moral vision of Scripture, you need to know these cities. Whether you're a player in the emerging global economy or an out-of-work laborer discarded in your company's mad rush for ever bigger profits, you need to know about Ambos Nogales. For Ambos Nogales is the reality behind the world's corporate glitter. It's the scar tissue underlying today's Wall Street "miracles."

When you arrive in Ambos Nogales, you'll find a rusty steel wall dividing Nogales, Arizona, from Nogales, Sonora—now two cities, though historically one. You won't have trouble finding the wall, for it rises twelve feet high and snakes almost four miles through the canyons of downtown Ambos Nogales.

As it climbs the hills that surround Ambos Nogales and then trails off into the desert, the wall that divides this city becomes a five-strand, barbed wire fence. But almost 400 U.S. agents persistently patrol the Arizona boundary between the United States and Mexico. Their mission? To ensure that this division will effectively perpetuate realities crucial to the globalization of the world's economies.

The wall, of course, is no restrictor of corporate entities, who make their own rules. It matters only to the people—who are forever defined by which side of the barrier they're on.

Walk with me now, through the port of entry from the United States into Mexico. In less than a minute, you move from the heart of North America to the heart of Latin America. The water here on the south side is unsafe to drink, filled with parasites and amebas. You see that raw sewage flowing through the streets and into Nogales Wash? During the next heavy rain, it will head north.

Children here often clamber to wash the windshields of cars waiting to cross back into the United States. Other times, they simply hold out their hands for loose change. If you were to stay here long, you'd find homeless kids wandering in gangs through underground sewer tunnels,

often terrorizing local residents.

Look around you. Those homes made of packing crates, cardboard, scrap lumber, and corrugated tin are packed together so tightly on the canyon walls that you could easily reach from one to another.

Most city streets are narrow, rutted dirt paths winding up the sides of the hills. The early morning air hangs thick in the canyon. Car exhaust and wood smoke (from home heating) conspire before moving slowly up the canyon and across the border.

Talk to a few folks, and you'll discover that once you've crossed to this side of the wall, the minimum wage instantly plummets from $4.75 per hour in the United States to less than $3.50 per day here. Is it any wonder that "families" suddenly become larger? The more working cousins, parents, aunts, uncles, and friends you squeeze into your two-room house, the better chance you have of paying the bills.

Do you see those children roaming the streets? They've finished their half-day in this town's grossly overcrowded schools. By the time they're seven or eight years old, most children are unattended. Their parents are working ten to fifteen hours a day in foreign-owned factories called maquiladoras.

What do their parents do? They sew women's underwear. They package surgical prep kits. They assemble electronic computer boards or power supplies. They sort coupons. They machine high-speculation antennas for the defense industry. In short, their jobs are connected to almost every aspect of your life in the United States.

This is a city of desperation. Few people have the luxury to question their participation in the global economy. They may live anywhere from five feet to five miles from the United States. But, thanks to the rigid divisions enforced by that wall, they struggle to raise their families without such basic amenities as running water, sewage systems, electricity, or weather-protected homes.

Cross back now into Nogales, Arizona, and take a look around you. On the surface, the people north of the border may appear to be the winners in the global economic adventure. But in reality, they are no more secure than their Latin American brothers and sisters. The paved roads, clean sidewalks, shiny fast food restaurants, the K-Mart and the Wal-Mart—they belie the reality. For Nogales, Arizona, is

Reprinted with permission from *The Other Side* magazine, Jan.-Feb. 1997.

also a city at risk, a city whose destiny is interwoven with Nogales, Sonora, that city just across the wall.

Nogales, Arizona, is a city of 22,000 people—downhill and downwind from its sister city of 350,000 to the south. Nogales has a higher particulate pollution count than any other city in the state of Arizona, including Phoenix, a city 136 times its size.

Residents of Nogales have more cases of lupus per capita than in any other place in the world. There are city blocks on tributaries of Nogales Wash where as many as nineteen people have either a rare bone-marrow cancer or lupus. The health problems are incredible.

Unemployment is also high here. Since December 1994, when the Mexican peso fell to half its former value, this small Arizona city has lost more than 1,000 jobs. Do you see those boarded-up buildings in the commercial district near the border? Those were once family-owned businesses, stores that had operated in Ambos Nogales for generations. No one has the money now to keep them in business.

For years, families divided by the border saw it as a minor inconvenience. Now, as they go about their daily business, they're confronted by suspicious and unyielding border guards. People on both sides of the border are moving ever closer to economic disaster. So crime, especially robbery, has skyrocketed. For those assigned to defend the border—and for those drug runners and smugglers who defy it—violence is endemic.

Nine years ago, I moved to the Arizona-Sonora borderlands, where I helped found Border Links, a nonprofit organization using experiential education to help North Americans better understand the complexities of the border region.

Working for BorderLinks has enabled me to establish long-term relationships with people on both sides of the border—from factory managers, politicians, and immigration officials to refugees, church leaders, and community activists. Knowing their stories and experiences is like looking through a magnifying glass at the effects of neoliberal economic policy.

Most of us in the United States are aware that the economic patterns that shape our lives are changing. We understand in some vague, undefined way that free trade, multinational (or even supranational) corporations, and hemispheric economic trading blocs now define our economies on every level from the personal to the international. We're encouraged to believe that these new economic realities are inevitable, that they will work only for the common good, and that there is some kind of inherent natural law that governs our economic interactions with one another.

Here at the border we can see more clearly the values underlying that economic paradigm. Monoculture is valued over diversity. Concentration of wealth is treasured more than an equitable distribution of resources. Global competition among workers has won out over sustainable wages in local economies. Economic growth has triumphed over environmental protection. And unbridled business opportunities always win out over democratic institutions. These values are so much a part of our day-to-day lives that we rarely question their validity.

For example, one block south of the port of entry in Nogales, Sonora, old school buses regularly fill with shoppers lucky enough to have documents to cross legally into the United States. These buses, their sides emblazoned with advertisements, are headed for the Safeway, Wal-Mart, and K-Mart in Nogales, Arizona.

No one who has the ability to cross the border would think of shopping in Nogales, Sonora. They know that they can buy better-quality goods at a lower price on the U.S. side of the border. Mexican teenagers and families with young children crowd the McDonald's, Burger King, and Jack in the Box, all within three blocks of the border, day and night.

These are signs of what Quaker philosopher and local rancher Jim Corbett has called "monoculture," a term once used for the most destructive kind of agriculture but now suitably relevant to our entire economic system.

We hardly notice the irony when Mexicans living a subsistence lifestyle cross the border in order to buy cheap goods at Wal-Mart, goods which were made by Mexicans for less than a living wage in Mexico. We're not even surprised to learn that in South Tucson, a community that is primarily Mexican-American, a family-owned Mexican restaurant was recently torn down to make way for a Taco Bell.

All of us, all over the world, face a daily advertising barrage from multinational corporations, encouraging us to have the same needs, brand loyalties, and economic aspirations. Such a culture is the foundation of the global economy. Unless vast numbers of us agree to participate in the monoculture, many corporations will find the continued growth of markets and profits impossible.

Another fundamental value of the global economy is the perpetuation and expansion of the unequal distribution of wealth. In the world of free trade, borders are critical because they control the movement of people. Borders incarcerate communities of desperation whose citizens are willing to work for slave wages.

It is no coincidence that at the same time the United States, Mexico, and Canada signed the North American Free Trade Agreement (NAFTA), the U.S. government doubled the number of Border Patrol agents in the Tucson sector and built the steel wall that runs through the center of downtown Nogales.

The correlation between "free trade" and an increasingly militarized border reveals the folly of "trickle-down economics." Corporations and free-trade economists would have us believe that competition for labor will eventually elevate the wages and standard of living of workers everywhere. But for that to be true, workers must be able to move from place to place in search of better living conditions and a higher wage. And there must be an appropriately finite supply of labor.

Neither condition exists here on the border. Indeed, the U. S. Border Patrol, acting as an agent of the new economic order, has become more vigilant than ever in stopping the free movement of workers. To maintain Mexico's "advantage" in the global economy, we're told, Mexicans must remain in Mexico. And they must be desperate enough to work for below-poverty wages.

Profits for international investors are the driving force of the global economy. The standard wage in the maquiladora industry in Nogales, Sonora, is roughly twenty-five pesos for a ten-hour day. At the current rate of exchange, that's less than $3.50 per day.

One group that helps new maquiladora operations get started in northern Sonora advertises that the average U.S. corporation will save more than $25,000 per direct employee in its first year of operation in Mexico.

The cost to the workers, of course, is unimaginably high. Several years ago, I had a conversation with a Mexican man at a church potluck in the border city of Agua Prieta, Sonora. Manuel was in his mid-fifties and had retired due to medical problems the year before. He began work in 1967 at one of the first U.S. maquiladoras to open in Agua Prieta. At the time, it was possible to support his wife and two infant daughters on his salary, while his wife stayed home to care for their children. They lived what he considered a middle-class life, simple by U.S. standards, but one in which their basic needs were met.

By the early 1990s, he was disabled, with only a par-

tial income. His wife and two adult daughters were working in maquiladoras. Although he had built his own home, and it was already paid for, his family, with slightly more than three incomes, found it impossible to make ends meet.

Profits of foreign corporations operating in Mexico have increased dramatically. But the buying power of a minimum wage salary there hasn't even come close to keeping up with inflation. At the time I talked with him, Manuel and his family, despite the income from three jobs, were still dependent on weekly food baskets from their church.

The global economy depends on pitting workers against one another as a way of maximizing corporate profits. In the world of free trade, corporations move manufacturing facilities from country to country at the drop of a hat, constantly looking for the most favorable wage conditions.

For example, in December 1993, General Electric was operating two plants in Nogales, Sonora. One manufactured all of GE's extension cords for the United States. It was operated by a man I knew to be one of the most responsible maquiladora managers in Nogales. He was creative in offering low-cost benefits that he knew could make a difference in his employees' lives: showers, purified water, laundry, a savings plan, and a cafeteria.

In January 1994, General Electric closed the plant, citing the high cost of labor. The average employee in the plant cost GE $1.26 per hour, including all benefits and taxes. GE began subcontracting its work through a Taiwanese businessman operating in the Philippines, where labor cost just 27 cents per hour and could be hired seasonally.

The irony is inescapable. Mexican workers, accused by organized labor of stealing jobs in the United States, had now lost those same jobs to Filipino workers desperate enough to work for an even smaller pittance.

The same mentality afflicts the power brokers' thinking about environmental protections. They argue that environmental protections are a luxury that first requires a substantial period of economic growth. In other words, the more successful the economy, the more money there will be, later on, to clean up the mess industrialization has made. Yet, after thirty years of maquiladora operation in the city of Nogales, Sonora, the environmental cost of unregulated industrialization and its accompanying population explosion is staggering.

Frankly, if the experience of Ambos Nogales is any indication, vague promises to "someday" clean up the environmental messes that inevitably arise in the rush to a global economy mean nothing. The residents of Ambos

Nogales know that no matter what the political rhetoric may be, a commitment to resolve environmental problems will always take a back seat to economic opportunity.

Pause for a moment—and think about those nineteen people on a single block in Ambos Nogales who have contracted rare environment-related diseases. Can you begin to understand the trepidation of those who live on the border?

Fears grow even larger when you factor in the new buzzword of those who negotiate free-trade treaties: the "harmonization" of standards. The theory is that it is unfair for one country to impose more stringent requirements on imported goods than other countries.

What it means, in practice, is that regulations of diverse areas regarding worker safety, environmental protection, and consumer safety are brought into conformity. Too often, "harmonization" will mean lowering the higher standard, rather than raising the lower one. So hard-won battles for environmental and worker protection in one country or local community can—and will—be lost in an effort to advance corporate profits.

Managers in Nogales' blue-chip company maquiladoras claim their companies hold their Mexican plants to the same standards as their company's operations in the United States. Yet such responses miss the point. Shouldn't the residents of Nogales have some voice in determining the environmental laws and policies that are needed in their own community? What if, given the devastation that's already been experienced, an even more stringent standard is needed?

And who enforces company-adopted standards? Certainly not the Mexican government. At the time NAFTA was being negotiated, there were only two Mexican officials to enforce environmental and worker safety standards for all of the businesses and industry in the entire state of Sonora.

Multinational corporations have become supranational far beyond the purview of any government. The resulting free-for-all defies everything we've learned since the Industrial Revolution about the need to define acceptable standards within which we expect businesses to operate.

Not only are there no democratic governmental institutions anymore that might enact and enforce such standards, but our governments have now become beholden to those very corporations and directed by their desires.

The value system underlying the global economic enterprise is determined by supranational corporations which have no allegiances to local communities or even nation states. Policies supporting those values are implemented by institutions such as the World Bank and the International Monetary Fund and by the politicians and governments who are held for ransom by the economic power of those institutions.

The bottom line for the people of the sister cities of Ambos Nogales—and eventually for all of us—is that the shapers of the global economy have neither the interest nor the experience to make the moral and ethical determinations that are needed to sustain us and our communities in the new world order. Even worse, those very institutions perceive it to be contrary to their interests to even begin to think along those lines.

The void created by the supranational corporations' lack of commitment to a sustainable future presents a bold challenge to church activists and grassroots community organizers across the Americas.

Jim Corbett calls the process of confronting the global economy "hallowing our life support systems." And he suggests that the more we are able to reconnect with the basic necessities of life and where they come from, the more the practice of living will itself become holy.

Jesus said that no one can serve both God and money. In an economy that honors only the latter, in a corporate system willing to enslave neighbors, divide cities, and destroy creation for the sake of ever greater profits, Christian communities need to rediscover what it means to be the people of God.

As daunting as the task will be, it's also exciting. Nothing since the Industrial Revolution has provided such a clear and overwhelming challenge. Clearly, the time has come to rethink how we will choose to be in community with one another—not just locally but globally.

Years ago I memorized a poem, though I've long since forgotten its author. One line goes, "Thank God our time is now when wrong comes up to meet us everywhere, never to leave us till we take the longest stride of soul we ever took."

The wall that tears through Ambos Nogales may not fall soon. The divisions that breed human desperation—and corporate profits—will not be foiled first thing tomorrow. And hearts that worship capitalism rather than God may not be transformed as hastily as we would hope.

But surely the time has come for all of us to take that "stride of soul" that will set our feet in a new direction, discovering together the journey that Christ himself has set before us.

Statistical Profile of the Maquiladora Industry

Information compiled from statistical reports of Mexico's Instituto Nacional de Estadística, Geografía e Informática (INEGI – National Institute of Statistics). The data below are current as of September 1998 (published December 1998). Updated data are posted periodically on the INEGI website: http://dgcnesyp.inegi.gob.mx/BDINE/J15/J150001.htm.

Total number of maquiladoras: 3,051

Total employees: 1,035,957

Total number of women workers: 472,423 (56% of total production workers)

Production workers: 841,409 (81% of total personnel)

Technicians: 120,895 (12% of total personnel)

Administrative employees: 73,653 (7% of total personnel)

Note: disaggregated data of the number of women in each employment classification are not available.

Maquiladoras located along the border: 2,283 (75%)
    Baja California: 1,045
    Chihuahua: 381
    Tamaulipas: 346
    Coahuila: 263
    Sonora: 248

Total maquiladora employees in border region: 821,592 (79%)

Number of Mexican states with maquiladoras: 27

Mexican states without maquiladoras (as of February 1998): Nayarit, Colima, Chiapas, Tabasco, Campeche

Mexican city with the most maquiladoras: Tijuana, 681

City with largest maquiladora workforce: Ciudad Juárez, 210,650

New maquiladoras established since NAFTA went into effect in Jan. 1994 (as of Sept. 1998): 908

Average number of maquiladoras established per month since NAFTA went into effect: 16

Growth in maquiladora workforce since NAFTA went into effect: 489,369

Maquiladora Labor Force by Branch of Industry

Branch of Industry	Number of Maquiladoras	Percent	Number of Employees	Percent
Electrical and electronic accesories and materials	470	15.78	253,730	25.27
Garment assembly and other textile products	832	27.94	205,020	20.42
Construction, reconstruction and assembly of transportation equipment (including accessories)	209	7.02	186,838	18.61
Other manufacturing establishments	451	15.14	114,054	11.36
Assembly of machinery, equipment, and electrical and electronic articles	138	4.63	91,322	9.10
Assembly of furniture and related wood and metal products	342	11.48	47,799	4.76
Service establishments	170	5.71	40,778	4.06
Chemical products manufacture	127	4.26	19,754	1.97
Assembly of toys and sporting goods	61	2.05	13,978	1.39
Selection, preparation, packing and canning of food products	79	2.65	10,675	1.06
Assembly and repair of equipment, tools, and components (excluding electrical items)	42	1.41	10,616	1.06
Manufacture of shoes and leather products	57	1.91	9,354	.93
TOTALS	2,978	99.98%	1,003,918	99.99%

TWO

WOMEN IN THE MAQUILADORAS

When Teresa Hernández, a *promotora* (organizer) for the Comité Fronterizo de Obreras (CFO), moved to the border from Mexico City to work in a maquiladora, her children were eight and ten years old. Teresa, a single mother, was relieved that her son and daughter were old enough to eat breakfast alone and get to school by themselves while she worked the first shift, from 6:30 in the morning until 3:00 in the afternoon.

Teresa explains that income from the maquiladoras is rarely enough to support a family, especially with only one family member working. "There are a lot of single women living here," Teresa says, "but even in most marriages both partners have to work."

In the afternoons when her shift ended, Teresa cleaned and ironed for a wealthy family for an extra 50 pesos a week. After that she had to do all the housework in her own home: clean, cook dinner, make lunch for her children to take to school the next day, wash and iron their uniforms. "But," she says, "we lived well."[1]

Women constitute a large majority of the maquiladora workforce. On the Mexico-U.S. border, the proportion of women in the maquiladoras reached a high of at least 80 percent in the early 1980s.[2] In recent years, labor shortages and the entry of heavier industries have prompted many firms to hire increasing numbers of male workers. Women, however, are still in the majority, constituting up to 70 percent of the workforce in light assembly industries[3] and 57 percent overall.[4]

While life in the maquiladoras is a struggle for all workers, the greater social subjugation of women increases their vulnerability to economic exploitation. The lower status of the female labor force is reflected in the maquiladoras' low wages, long hours, and poor health conditions. Around the world, women have fewer options for paid employment than men, face the overt or tacit threat of violence both inside and outside of the home, and bear the lion's share of responsibility for caring for children, the elderly, and the sick. As several of the readings in this chapter document, maquiladora women are also subject to sexual violence and abuse. This is the social reality that underlies the stereotypical image of the "docile" woman worker.

I went looking for work every day. When one plant was hiring they told me to come every morning and they kept me there until 8:00 at night. Every day they gave us one five-minute test: vision, blood, ears, X-rays, pregnancy test. They asked me how many children I had, how many years I'd been married, what my husband did for a living, how much he earned. They asked what I'm like, whether I had a temper, did I complain much. I said I'm very calm. Every day for two weeks I paid a lot of money to take two buses to get there, wait most of the day with about sixty other people, and then go home. After two weeks they put a list up of the fifteen people they'd chosen, and I was on it. It takes a long time to get a job. They do that to see if you really want to work.[5]

— *Elsa, worker at an electronics plant in Reynosa, Tamaulipas*

A dearth of paid employment for men is one consequence of the maquiladora industry's preference for hiring women. Such trends have brought about a restructuring of social roles that reverberates through the entire community. Gregoria Rodriguez, an epidemiologist in the Texas border region, argues that rapid changes in traditional social structures, coupled with economic destitution, have led to increased rates of alcoholism and domestic violence.[6]

In other cases, women are left to care for their families alone, as single heads of households. With or without a partner, maquiladora women often lack a strong support network, as many are migrants from Mexico's interior who have left everything behind in order to earn a meager wage. Women's classic "double shift"—at the factory and at home—must be shouldered without the traditional support of an extended family. Cuts in government spending for health and social services only exacerbate the problem.

In the United States, women are also disproportionately affected by the flight of industry across the border. In El Paso, Texas, for example, garment factories owned by Levi Strauss have closed down and moved to Mexico in search of cheaper labor. Women, who make up 85 percent of the city's garment workers, have been forced to take jobs in the service industry, suffering a cut in pay and status.[7] According to researchers, the greatest number of NAFTA-related layoffs in the United States have occurred in the electronics and apparel industries, both of which employ a predominantly female labor force.[8]

Women in the maquiladoras are far from passive victims of circumstance, however. As women begin to organize in the workplace and in communities, many strengthen their self-confidence and build stronger ties of solidarity.

From individual acts of resistance on the shop floor to international campaigns, women stand at the center of maquiladora activism.

Notes

1 Interview with Anya Hoffman, Matamoros, Tamaulipas, June 1997.

2 Kathryn Kopinak, "Gender as a Vehicle for the Subordination of Women Maquiladora Workers in Mexico," *Latin American Perspectives* (Boulder), Issue 84, Vol. 22, No. 1, Winter 1995, p.31.

3 "No Guarantees: Sex Discrimination in Mexico's Maquiladora Sector," Human Rights Watch Women's Rights Project, Vol. 8, No. 6 (B), August 1996, p.12.

4 Data from Mexico's Instituto Nacional de Estadística, Geografía e Informática (see Statistical Profile of the Maquiladora Industry, page 18). A detailed statistical breakdown of the percentage of women in various industries or job classifications is not available.

5 Interview with Anya Hoffman, Rio Bravo, Tamaulipas, June 1997.

6 Interview with Anya Hoffman, Edinburg, Texas, June 1997.

7 Beatrice Johnston-Hernandez, "Women Fight Free Trade," *Third Force*, Volume 2, No. 2, May/June 1994, p. 36.

8 Sarah Anderson, et al. "No Laughter in NAFTA: Mexico and the United States Two Years After," a joint report by the Institute for Policy Studies, the Development Gap, and Equipo Pueblo, Washington, DC, IPS, December 1995.

READINGS

The first selection in this chapter, Women on the Border: Needs and Opportunities, summarizes how women bear the brunt of economic integration, arguing that the border is a prime test case for the project of economic restructuring that consumes both the U.S. and Mexican governments.

In "Death Comes to the Maquilas," El Paso-based writer Debbie Nathan untangles the story of a series of murders of maquiladora women in Ciudad Juárez, which began in 1995. Her account reveals how the threat (and the reality) of sexual violence are an inevitable accompaniment to the sexualization of factory life.

Sex discrimination and sexual harassment have been the focus of some highly significant cross-border initiatives. Reprinted here are the summary and recommendations from a 1996 study by Human Rights Watch–Americas, which documented extensive discrimination by maquiladora firms against pregnant workers, in violation of Mexican law. By illegally excluding pregnant women from hiring, corporations have sought to avoid paying for legally mandated maternity benefits. Following the release of this study, Human Rights Watch, the International Labor Rights Research and Education Fund, and Mexico's National Association of Democratic Lawyers filed a complaint under NAFTA's labor side accord. The National Administrative Office, which administers the side accord, found considerable merit in the complaint and called for interministerial consultations to review the issue. A follow-up report, issued in December 1998, documented continuing instances of discrimination and charged the Mexican government with failure to take any meaningful action to investigate the charges or correct the problem. Mexican women's groups, meanwhile, have launched a campaign against the practice of requiring pregnancy tests as a condition of employment, and held a national tribunal on the topic in October 1998.

A fight against sexual harassment at a Tijuana maquiladora, a subsidiary of the California firm National O-Ring, led to a landmark case in Los Angeles, when for the first time a U.S. court asserted jurisdiction over the activities of a U.S.-based firm in Mexico. In an excerpt from his 1995 article "May Day on the Border," labor writer David Bacon recounts the details of the National O-Ring case. This case was ultimately resolved in favor of the plaintiffs in January 1996, and the company was forced to pay $450,000 to the workers. However, although 118 women had initially joined the suit, most had dropped out by the time the case was finally resolved, accepting smaller settlements from the company.

A final selection, "For Mexican Women, Sexism Is a Daily Battle," is reprinted from the Providence (RI) Journal-Bulletin, *an example of the upsurge in journalistic interest in the maquiladoras prompted by the NAFTA debate. While we would dispute this article's implication that sexism is no longer a problem for U.S. workers, we have included it for its vivid portrait of the concerns of women in the maquiladoras.*

Women on the Border: Needs and Opportunities

The U.S.-Mexico border—the physical juncture of North and South—is a region where the social dynamics of economic integration are held in sharp relief. As such, the border provides a prime opportunity to examine the benefits and problems associated with the project of economic restructuring that consumes both the U.S. and Mexican governments. Examining the status and needs of women on the border is equally illuminating, for women on the border, like women in other parts of the developing world, bear the brunt of the structural inequities that are becoming increasingly apparent in the predominant neoliberal, export-oriented development model.

The complex "reality" of the border defies a one-shot characterization of women in the region. Enormous differences exist in the experiences of women on the U.S. versus the Mexican side, of course, and factors such as age, class, ethnicity, and migrant status interact with dominant cultural patterns on both sides of the border to produce a kaleidoscope of women's lives. But women on both sides of the border share certain experiences and realities that cut across lines of race, ethnicity, and class.

Many of the problems entailed by economic integration affect men and women indiscriminately. In Mexico, for example, population growth fueled by the promise of maquiladora jobs has far outpaced the construction of public infrastructure, resulting in severe environmental and public health concerns. In the United States, industries that have shut down and relocated to Mexico have laid off both male and female workers.

Yet women bear the brunt of the high levels of poverty that plague both sides of the border. Researchers have calculated that over 30 percent of the U.S. border population and over 60 percent of the population in Mexican border municipalities have incomes below the poverty line; that is, incapable of supplying the basic needs of a family of four. Women must perform the daily miracle of providing for the family on wages that cannot possibly meet basic needs. In Mexico, this onerous task was made all the more difficult by the devaluation of the peso in 1994, which robbed Mexican workers of over half their pre-crisis purchasing power.

On both sides of the border, women are more severely affected by cutbacks in social spending associated with economic restructuring. In Mexico, austerity measures threaten vacation pay, daycare, and family leave programs. Ongoing reductions in government food subsidies have also had significant impacts on women. In the United States, recent cuts in the welfare program will add countless new members to the ranks of women living in poverty. Both countries have reduced spending levels for education and public health.

For many, poverty on the border is most dramatically illustrated by the proliferation of makeshift housing in unplanned communities that lack basic amenities such as paved roads, electricity, public water, or sanitation services. On both sides of the border, women feel more acutely the effects of the lack of basic services in the border's poorest colonias, which presents them with obstacles that are prosaic but nevertheless momentous—keeping the house clean when neighborhood streets are a muddy soup, cooking a meal without running water, tending to a sick child when the cost of medicine is prohibitive. In addition, women living in colonias in Texas and New Mexico, many of whom are recent immigrants, lack the community and kinship networks that offered a small buffer to such dismal poverty in Mexico.

In Mexico, one result of these trends is the rising number of women who must work outside the home. In addition, increasing numbers of Mexican women are heads of households or primary breadwinners for their families. The logistics of feeding a family on meager wages has traditionally fallen to women; now women must increasingly earn the meager wages in the first place. In the United States, such changes in household structure are less recent and more pronounced. But on both sides of the border, these changes imply significant restructuring of both household and societal power relations.

Women who enter the job market have fewer options than men, constrained by a general lack of education and marketable skills, as well as societal definitions regarding the type of employment appropriate for women. Frequently, their only recourse is participation in the informal economy. Women are the majority of participants in the informal border economy, engaged in a variety of activities, from selling tacos to washing other peoples' clothes. In addition,

Originally published in *borderlines*, Vol. 5, No. 4, April 1997. Reprinted by permission of the Interhemispheric Resource Center, PO Box 2178, Silver City, NM 88062.

piecework in the home is a growing trend, as firms ever seek to reduce costs and avoid troublesome unions. Women in the informal sphere are disadvantaged by a general lack of access to capital and decision making about the allocation of resources. As a result, they are often unable to obtain loans or other financing that would enable them to expand their businesses and better provide for their families.

In Mexican border states, one of the main opportunities for employment is offered by maquiladora factories. . . . Although declining since its peak at 80 percent in the 1980, female participation in the maquila work force still logs in at about 60 percent. . . .

Women face specific gender-based forms of exploitation throughout the maquiladora industry, including widespread pregnancy-based discrimination and sexual harassment. It is no accident that the majority of the maquiladora work force is female. Managers at the plants habitually justify such bias with the claim that women's patience and nimble fingers make them more suited for the long hours and repetitive motions entailed by assembly-line work. But actually women workers are preferred because it suits the industry's economic interests. Hiring predominantly young, politically inexperienced women allows management to keep wages low, dominate employer/employee relations, and impose abominable working conditions. Women workers have little access to job mobility in the maquila industry: the better-paid, skilled positions, such as supervisors or managers, are almost entirely reserved for men.

Many researchers have argued that women's participation in the maquiladora industry has brought empowerment, as women gain skills, independence, and access to wages. It is probably true that maquiladora work serves to heighten women's consciousness as workers, and provides them with a degree of economic autonomy vis-à-vis male members of the household. But in order for the maquiladora program to contribute to Mexico's long-term development, and for the benefits to women to be more than merely attitudinal changes, women workers of all ages must have access to specific policies that enable them to translate their maquila work experience into opportunities for other employment and an improved standard of living, either through educational programs or access to training on the job. And perhaps most fundamentally, both men and women workers need democratic and independent union structures capable of challenging multinational impunity and strengthening the position of the Mexican working class.

In the United States, the majority of women work in the service sector. The boom in trade since NAFTA has created pockets of economic prosperity along the U.S. border, but many of the jobs generated for women tend to be nonunion, low skilled, minimum-wage, service sector positions largely incapable of lifting workers out of poverty. These are the jobs that spring up to fill the void left by factories that have shut down and moved across the border or even further south. El Paso, for example, has seen over two dozen manufacturing plants relocate abroad in search of cheaper labor. It is also the sixth most destitute city in the United States: 15 percent of its working population earns less than the minimum wage, and unemployment for the city is twice the national average. Along the length of the U.S. border, Hispanic and immigrant women disproportionately fill the ranks of the working poor.

Immigrant women on the U.S. border find work as domestic servants in the larger urban centers, or as agricultural workers in the border's rural counties. Women's immigrant status and class standing as workers on the lowest rung of the occupational ladder mean they are especially vulnerable to exploitation. Undocumented employment offers little enforcement of minimum wage or benefits laws, no contract between employer and employee, and almost no protection against being fired at will.

The number of immigrant women coming to the United States from Mexico is rising. According to figures from Mexico's National Human Rights Commission, the percentage of female migrants to the United States has increased from less than 8 percent in 1969 to almost 30 percent in 1990. Women often migrate for familial reasons, as part of a household unit that makes the collective move to another country. But mounting evidence suggests that economic necessity spurs women's migration to the United States at least as frequently as familial relations. As women in Mexico assume more responsibility for family income, the wage disparities between the United States and Mexico become a particularly strong incentive for immigration northward.

Human rights advocates on both sides of the border fear that as the number of women migrants increases, they are being subjected to a simultaneous increase in sexual violence and abuse, both by U.S. Border Patrol Agents and by the "*coyotes*" who ferry immigrants across the border for a fee. Violence against women is rampant on both sides of the border, and its targets are not limited to illegal immigrants. Many healthcare workers mention violence as one of the primary health hazards faced by women on the U.S.-Mexico border. Most often, the abuser is the woman's husband or partner. Ester Chávez, a women's rights advocate in Ciudad Juárez, says that while lack of education is partly to blame, the border's battered women must be placed within an economic context. "Men are frustrated and take it out against both women and children," she says. And increasingly, border women are falling prey to a trend of sexual violence. Chávez notes that Ciudad Juárez has the highest number of rapes and molestation in all of Mexico. The apparent serial killings in Juárez—nineteen young female victims raped and murdered in the last year-and-a-half— are only the most shockingly newsworthy example of this trend.

Rising violence against women is likely fueled by a general sense of insecurity about economic and social changes entailed by integration and industrialization. Women's increased participation in the work force and their heightened role in the economic decision making of the family have begun to chip away at male authority. In part, the rising violence against border women is an unsurprising, though deplorable, backlash against these changes.

But the dynamics of change prevalent in border life also point to a brighter future for the border's women. The new and evolving circumstances of border life present vast opportunities in terms of organizing women. Indeed, women are at the forefront of much of the organizing and resistance that is occurring in the border region. In the maquiladoras, women are engaged in organizing on the local level, running independent slates of candidate within the conventional union system or setting up committees to function as alternatives to company unions. Women are challenging sexual discrimination and harassment as well:

workers at Tijuana's EMOSA plant successfully sued their supervisors for damages in a U.S. court, and workers at a Korean-owned plant near Mexicali have formed a committee in response to sexual abuse suffered there.

Much of the organizing done by women moves beyond the boundaries of old models, particularly when it comes to union campaigns. Women's organizing efforts seek to erase artificial lines between workplace, community, and home by drawing upon the connections and interrelationships among the different facets of their lives. Organizations like the Comité Fronterizo de Obreras go out into the community in order to educate residents about labor rights, rather than merely focusing efforts on a particular factory. Others, like La Mujer Obrera in El Paso, operate out of community centers that offer a variety of classes and services targeted to the needs of border women.

It is precisely such an integrated approach to the needs and capabilities of border women that offers the best opportunity for improving living and working conditions in the region. Women on both sides of the border have urgent and tangible needs. Some are as easily curable as providing plastic gloves or better ventilation systems in the workplace. Others require more effort, but are nevertheless feasible, such as adequate prenatal care or access to clean drinking water. But these tangible needs should not be disembodied from the larger problems facing border women. Women's lack of employment alternatives, access to capital, and gender-based discrimination and violence require more far-reaching solutions. Above all, courage is needed to challenge the dominant development model and the prevailing economic rationale currently driving the integration process.

Death Comes to the Maquilas: A Border Story

By Debbie Nathan

On a scorching day in August 1995 in Ciudad Juárez, Mexico, a trash picker combing an illegal dump site discovered the half-naked corpse of a young woman. Police eventually identified her as Elizabeth Castro, a seventeen-year-old from a poor neighborhood who had last been seen alive downtown a few days earlier. Since then in the same desert area—just a few miles south of El Paso, Texas—eleven more female bodies have been found. Most were adolescents as young as fourteen. All were slender and dark-skinned, with shoulder-length hair. Many bodies were too decomposed to determine the cause of death, but the better-preserved victims were raped and strangled or stabbed. Most were partly unclothed, with their underpants torn. Some had their wrists bound; on some, a breast was mutilated or severed. Of the victims police have identified, all came from impoverished families. Last spring, seven more bodies turned up in another desolate part of town. Again, they were half-naked, bound, and mutilated. They had slim figures and longish hair, and the identifiable ones were poor.

These nineteen victims constitute the biggest mass sex murder case in Mexican history, and the nation is horrified. In Juárez, everyone has responded—from a conservative mayor embarrassed by the violence, to women's activists, who have played it up to bolster campaigns against more common forms of sexual assault. Several suspects have been arrested, yet in the public mind the murders remain a mystery. Partly this is due to police corruption and ineptitude. But more deeply, the continuing whodunit reflects a lack of understanding of how sexuality and violence intertwined for the victims, whose lives and deaths centered around their work on the global assembly line.

Many of the dead young women had jobs in maquiladoras—or maquilas, as they're popularly known—transnational assembly plants that have blanketed Mexico's northern border since the mid-sixties, displacing jobs from the United States and recycling them for wages that currently equal about $23 a week in take-home pay. Some 170,000 Juárez residents have jobs in the plants. Half are female, and most are so young (as young as fourteen, even though Mexican law says they must be sixteen) that inside the factories and outside, they are still called *muchachas*—girls.

Six days a week, thousands of them leave their shantytown neighborhoods, cram into aging buses, transfer downtown and eventually reach vast industrial parks. There they put in forty-eight-hour weeks soldering electronics boards, plugging wires into car dashboards, binding surgical gowns, and sorting millions of cosmetics discount coupons mailed by North Americans to PO boxes in El Paso. The work they do is highly repetitive and requires little training. Their labor is easily replaceable, and turnover is astronomical, often 100 percent a year or more.

These are the girls of what author Jeremy Seabrook calls the "Cities of the South"—those sprawling new enclaves of Third World capitalist glitz, surrounded by slums full of workers who feed the local neon and the consumer appetites of the North. Navigating this territory, factory girls are subject to unprecedented sexual harassment and violence, of which serial killing is only the most horrific extreme. It has always been risky for women to move through cites on their own, and in Juárez everyone acknowledges the connection between work and danger. But few talk about work and pleasure; few recognize that when maquila girls' shifts end, they are loosed to sample freedoms their mothers never imagined.

Miles from their neighborhoods and with paychecks in hand, they have access to urban diversions that their brothers always had but that "proper" girls used to be denied: public nightlife, friendship based on affinity rather than kin and, most momentously, sex. According to University of Chicago sociologist Leslie Salzinger, who has worked on Juárez assembly lines, even girls who still live at home with their parents enjoy these pleasures.

Indeed, Salzinger says, many girls have told her that they take maquila jobs not for survival but for independence: to buy clothes with their own money and to get out of their houses and socialize. (Affluent kids do this at school, but for the working class, education is a luxury. Mexico guarantees public schooling only to sixth grade.)

So poor teens go to work. But unlike their older North American sisters, who dress for the assembly line in no-nonsense T-shirts and sneakers, most maquila girls don

Reprinted with permission from *The Nation* magazine, Jan. 13/20, 1997.

miniskirts, heels, and gobs of lipstick and eye shadow. Their flashiness is hardly incidental to their jobs. Instead, it is a fundamental feature of those maquilas that make a priority of hiring females: the reinforcement and updating of a rigid version of "womanhood."

The process begins even when a girl is still looking for a job. *Se Solicita Mano de Obra Feminina*—Female Labor Wanted—blare the newspaper want ads. Managers say that females have more nimble fingers, deal better with boredom, and are "more docile"—i.e., less inclined to engage in disruptive behavior, including union organizing. When maquilas first came to the border, men were virtually excluded as line workers. Labor shortages have since led to their hiring, but in many plants women still predominate, particularly in electronics assembly.

While gentle hands and natures are a plus for transnational exploitation, fecundity is a minus. Typically, maquilas will hire women only after they've taken a pregnancy test (this is implicitly illegal, according to Mexican labor law) that comes out negative. In many plants, management inspects workers' sanitary napkins for monthly menstrual flow. Meanwhile, in-plant health services are sparse except for generous provision of birth-control pills.

There are also discriminatory job classifications. At an electronics plant Salzinger worked in, stuffing computer boards is a task exclusively assigned to women; cabinet assembly and screen installation are reserved for men because the company deems this "heavy" work. Meanwhile, almost all technicians, supervisors, and managers—who make the most money—are men.

Identification numbers distinguish men from women. So does work clothing, with women assigned light blue smocks and men navy. Women are monitored more rigorously than men, by Mexican supervisors who pace the assembly lines, staring, flirting, and asking for dates. The foreign manager also walks the lines and chats up his favorites. Invariably they are the youngest, prettiest girls, and under their smocks, they are usually dressed to the nines. These girls are groomed for annual industry-wide "Señorita Maquiladora" beauty contests, complete with evening gown and swimsuit competitions.

This sexualization of factory life, as Salzinger calls it, creates a dense web of intrigue. Dating, boyfriends, clothing, and gossip about whom the manager has the hots for are constant sources of conversation and palpable tension. Indeed, sexualization allies workers with management and alienates them from one another. It also makes horribly

tedious, draining work bearable, as the maquila becomes a fantasy world.

Not surprisingly, Eros overflows the plants, especially on weekends after work. Instead of going straight home then, many employees stop at a strip of downtown bars with names like Alive, La Tuna, and Noa Noa. Several clubs advertise free admission for girls, as well as "Most Daring Bra" and "Wet String Bikini" contests with prizes of $30 to $45— more than a week's pay on the assembly line. Others feature Chippendale-style male striptease dancers. All provide huge sound systems, and dance floors are packed with couples doing everything from disco slamming to *la quebradita,* which mixes the two-step with pelvis grinding, techno-tango gyrations.

Prostitutes do business in some bars, and in more casual fashion, so do many maquila girls. This is hardly novel for industrial workers in Dickensian circumstances. A century ago, New York City's factory girls were roaming dance halls and amusement parks, picking up unknown young men and trading sexual favors for romance and the "treats"—like clothing and entertainment—they couldn't afford.

In Juárez, police investigating the first serial murder wave determined that several victims had frequented the downtown bars. A break in the case came when a teenager revealed that she had met a man at one and gone home with him, where he tried to rape her and told her she would end up like the women in the dump. He was arrested, and after his picture appeared in the news, witnesses told police they'd seen him with some of the girls later found in the desert.

The suspect, jailed since October 1995, is Sharif Abdel Latif Sharif. A 50-year-old Egyptian, he has lived most of the past two decades in the United States. "Give me a f-ing break!" Sharif snorts in English, to the delight of Juárez reporters. He indignantly denies any connection to the corpses in the dump, but Sharif also says he has come to know "all the prostitutes downtown" since he moved to Juárez two years ago. Before that, he racked up an extensive record for violent sexual assault in the United States, including six years in a Florida prison for savagely beating and raping a woman. Following another charge in 1993, Sharif fled Midland, Texas. He had been working there as a chemist, and he beat his rap by helping his employer set up operations across the border. He relocated to Juárez and settled in a posh neighborhood.

With his athletic build, olive skin, and dapper mustache, Sharif looks like a Spanish-language soap opera star—the kind who plays the rich, handsome father. Police say Sharif befriended his victims in the downtown bars, then cruised their workplaces or bus stops, offering them rides in his shiny white Grand Marquis. Maquila workers tell me it's common to accept such propositions, even from strangers, to save car fare and the dreary bus trip home. And for girls whose families and friends can barely afford seventies junkers, tooling around in a late-model vehicle is a thrill, especially with an attractive man.

Witnesses also saw some victims chatting or taking rides from young Mexican men dressed in cowboy hats and boots; this led investigators to suspect that Sharif had accomplices. It took a long time to figure all this out, though, because the victims' parents had no idea their daughters frequented bars, and their friends were loath to admit it. In Mexico, the thinking goes, good girls don't go to bars or watch male strippers or display their bras for money. And they would never think of leading *la doble vida*—the double life of assembly work by day and casual prostitution by night.

Parents who harbor these beliefs are clinging to memories of their youth, when poor but decent Mexican daughters were still cloistered until marriage. Understandably, they are comforted by industry's characterization of the maquila as a chaste, surrogate "home" for their daughters. But U.S. organizers seem equally naive. A few summers ago, when I helped with a solidarity tour for North American union women who'd lost their jobs to transnational flight, one guest expressed dismay at the girls' makeup and high heels: "They sure don't look like they're working," she huffed. "They don't even look poor."

Disapproving of girls' involvement with night life and sex constitutes "hypocritical moralizing," says Esther Chávez. An accountant in her fifties, she is spokeswoman for Juárez's Coalition of Nongovernmental Women's Organizations, which does groundbreaking work to combat sexual and domestic violence. Like Chávez, some coalition leaders are affluent. Some are former maquila workers who were blacklisted for trying to unionize, but who continue their organizing efforts from outside the plants. Others are human rights advocates who've spent years protesting police brutality and torture.

Chávez and other activists understand casual prostitution as a response to poverty, and they see the serial killings as the spectacular tip of an iceberg of sexual assault against border women. In October alone, there were thirty-two reported cases of rape and molestation. According to Chávez, Juárez logs the highest rate of these crimes

in Mexico, and authorities think they are a mere twentieth of the total. Only a fifth go to prosecution. Most victims are eighteen or younger.

Many coalition activists attribute the high sexual assault statistics to gender inequality, and some mention the maquila industry's complicity in fostering it. However, coalition organizers focus far more narrowly. Even before the first of the mass murders surfaced two years ago, Juárez feminists were petitioning the city and state administrations for kiosks where the public could report sexual assaults and for a woman-staffed sex-crimes unit in the district attorney's office.

It's easy to see how a crime as revolting as serial murder could inspire a law-and-order approach. That's what has happened in Juárez, particularly since the second group of bodies—many of them freshly dead—began turning up last spring, after Sharif had been locked up for months. The populace was terrified, and the women's coalition sprang into action. It organized marches, held press conferences, and sent the United Nations a report describing the killings as a violation of women's human rights.

Feminists weren't the only ones pressing for a resolution to the case. Juárez police answer to a mayor and a state governor who are members of the Catholic-based, conservative National Action Party. The PAN has gained power in Juárez and other northern Mexican cities recently, but the infamous and powerful PRI—the Institutional Revolutionary Party—is constantly looking for ways to discredit its rival. By spring, the local PRI was noisily mocking PAN leaders' failure to protect the city's women. To make matters worse, the PANista Attorney General failed to win even one murder indictment against Sharif; a judge ruled there wasn't enough material evidence.

Finally, late one Saturday night in April, a phalanx of police surrounded several maquila-worker bars and arrested more than 100 people, including dozens of underage girls. Police now claim that nine young men, members of a gang called the Rebels, committed the murders along with Sharif. Most wear cowboy clothes; some worked as male strippers and musicians in the bars, where they are said to have done a brisk business in illegal drugs, bootleg liquor, and pimping. The police allege that they were paid by Sharif to recruit and kill victims—even after he was jailed, when he calculated that new corpses would make him look innocent.

A rich foreign boss, a crew of native-born male supervisors, a high-turnover supply of females. Is this a true-crime scenario or a maquila-saturated city's freaked-out, global-assembly-line fantasy: mass production as mass murder? Serial killers are popularly portrayed as lone, Ripper-style offenders, but multiple murderers may actually account for as many as a fifth of all cases, according to Penn State history professor Philip Jenkins.

A Sharif & Co.-type enterprise is thus imaginable, and there are indications that some of the accused may have been involved. One purported Rebels member was seen visiting Sharif in jail. Tests done on another's car supposedly have found blood. The gang's so-called leader, a beefy 26-year-old who police say is nicknamed "The Devil," was seen at a bar with a victim, and authorities say bite marks on her corpse match his dentition. At least two women have reported that they were kidnapped and/or raped by gang members but managed to escape.

On the other hand, the case is seriously flawed. The biggest problem is the inability of the police to identify most of the dead women so they can investigate possible connections. Speculation is that these Jane Does were newcomers to the city: poor girls who journeyed north to work in the maquilas or cross to the United States. Artists' sketches of facial reconstructions appear in the papers, along with itemizations of victims' clothing that constitute inventories of the globalized textile market these girls both worked and consumed in. ("Lee jeans size 3M, Hanes panties," reads one list. To the sad bemusement of garment-worker organizers, police surmised that another victim was Central American because a label in her clothing said "Made in Honduras.")

More disturbing is that in addition to the nineteen bodies associated with the serial murders, the women's coalition recently tallied old press items and police records and discovered that fifty-three other raped and murdered female corpses have been found scattered about Juárez in the past three years. Are their deaths related? Are there other sex murderers?

Even the "hard evidence" is fraught with problems. Mexican police have claimed they found blood and semen in suspects' cars, but authorities in El Paso, where the vehicles were sent for testing, have denied detecting body fluids. A representative of the Mexican Human Rights Commission reports that suspects were arrested without warrants, denied lawyers, and injured during questioning; defendants say the police beat them, stuck their heads into toilets, held pistols to their heads, and threatened to kill them unless

they confessed. Bar habitués report being kidnapped by cops and subjected to the same treatment to force them to incriminate suspects. The human rights commission finds these claims credible since Mexican police are notorious for using Inquisition-style methods. (The police insist the Rebels were freely confessing until the human rights representative gave them legal advice. At a recent indictment hearing, a judge agreed—and finally charged Sharif with the murder of Elizabeth Castro, the teenager whose corpse started the case.)

Feminists like Chávez wonder uneasily whether they've opened a Pandora's box of false accusations and sexist moralizing. But they're reluctant to criticize the investigation. One reason for the activists' silence is their reluctance to fuel PRI squabbles with the PAN. More significant is that their outcry about the murders has finally achieved gains from the government, including the woman-staffed sex-crimes unit in the district attorney's office and discussions about opening a state-run battered women's shelter. So activists who were once vocal critics of police brutality—including against women maquila workers trying to unionize—are now quiet.

Left in the lurch, maquila girls have their own opinions. Some are commonsensically skeptical: "I don't believe the police," one factory worker comments. "They keep contradicting themselves." Others are frighteningly ignorant about sex murderers: "The young men they've accused can't be guilty," opines another, heavily made-up young woman, "because they're poor and the killer is probably rich." There are wild conspiracy theories in which the killers are military or police or organ traffickers. And of course, that they are foreign maquila managers—because, as another worker notes, "they know so much about the victims' habits."

Managers do know the girls, at least better than labor unionists and feminists do. Organizers need to catch up. They might start by campaigning to abolish discriminatory hiring, job classifications, and everything else based on M and F—including the pregnancy tests. They could work with women's advocates to organize mother-daughter classes in sexuality and self-defense. Such actions would recognize young maquila women's right to equality, dignity, and pleasure. They would also help sever the link between murderous sexual assault and the more insidious—and far more widespread—violence of work on the global assembly line.

No Guarantees: Sex Discrimination in Mexico's Maquiladora Se[

By Human Rights Watch

SUMMARY

Maquiladoras, or export-processing factories, along the U.S.-Mexico border account for over US$29 billion in export earnings for Mexico and employ over 500,000 workers. At least half of the Mexicans employed in this sector, mainly in assembly plants, are women, and the income they earn supports them and their families at wages higher than they could earn in any other employment sector in northern Mexico.

These women workers routinely suffer a form of discrimination unique to women: the maquiladoras require them to undergo pregnancy testing as a condition of employment and deny them work if they are pregnant; if a woman becomes pregnant soon after gaining employment at a maquiladora, in some instances she may be mistreated or forced to resign because of her pregnancy. Maquiladora operators target women for discriminatory treatment, in violation of international human rights and labor rights norms. And despite its international and domestic legal responsibility to ensure protection for these workers, the Mexican government has done little to acknowledge or remedy violations of women's rights to nondiscrimination and to privacy. In addition, the Mexican government's failure to remedy discrimination in the maquiladoras infringes on women's right to decide freely and responsibly on the number and spacing of their children. In fact, government employees responsible for overseeing compliance with and enforcement of Mexico's federal labor law—which explicitly prohibits sex discrimination—inconsistently condemn such discriminatory practices; view themselves as incapable of enforcing the law; and, in one instance, defended the pregnancy-based discrimination as reasonable or legitimate.

Pregnancy as a condition is inextricably linked and specific to being female. Consequently, when women are treated differently by their employers or potential employers because they are pregnant or because they may become pregnant, they are being subjected to requirements for employment to which men are not. Thus pregnancy-based discrimination constitutes a form of sex discrimination, by targeting a condition only women experience.

It is difficult for workers—poor, under-educated, and female in a society with 6.3 percent official unemployment (Mexico's official, national unemployment figures are widely acknowledged by the U.S. Commerce Department and other U.S. agencies as being significantly underestimated)—with so few job alternatives to contest maquiladora policies. Most of the women Human Rights Watch interviewed had not finished primary school and had very little work experience outside the manufacturing sector. As a consequence, these women emphasized that their only other opportunity for work is in domestic service, which pays poorly, allows them very little control over their schedules and working conditions, and provides no health insurance or social security. Women repeatedly expressed unwillingness to challenge discriminatory practices in the maquiladoras, given the lack of other comparable employment opportunities.

For the Mexican government, there are economic disincentives to regulating closely the conduct of these companies, given the number of people the maquiladora industry employs and the amount of foreign currency earnings it produces.

In March 1995 the Human Rights Watch Women's Rights Project sent a mission to Mexico to investigate discrimination against pregnant workers or women who might become pregnant in the maquiladora sector. We interviewed women's rights activists, maquiladora personnel, labor rights advocates, Mexican government officials, community organizers, and victims of sex-based employment discrimination in five cities: Tijuana, in Baja California state; Chihuahua, in Chihuahua state; and Matamoros, Reynosa, and Rio Bravo, in Tamaulipas state. We interviewed women who currently or in the recent past worked as line workers or assemblers in forty-three maquiladora plants along the border....

Where possible, Human Rights Watch has contacted parent companies implicated in this report to alert them to our findings and seek their responses. We have received written responses from Zenith, American Zettler, W. R. Grace, Carlisle Plastics, Pacific Electricord, and Sanyo. The

Summary and recommendations from a report by the Women's Rights Project of Human Rights Watch, Washington, DC, April 1996. Reprinted by permission of Human Rights Watch.

responses range from a complete disavowal of any discriminatory behavior (American Zettler) to promises to investigate the allegations immediately and rectify the practice where appropriate (Sanyo), to admissions that pregnant women are in fact screened out of the applicant pool as a way to avoid paying for maternity leave (Zenith)....

Maquiladora employers discriminate against pregnant female employees, or women who might become pregnant (women of childbearing age, sexually active women, women who use contraceptives), largely to keep costs down. Starting in the 1960s, many U.S. and other companies relocated production to northern Mexico to take advantage of favorable tariff structures for importing unassembled goods and exporting finished products; low wages; and an abundance of available workers. Hiring or employing pregnant women could entail higher costs because Mexico's federal labor law contains explicit maternity provisions. According to the federal labor code, companies are required to protect pregnant women from executing tasks that would cause danger to their health in relation to the fetus; pay pregnant women maternity leave of six weeks before delivery and six weeks after delivery; allow new mothers two paid extra breaks of half hour each to breast feed their infants; and allow pregnant women to take an extra sixty days off while receiving 50 percent of their salary, if they so desire, apart from the twelve weeks of maternity leave, so long as no more than one year after the birth has passed. Thus, while many maquiladoras seek to hire women workers because they are believed to work harder and to be especially equipped emotionally and anatomically to execute such work, employers attempt to weed out potentially costly women workers from the applicant pool and at times force to resign those who become pregnant soon after beginning to work.

In maquiladoras along the U.S.-Mexico border, from Tijuana to Matamoros, we found, with few exceptions, that in the course of the hiring process employers require women applicants to submit to pregnancy exams, most commonly given through urine samples. These exams are administered by doctors or nurses employed at individual maquiladoras or by private clinics contracted by companies. Maquiladora staff also try to determine a woman's pregnancy status by asking intrusive questions about the woman applicant's menses schedule, whether she is sexually active, or what type of birth control she uses. Once a woman is hired to work in a maquiladora, should she become pregnant shortly after starting to work, maquiladora managers sometime attempt to reassign women to more physically difficult work or demand overtime work in an effort to force the pregnant woman worker to resign. The results of Human Rights Watch interviews suggest that the longer a woman is employed in a maquiladora the more able she might be to rely on her relationship with her supervisor to avoid being fired if she becomes pregnant. Nonetheless, there are no guarantees.

The women affected by pregnancy discrimination in the maquiladora sector are among the poorest, least experienced, and least educated in the workforce. Most women who work in the maquiladoras do so because their lack of schooling and previous significant work experience renders them unqualified for most other jobs and because work in the maquiladora sector affords them a better wage than they might earn in other sectors. Screened out of the applicant pool and denied jobs in the maquiladora sector, these pregnant women would be rendered virtually unemployable. Women applicants are often single mothers or their families' primary wage earners. Their desperation to get or retain maquiladora jobs combined with ignorance of the law make them reluctant to contest the discriminatory testing or forced resignations. Furthermore, Human Rights Watch is greatly concerned that such discriminatory treatment may directly compromise women workers' regulation of their pregnancies by forcing them into a situation of fearing the loss of their jobs if they become pregnant. In cases when women workers become pregnant, the fear of losing their jobs often compels women to hide their pregnancies, and risk their and their fetuses' well-being. In many instances women find themselves in the untenable position of choosing between their jobs and their rights.

Such employment practices constitute discrimination on the basis of sex, an invasion of a woman's privacy, and, in some instances, an undue limit on a woman's ability to decide freely and responsibly on the number and spacing of her children. By failing to address and remedy these practices the Mexican government fails to fulfill its human rights obligation to protect those under its jurisdiction from human rights abuses; promote respect for human rights within its borders; and ensure that those under its jurisdiction are able fully to enjoy and exercise their rights under the International Covenant on Civil and Political Rights (ICCPR), the Convention to Eliminate All Forms of Discrimination against Women (CEDAW), the American Convention on Human Rights, the American Declaration of the Rights and Duties of Man, the International Covenant on

Economic, Social and Cultural Rights (ICESCR), International Labor Office (ILO) standards, and the North American Agreement on Labor Cooperation. Such discriminatory treatment also contravenes Mexico's domestic laws prohibiting discrimination and guaranteeing the protection of women's reproductive health.

Women victims of sex discrimination in the maquiladoras have few tenable options for legal redress. Various states within Mexico have a human rights commission, and these are tasked, under their charters, to investigate human rights abuses involving public officials, but they cannot investigate private sector labor issues. Government mechanisms such as the Inspector of Labor's Office, which is responsible for assuring compliance with federal labor law; the Labor Rights Ombudsman's Office, which is responsible for offering workers free legal advice and assisting them in the resolution of labor disputes; and the Conciliation and Arbitration Board (hereafter CAB), which adjudicates worker disputes and issues binding resolutions, are not legally empowered to address sex discrimination in the hiring process and fail consistently to condemn such discrimination in those instances where women are already employed. Furthermore, none of these offices collects data on cases and their resolution disaggregated by gender or gender-specific claims.

To end the widespread discrimination against women in the maquiladora sector and the related denial of their right to privacy and, in some instances, to decide freely and responsibly on the number and spacing of their children, Human Rights Watch calls on the government of Mexico, the state legislatures, the Mexican commissions for human rights, the government of the United States, corporations that operate maquiladoras, and corporations that use maquiladoras as subcontractors, to take the following steps:

RECOMMENDATIONS
Human Rights Watch urges the Government of Mexico to:
- Uphold international human rights obligations to guarantee the right to nondiscrimination, the right to privacy and the right to decide freely and responsibly on the number and spacing of children without discrimination.
- Acknowledge and publicly condemn pregnancy discrimination as discrimination based on sex.
- Publicly condemn employment practices and procedures

that discriminate against women in their intent or impact.
- Enact federal legislation that explicitly prohibits any company, public or private, from requiring that women give proof of pregnancy status, contraceptive use (or any other information related to reproductive choice and health) in order to be considered for, gain, or retain employment.
- Fortify existing labor-resolution mechanisms by staffing the offices of the Inspector of Labor, the Labor Rights Ombudsman, and the Conciliation and Arbitration Boards with employees who are well informed about federal labor law and by putting resources at the disposal of these offices so that they may enforce federal labor law.
- Amend the rules governing the work of the Office of the Inspector of Labor, the Office of the Labor Rights Ombudsman, and the Conciliation and Arbitration Board so that these offices can investigate and adjudicate cases of discriminatory nonhiring as well as disputes involving an established labor relationship.
- Under the authority of the Secretary of Labor and Social Security, establish labor offices at the state and local level that have full powers to investigate and remedy discrimination in the hiring process, in compliance with obligations under the Convention to Eliminate All Forms of Discrimination Against Women (CEDAW).
- Oblige the Office of the Inspector of Labor, the Office of the Labor Rights Ombudsman, and the Conciliation and Arbitration Boards to maintain statistics on their investigations, case loads, and decisions, where appropriate, disaggregated by gender and the type of claim filed.
- Establish and enforce penalties, including fines, to punish companies, foreign or domestic-owned, engaged in pregnancy-based sex discrimination, in accordance with CEDAW provisions.
- Investigate vigorously all allegations of sex-based discriminatory employment practices and punish those responsible.
- Include specific information on efforts undertaken to eradicate discrimination against women in the workplace, including specific measures to end the testing of women for pregnancy, and the use of such information to make discriminatory hiring or firing decisions in its country compliance reports under CEDAW.
- Encourage state legislatures to amend the charter of the state human rights commissions so that it includes the

ability to investigate private action as it relates to the state's human rights obligation to combat sex discrimination.

- In compliance with the International Labor Office's Convention Concerning Discrimination in Respect of Employment and Occupation [Convention No. 111], Mexico should:
  - Pursue national policies to promote equality of opportunity and treatment in employment and occupation;
  - Take practicable measures to foster public understanding and acceptance of nondiscrimination; and
  - Receive and examine complaints of abrogation of nondiscrimination principles.
- Mexico is also obligated, under the North American Free Trade Agreement's North American Agreement on Labor Cooperation, to:
  - Promote elimination of employment discrimination;
  - Ensure that its labor laws are enforced;
  - Initiate, in a timely manner, proceedings to seek appropriate sanctions or remedies for violations of its labor law; and
  - Publicize the content of its labor law regarding nondiscrimination, thereby upholding its obligations under the NAFTA's Article 6, which states, "Each Party shall ensure that its laws, regulations, procedures, and administrative rulings of general application respecting any matter covered by this Agreement are promptly published or otherwise made available in such a manner as to enable interested persons and Parties to become acquainted with them."

Human Rights Watch urges Mexico's state legislatures to:

- Amend the charters of state human rights commissions so that they are able to investigate and report on unremedied private sector employment sex discrimination.

Human Rights Watch urges Mexico's state commissions for human rights to:

- Recognize that unremedied private sector employment sex discrimination is within the mandate of the state commissions for human rights because it is a violation of a woman's right to nondiscrimination and infringes on her ability to decide freely and responsibly on the number and spacing of children;
- Incorporate the monitoring of discrimination against women in the private sector labor force into the cases

they investigate and report on; and

- Monitor and report on steps taken by Mexico to comply with nondiscrimination requirements of international human rights law in a manner that would promote the eradication of discrimination against women in the work place.

Human Rights Watch urges the United States Government to:

- Take up the case of pregnancy-based sex discrimination and encourage the Mexican government to take immediate steps to combat it, in any interaction with the Mexican government; and
- Encourage the Government of Mexico to meet its obligations under the North American Free Trade Agreement's North American Agreement on Labor Cooperation, including the enforcement of its own labor law and the elimination of employment discrimination.

Human Rights Watch urges private corporations that own maquiladoras to:

- End the practice of requiring women applicants to provide proof of pregnancy status or contraception use or information about sexual habits in order to be considered for or to obtain employment in the maquiladoras;
- End the practice of denying pregnant women applicants work by screening them out of the applicant pool;
- Explicitly prohibit pregnancy exams for women applicants or any other such method that would invade a woman's privacy regarding her pregnancy status and right to nondiscrimination;
- End harassment, intimidation, and forced resignation of female employees who become pregnant;
- Reprimand personnel officers and other maquiladora employees who continue to discriminate against women workers by subjecting them to practices to determine their pregnancy status, including the practice of obliging them to provide proof of that status;
- Explicitly prohibit discrimination based on sex in all company materials, including materials in Spanish that are easily accessible to both management and workers at all Mexico-based company branches; and
- Accommodate pregnant women during their pregnancies, as per international standards and Mexican domestic law, by giving them seated work; allowing them to take maternity leave; and allowing them temporary transfers to less physically taxing work.

Human Rights Watch urges corporations that use maquiladoras as subcontractors to:

- Require proof that subcontracting factories are being operated without discrimination, as a condition for a continuing contractual relationship; and

- Monitor subcontractor plants on an ongoing basis, by, at a minimum, requiring periodic, timely certification that plants are being operated without discrimination; establishing an independent, impartial group wholly unconnected to the factory to monitor compliance; and periodically visiting the subcontractor plants to review the hiring process and solicit information from workers on the absence of discrimination.

May Day on the Border
By David Bacon

May Day, celebrated around the world to honor the labor movement, is traditionally the occasion for massive parades by Mexico's official labor movement. In 1995, however, concerns about popular discontent following the peso crash of December 1994 prompted the country's official labor movement to cancel May Day celebrations. The excerpt below is part of a longer article recounting the militant response by independent unions and labor activists, which demonstrated without official sanction.

TIJUANA (5/19/95)—"You can imagine how desperate we are, since we're so poor, and without a law to protect us. Here, if you have no money, the government won't enforce the law. We really have very good laws in Mexico, but a very bad government."

As she said these words, Yolanda Vásquez stood in the middle of a dusty street in Tijuana, voices pouring out of bullhorns, swirling around her. She held a placard in her hands. It said in Spanish "For the dignity of women in the maquiladoras." Other women stood with her in Tijuana's first unofficial May Day march. Their placards made similar appeals. Another said simply "We demand the companies obey the law."

Vásquez, a maquiladora worker for the last five years, expresses an opinion heard over and over among ordinary workers in Mexico—their problems, as they view them, aren't with the law, but with its lack of enforcement. In her case, those problems include sexual harassment, the closing of the plant where she worked, blacklisting, and wages which have fallen to a tenth of the minimum wage paid just a few miles away, on the other side of the border....

Yolanda Vásquez was a worker at a maquiladora called Exportadora de Mano de Obra. Exportadora was started eight years ago by National O-Ring of Downey [CA], a division of a large U.S. corporation, American United Global. Dan Melendez, a spokesperson for National O-Ring, says that his company never actually owned Exportadora. Nevertheless, he freely admits that Exportadora's wages, personnel policies, and the work itself were controlled from Downey. The Exportadora plant employed about 180 workers, who did finishing work and inspection on rubber o-rings.

Last summer Exportadora held its annual picnic. Vásquez says that in the middle of the picnic, an announcement was made over the microphone that there would be a bikini contest among the plant's female workers. "It took us by surprise, because there had never been one before," Vásquez says.

Melendez alleges that there had been a bikini contest every year. He called it "a benefit for the workers." National O-Ring has never asked its workers in Downey to have such a contest, nor has it ever had a company picnic for them.

When Vásquez and her coworkers balked at the idea of stripping and putting on bathing suits for company managers, she says she was told that company president John Shahid, who was at the picnic, wanted them to do it. The contest was videotaped.

Later in the fall, workers asked for meetings with the company to express their discontent. Vásquez says they wanted to protest their treatment, including the bikini contest and the videotaping. They also wanted improvements in the wages and conditions at the plant. When they finally met with Shahid, and asked him for a raise, he took the money he had in his pocket, about $15, and threw it on the table. "We told him we didn't want money like that, that we wanted our pay increased," Vásquez remembers. "So he asked us what we would give him in exchange. We said we'd give him our work, like we always did. But he told us that he wanted love."

Shahid did not respond to requests for an interview. Melendez says that workers were told the company had bought land and had begun building another plant for Exportadora in Tijuana. When it opened, he told them, some of their demands for better conditions could be met. He says he also told them he was conducting a survey of the wages in other maquiladoras, to see if the wages at Exportadora were too low. In Tijuana, however, as in other cities along the border, all the maquiladoras belong to an association, in which employers agree on wage rates. This is common knowledge among maquiladora workers.

The women at Exportadora went to the Mexican labor board to complain about the bikini contest and their treatment. A labor board investigator asked the company

Excerpted with permission from the *Nation* magazine, Nov. 13, 1995.

for a copy of the video, but when he received it, it was blank. Enraged, he recommended to the workers that they file sexual abuse charges with Tijuana's public prosecutor, which they did. Two days after those charges were filed, the work coming from Downey dried up. Each day the Exportadora plant normally received 200 boxes of o-rings for processing. First it was cut to fifty, the next day to ten, and finally, on the last day, workers were just told to go home.

Melendez accuses the workers of slowing down the work in Tijuana as a protest over their conditions. "We demanded that they increase their productivity, and when they wouldn't, we closed the plant," he says. Since then, National O-Ring has abandoned plans to build a new plant in Tijuana, and has moved the work back to Downey. The Tijuana workers made about $20 a week. Melendez wouldn't say what wages are paid in Downey, but minimum wage is $170 for a forty-hour week.

When National O-Ring workers lost their jobs, they did something new, however. With the aid of San Diego union activists in the Committee to Support Maquiladora Workers, they found a lawyer in Los Angeles. Then they filed suit in Superior Court, alleging that they had been sexually harassed and punished with the closure of their plant after they protested.

The suit is unprecedented. It marks the first time workers in Mexico, aided by supporters in the United States, have filed suit in a U.S. court to defend their rights. Exportadora workers reasoned that if they couldn't get Mexican authorities to enforce the law, they would try to use the legal process on the other side. After all, National O-Ring is a U.S. company, and John Shahid is a U.S. resident.

Whether the case is won or not, Vásquez feels that it sends an important message to U.S. companies. "Companies like National O-Ring and people like Shahid come to Mexico to make money," she says. "They think they can do anything they want with us because we're Mexicans. Well, it's our country, even if we're poor. Not theirs." . . .

For Mexican Women, Sexism Is a Daily Battle

By Nora Lockwood Tooher

In Mexico, sexism goes hand-in-hand with industrialization. As widespread as pollution, the exploitation of women workers is rampant in Mexico's maquiladoras. And sexual harassment happens all the time.

Just ask Adelia Ramírez Hernández. Ramírez, nineteen, earns seventy-eight cents an hour assembling color televisions at a Zenith Electronics Corp. factory in Reynosa, one of the centers of the maquiladora region.

She works forty-five hours a week, from 3: 30 in the afternoon until 12:30 in the morning. Her weekly take-home pay: $30.16 a week. She says her Mexican supervisor "screams to the people and speaks badly. He makes some of the women clean his shoes." Young women workers, she says, are "constantly asked to go out with supervisors. . . . Women who befriend the supervisors don't have to work as hard."

John Taylor, a Zenith spokesman in Glenview, Illinois, says the company has "strict policies forbidding such harassment," and disputes Ramírez's account of harassment. Zenith has training programs in Mexico, he says, to help supervisors understand "that sexual harassment will not be tolerated." Because of cultural differences, he says, there have been some instances of sexual harassment in Mexico. But, Taylor says, "When these kinds of things are brought to our attention—and it's not widespread—we take swift action."

Women workers and labor organizers tell a different story. So far, opposition to the North American Free Trade Agreement has been focused on wages and pollution. No one talks much in Washington about the treatment of women workers. But in Mexico, where *machismo* reigns, women say they are routinely subjected to instances of sexism that are either socially unacceptable or outright illegal in the United States.

Nearly two-thirds of Mexico's 500,000 maquiladora workers are women, according to CIEMEXWEFA, an economic forecasting group that tracks the maquiladora industry. Most of them, U.S. labor activists say, are between the ages of sixteen and twenty-four. That's not all that sur-

prising, considering that 57 percent of Mexico's population is under age twenty-nine. But that doesn't explain why there are so many women in the factories.

Factory owners say the assembly jobs are more suited to women because women have better manual dexterity. But labor organizers and feminists in Mexico and the United States say that maquiladoras like to hire young women because they are less likely to complain or organize than men, and because women are more easily exploited

Phoebe McKinney, director of an American Friends Service Committee program for maquiladora workers, says the high proportion of young women in maquiladoras is part of a pattern by huge multinational corporations to locate "in areas of the world where there's a vulnerable work force, and the vulnerable and exploitable work force is women."

One maquiladora in Ciudad Juárez puts color-coded lollipops over the heads of women workers to encourage them to meet production quotas. The lollipops serve as signals of how fast a woman is working. McKinney, who says she can't get that image out of her mind, calls it an example of the "infantalization of women."

Ten-Hour Days

Idalia Vásquez, nineteen, sleeps on the floor of a small shack in Colonia Roma in Reynosa. Across from McAllen, Texas, Reynosa's population has doubled in the last decade to 750,000, as hundreds of thousands of Mexicans have flocked to the northern border, looking for jobs.

It is a Thursday evening in spring, and Vasquez's family says she is tired after working all day at Erika, a U.S. factory in Reynosa that makes disposable bags for IVs. Vásquez supports ten relatives who live with her. As she sleeps, her mother and other relatives sit outside in the dusk.

Later, Vásquez awakens and goes for a walk around the colonia with her mother. Vásquez started working at Erika when she was fifteen, and earns $54.83 a week, working 6:30 a.m. to 4:30 p.m. five days a week. She says her job is to put a little hose in a jar that has chemicals in it. Then, she attaches it to another piece. "Sometimes women faint because of the smell," she says.

Originally published in the *Providence* (RI) *Journal-Bulletin*, Sept. 29, 1992, as Part 3 of the series "The Price of Free Trade." Reprinted by permission.

Poor Working Conditions

Wearing a red-and-white striped, sleeveless dress, Veronica, nineteen, stands barefoot in the dirt in front of her mother's house in Colonia Esperanza. It is twilight and the crickets are beginning their evensong. Veronica, who does not want her last name used, works at a Converse factory in Reynosa, where she earns eighty-one cents an hour, sewing soles onto sneakers for export to the United Sates.

Veronica works forty-eight hours a week, for which she is paid $38.88. She gets a half-hour break for lunch each day, but is not paid for that time. She started working for Converse when she was fifteen, and says that her pay is $6.12 more a week than when she started four years ago.

She works 7:00 a.m. to 4:30 p.m., Monday through Friday. To avoid paying for two buses, she walks a mile to the highway each morning. Inside the factory, she says, there is a lot of lint in the air. The women are given face masks to wear, but they are uncomfortable.

AT&T: A Rare Example

In an AT&T factory in Guadalupe, near Monterrey, an American plant manager explains why, like other maquiladoras, his factory employs mostly young women. The manager, Jim Cole, says it is because of the "type of jobs" in the assembly factory. "I don't want to make this sound sexist, okay, but it's probably lesser technology ..."

Training workers has not been difficult, he says: "I find these workers, they're so willing to work, and they're willing to learn." Well-intentioned, Cole manages one of the better factories in Mexico. He also tries to treat his employees fairly, and does not consciously discriminate against women employees. Still, as he walks past rows of women workers putting connectors on the end of wire cables, he points to one woman, and says with a smile, "That's one of the prettiest little señoritas you'll see south of the border."

Despite his comment, Cole prides himself on giving women employees equal opportunities. His protégé, Magdalena Sigona de A., one of Cole's purchasing officers, says she believes she has more opportunities with a U.S. company than a Mexican firm. Wearing the red-and-white skirt and blouse worn by AT&T's women office workers, Sigona, 35, says she was recently promoted and given a raise from $522 a month to $1,077, a huge salary compared with most other women workers.

The company also paid to send her to Oklahoma with her husband, Claudio, and their son, Claudio Jr., four, for training—the Sigonas' first trip to the United States. Mem-

bers of Mexico's small middle class, the Sigonas own two new cars and a two-story house that has air conditioning, two televisions, a computer, and a roomful of toys for Claudio Jr.

But Sigona has also felt the sting of Mexican sex discrimination, and exemplifies the difference in equality between the sexes in the United States and Mexico. She was fired from her job as a secretary at a Mexican-owned company after she married. In Mexico, married women are traditionally viewed as poor workers because they are likely to want more time off.

But after staying home for a while, Sigona wanted to return to work to help with the family finances. She asked her husband, Claudio, for permission, something that is also the norm in Mexico. Although reluctant, Claudio says he gave her his permission, and 18 months ago, she was hired by AT&T.

Mandatory Birth Control

Lidia Chavarría says she was required to take a pregnancy test before she was hired at Levimex, a Tijuana maquiladora owned by Leviton Manufacturing Co. Leviton closed its South Kingstown plant in 1989 and laid off 200 Rhode Island workers so it could move to Mexico, where wages are far lower.

"In the maquila," Chavarría says, "the attorney asks if you have children and if your husband permits you to work. They did a pregnancy check even though I told him I had an operation." Levimex workers, she says, are given contracts for one month, three months, and one year. Each time the contract is renewed, she says a worker has to take a test proving she isn't pregnant.

Carmen Valadez, a women's labor organizer in Tijuana, says company doctors routinely administer pregnancy tests and distribute birth control pills. Women workers, she says, are "forbidden from having children by the maquilas." And, Valadez says, many maquiladoras, like Levimex, require women employees to submit a "certificate of nonpregnancy" to get their employment contracts renewed.

Factory owners say they are merely doing their part in Mexico's aggressive family-planning program. Requiring pregnancy tests and dispensing contraceptives helps control unplanned births, they say. (Abortion is illegal in Mexico.)

Sylvia Galarza, who works in Tijuana with MEXFAM, a Mexican family-planning group that receives support from Planned Parenthood, praises the maquiladoras for allowing groups like hers into Mexican factories to provide contraceptives and birth-control counseling. Galarza says women are glad to have access to birth-control information and contraceptives on the job, rather than taking a day off from work to go to one of the government's nationalized heath clinics.

One of the justifications for mandatory pregnancy testing is that the turnover rate in the maquilas is high—up to 100 percent a year. And training workers is costly, as much as $625 per employee, according to a maquiladora trade organization. "It's nothing to do with trying to control the fertility of the worker," Galarza says. "I have never ever encountered a controversy about family planning."

But Mexican activists such as Valadez—while favoring family planning and women's access to contraceptives—say these birth-control programs are simply another way foreign companies control their women workers. In 1978, when Valadez was eighteen, she worked at a maquila in Tijuana. "The first thing they asked was if I took birth control pills." She says a company official told her: "We'll give them to you every month."

A Fight for Improvement

A group of Mexican women is working to change the way women are treated in the maquiladoras. It is called Comité Fronterizo de Obreras (Border Committee of Women Workers).

At nights and on weekends, CFO organizers like Tanny Gaspar Labastida and Olga Jiménez Calderón visit colonias or invite women workers into their home. In sessions resembling Bible study groups, workers memorize sections of the Mexican labor law, Ley Federal del Trabajo. The women role-play worker and supervisor and learn how to work together to obtain better treatment.

Unlike the major Mexican unions that are tied to the government, the CFO is an informal, grassroots group. Financed in part by U.S. labor groups, the CFO estimates it has contacted about 10,000 women workers and their families during the last twelve years.

At the home of Gaspar and Jiménez in Reynosa, three women who work for General Motors sit on the couch in the dark on a warm evening. They show their paychecks and talk about working conditions. Two days later, Gaspar and Jiménez visit Ramírez, the Zenith worker, in her grandparents' home in a well-kept neighborhood in Reynosa. Gaspar reviews a section of the Mexican labor law with Ramírez, who talks about her job and the conditions in the factory.

On one of the handouts CFO organizers give women workers is this question: "Can the management make distinctions based on the age or sex of the person?" The answer from the Mexican labor law is clear: "There should be no distinction made based on the age or sex of the person." Ramírez, who wears a blue-green Zenith T-shirt, has already learned to quote the section forbidding sexual harassment.

That's why, she says, her supervisor doesn't proposition her. A lot of her coworkers "are angry and don't like it," but don't say anything. They are afraid, she says.

THREE

HEALTH AND
ENVIRONMENTAL ISSUES

Between 1988 and 1992, twenty-five children were born with a neural tube defect known as spina bifida in the border towns of Brownsville, Texas and neighboring Matamoros, Tamaulipas. Another thirty children were diagnosed during this period with anencephaly, a rare and invariably fatal birth defect in which a full-term baby is born with incomplete or missing brain.

Although this cluster of birth defects was investigated by the Texas Department of Health and the federal Centers for Disease Control, the results of the investigation were inconclusive. Meanwhile, twenty-seven parents of anencephalic babies on the U.S. side of the border sued eighty-eight maquiladora firms and the Brownsville Public Utility Board, charging that pollution from maquiladora plants was responsible for these birth defects. Although the defendants insisted they had abided by environmental regulations, the lawsuit was settled for $17 million in 1995, shortly before it went to trial.

This settlement offered a measure of vindication, as well as monetary compensation, to the Brownsville parents. Families of anencephalic babies in Matamoros, for their part, continue to struggle with the human and financial burden of caring for their fatally ill children. Clusters of anencephaly have also turned up in towns like Del Rio, Texas (across the border from the maquiladora center of Ciudad Acuña), and Colonia Chilpancingo, in Tijuana, where twenty anencephalic births were reported in 1993 and 1994.[1]

• • •

I work with hot metal and management is supposed to give me a pair of gloves, but sometimes they don't. One day the material came down the line before the gloves and I did nothing, and the entire line of workers stopped with

me. The supervisor asked me why I wasn't working, and I said I wouldn't work without gloves. He said, fine—if you don't want to work I'll change your post. He put a new woman in my place and didn't give her gloves, but she didn't know any better and worked without them."[2]

*— Celia**

Maquiladora workers voice constant fears about their safety on the job. In the electronics industry alone, workers are exposed to a variety of substances which include xylene, trichloroethylene, zinc and lead oxides, and nitric acid. Not only electronics assembly but other industries as well expose workers to the materials used in thinners, paints, solvents, resins, solders, dyes, flux, and acetone. Exposure to such substances without proper protection can cause cancer, reproductive problems, skin diseases, vision problems, respiratory impairments, gastrointestinal and nervous disorders, and headaches and fatigue.

Maquiladora workers in many industries also risk injuries to their fingers, hands, and feet; stress-related conditions; and circulatory and muscular problems caused by repetitive motion and standing for ten-hour workshifts. Health-and-safety training and the provision of protective equipment fall far short of Mexican legal requirements throughout the industry.

It is difficult to collect reliable data on health issues inside the plants because most managers will not allow researchers access to their facilities and workers, says Garrett Brown of the Maquiladora Health and Safety Support Network.[3] Gloria, a worker at the General Motors plant in

---

* Celia makes windshield wipers at Delnosa, an auto parts maquiladora owned by the Delco Electronics division of General Motors, Mexico's largest private employer.

Reynosa, Tamaulipas, explains that workers are not allowed to bring a camera into the plant, even if they want to take a picture of friends on the line, because management is afraid that a safety hazard will show up in a photo.[4]

Management's response to organized work stoppages in a Reynosa plant has led to further safety violations. "The new supervisor locked the emergency doors so no one leaves before the shift is over," says Gloria. "We're not in jail, we're working." Working without access to emergency doors, an obvious danger, is illegal under Mexico's labor code.

Julia, who works at Deltrónico making car radios, is concerned about her hearing. After each radio is made, Julia makes sure that it functions correctly. She works all day with earphones, listening to see that the radio plays all frequencies and performs all functions and that all the buttons work.

"I listen to deep sounds, sharp sounds, all day it's the same," she says. At a meeting of the Comité Fronterizo de Obreras (CFO), Julia plays the tape she must test on every radio. The first sound is more than sharp, it is piercing, and it seems to last for longer than thirty seconds. In spite of the discomfort, Julia thinks her job is better than those of other workers who are not given chairs and are forced to work while standing.[5]

A "Breeding Ground for Disease"

Within maquiladora communities, even those who do not themselves work in the factories are adversely affected by the industry. According to a report by the American Medical Association, the border area has become a "virtual cesspool and breeding ground for infectious diseases."[6] As noted in chapter 1, the tax exemption afforded to maquiladora firms leaves border towns unable to invest in infrastructure for their rapidly growing populations. As a result, most maquiladora workers live without access to basic services.

Without an adequate sewer system, water sources are contaminated with garbage and human wastes. According to a 1991 survey in *U.S. News and World Report,* canals and rivers containing raw sewage were causing widespread gastrointestinal illness, hepatitis, and other health problems. A 1996 report from Public Citizen states that "two years after NAFTA the hepatitis rate in the border region remains at two to five times the U.S. national average."[7]

Next to a colonia in Matamoros, foaming liquid gushes into a canal. Near the bank, an old tire floats atop oily sludge. Colonia residents transport drinking water laden with toxic wastes in empty gallon drums once used as chemical containers. The growth of electronics, chemical, and furniture plants on the border since the 1980s has greatly increased the amount of industrial solvents polluting the environment.[8]

Many U.S. officials blame the slow cleanup of hazardous waste sites on Mexico's economic crisis and the corresponding lack of resources. While it may be easy for those in the United States to hold Mexico responsible for the precarious status of environmental cleanup, the truth is that U.S.-based corporations have been the principal contributors to the problem in the first place. Although the La Paz Agreement, signed by Mexico and the United States in 1983, requires hazardous waste created by U.S. corporations to be transported back to the United States for disposal, many companies avoid paying disposal costs by dumping toxic and other waste into Mexico's rivers and marine waters.[9] Under NAFTA, even this limited protection will be eliminated as of the year 2000, and hazardous wastes produced by the maquiladoras will be under the sole authority of Mexico's underfunded and inadequate regulatory apparatus.

Even when financial resources are available, border cleanup still proceeds at a snail's pace. The prosecution of those responsible for the Alco Pacífico site in Tijuana (where thousands of tons of toxic waste were abandoned when the company went bankrupt) resulted in a $2 million court settlement in 1993, earmarked for remediation of the site. Yet it took four years for cleanup to even begin. During all that time a mountain of lead was left uncovered in a residential area, near a dairy farm.[10]

NAFTA and Environmental Protection

Both the U.S. and Mexican governments affirm their commitment to environmental preservation, while failing to provide adequate resources to implement existing policies. Further, only those initiatives that do not hinder the pace of trade are capable of garnering official support. Sustained lobbying by environmental activists and human rights groups won an environmental side agreement to the North American Free Trade Agreement (NAFTA), known formally as the North American Agreement on Environmental Cooperation (NAAEC). This measure was ostensibly to alleviate the environmental impact of industrial development fueled by the trade agreement. (See chapter 6 for a discussion of NAFTA's labor side accord.)

Under the NAAEC, a trinational Commission for Environmental Cooperation (CEC) has been established. According to CEC Executive Director Victor Lichtinger, this body hopes to ensure high levels of environmental protection, foster public discussion of environmental concerns, advise trade representatives from the three countries, and facilitate enforcement of environmental laws.[11] Critics have highlighted structural problems that limit the CEC's authority and effectiveness. It is extremely difficult for the CEC to impose trade sanctions on countries that lower or ignore environmental standards: the process can only be initiated by a government, not by nongovernmental organizations; there is an unusually demanding burden of proof; and fines are capped at $20 million, even if the cost of the damage is far greater.[12] In the eyes of many observers, such flaws leave the NAAEC without teeth.

"'The typical strategy for the last twenty years has been to give companies permission to discharge, and then try [to] manage those emissions. [Now] we need to be working on the front end of things—to reduce the use of toxic chemicals and ensure more efficient use of the materials that are used,' says Eileen Sheehan of the U.S. Environmental Protection Agency."[13] Government funding, however, is still focused on dealing with environmental problems after they develop, rather than prevention.

Two additional environmental institutions were created by the United States and Mexico to address problems along the border: the North American Development Bank (NADBank) and the Border Environment Cooperation Commission (BECC). NADBank was created to "assist local communities in developing and financing environmental infrastructure while promoting sustainable development in the border region,"[14] and the BECC is charged with collecting and evaluating applications for NADBank financing.

Because of provisions that require borrowers to prove their ability to pay back loans, this funding is unavailable to those who need it most. In Nuevo Laredo, in the state of Nuevo Leon, for example, the death of a thirteen-year-old boy from a brain infection caused by an ameba found in untreated water led to plans for a wastewater treatment plant. Construction on the plant was halted, however, because the Nuevo Laredo municipal government could not afford to pay the required 10 percent share of project costs.[15]

While many organizers hope that BECC and NADBank will one day become useful tools for supporting sustainable development, it seems unlikely that this will happen in the near future. Argues Harry Browne of the In-

terhemispheric Resource Center: "NADBank and BECC are primarily products of political horse-trading rather than comprehensive environmental planning, and they are incapable of meeting many challenges posed by transboundary pollution and water depletion."[16]

Activist Responses

How can workers and their communities address environmental and health problems? Fighting for enforcement of health-and-safety provisions of Mexico's labor code has been a major focus of shopfloor actions by maquiladora workers. Typical demands include the installation of local exhaust ventilation to remove airborne contaminants; the provision of personal safety equipment; and rank-and-file representation on the Comisiones Mixtas, joint health-and-safety committees mandated under Mexican law.

Cross-border activism traces its roots to a moment more than twenty years ago when a staffperson for the United Church of Christ responded to a plea by maquiladora workers for help in translating an English-language safety data sheet that was packaged with solvents used in their factory. Today, many cross-border initiatives offer training to maquiladora workers in occupational health, using techniques such as risk mapping. The Maquiladora Health and Safety Support Network connects occupational health specialists with groups of maquiladora workers along the border to provide Spanish-language health-and-safety trainings. Training has also been provided to Mexican physicians. At the training sessions, workers and doctors learn how to recognize and control hazards. They study toxicology and workers' rights and develop action plans.

The Coalition for Justice in the Maquiladoras (CJM) has been pressuring maquiladora firms to provide workers with safety information on the materials and chemicals they are working with. However, until the factories are forced by their governments to comply with this basic request, few maquiladoras will do so. To help workers educate themselves on the dangers of the workplace, the CJM has published a *Manual de Seguridad Ocupacional* (Occupational Safety Manual), which discusses risk management in conversational Spanish.

AFSC, for its part, has supported Mexican groups to train workers in health-related issues. As part of this effort, the Mexican nongovernmental organization Servicio, Desarrollo y Paz (SEDEPAC—Service, Development, and Peace), has developed workshops in which women workers discuss issues of labor, reproductive, and community health. The CFO has also provided trainings in health and safety to its membership, and in 1998 initiated a process of participatory diagnosis of health problems in the maquiladoras. In conjunction with this training program, AFSC has also sponsored publication of a review of existing scientific and professional literature on health and environmental issues in the maquiladoras.[17]

Notes

1 David Bacon, "May Day on the Border," *The Nation,* Nov. 13, 1995.

2 Interview with Anya Hoffman, Rio Bravo, Tamaulipas, June 1997.

3 Interview with Anya Hoffman, June 1997.

4 Interview with Anya Hoffman, Reynosa, Tamaulipas, June 1997.

5 Interview with Anya Hoffman, Reynosa, Tamaulipas, June 1997.

6 Michael Satchell, "Poisoning the Border," *U.S. News and World Report,* May 6, 1991, p. 34.

7 Global Trade Watch, "The Border Betrayed 1996," Public Citizen, Washington, DC, 1996, p.7.

8 Edward J. Williams, *The Maquiladora Industry and Environmental Degradation in the United States-Mexico Borderlands,* rev. ed. (Tucson: University of Arizona, 1995).

9 Mary E. Kelly, "Free Trade: The Politics of Toxic Waste," NACLA *Report on the Americas,* Vol. XXVI, No. 2 (September 1992), p.5.

10 "Free Trade, Hazardous Waste," *borderlines,* Vol. 5, No. 6, June 1997.

11 Sarah Anderson, et al., "NAFTA's First Two Years: The Myths and the Realities," Institute for Policy Studies, Washington DC, 1996, p.27.

12 Ibid., p.28.

13 "Free Trade, Hazardous Waste," *borderlines,* op. cit.

14 Harry Browne, ed., *Cross Border Links: 1997 Environmental Directory* (Silver City, NM: Interhemispheric Resource Center, 1996), p. ii.

15 Global Trade Watch, op. cit., p. 15.

16 Browne, op. cit.

17 Alayne Unterberger and Ken Sturrock, "Health Status of Maquiladora Workers: What They Don't Know CAN Hurt Them," AFSC, 1998.

READINGS

The issue of safety on the job is illustrated in "Somebody Has to Stop This!," personal testimony by a worker from Matamoros that is reprinted from the newsletter of the Coalition for Justice in the Maquiladoras.

The Texas Center for Policy Studies (TCPS), based in Austin, has been a leading force in the fight against toxics at the border. In "Free Trade: The Politics of Toxic Waste," Mary E. Kelly, the center's executive director, offered a comprehensive overview of the issue, published at the opening of the NAFTA debate in 1992.

Two 1998 articles from borderlines, *a newsletter of the Interhemispheric Resource Center, analyze how the issues have evolved in the post-NAFTA era. "Workers' Health Is on the Line" discusses the many dangers maquiladora workers are exposed to and some of the steps workers' groups have taken to protect their health and safety. In "Hazardous Waste Management on the Border," TCPS documents the existence of a continuing problem of major proportions and the failure of the regulatory mechanisms that were put in place to address it.*

"Someone Has to Stop This":
Testimony of an Autotrim Worker in Matamoros

My name is Pedro Elias Medellín. I'm twenty-six years old, married, and have a four-year-old son. I have only studied through the first year of high school. I work in a maquiladora called Autotrim de México, located in Matamoros. We cover steering wheels and mold plastic car accessories. There are about 1,100 employees at the plant, and we all work a day shift. I assemble and sew the steering wheel cover by hand. The sewing is difficult because the leather that we use is quite hard. We have to work quickly with our hands, and I am responsible for sewing twenty steering wheel covers per shift.

After having worked for nine years at the plant, I now suffer from an injury in my right hand. I start out the shift okay, but after about three hours of work, I feel a lot of sharp pains in my fingers. It gets so bad that I can't hold the steering wheel correctly. But still the supervisors keep pressuring me to reach 100 percent of my production. I can only reach about 70 percent of what they ask for. These pains began over a year ago, and I am not the only one that has suffered from them. There are over 200 of us who have hand injuries and some have lost movement in their hands and arms. The company has fired over 150 people in the last year for lack of production. Others have been pressured to quit. Lately, the company has been negotiating with the injured workers, taking advantage of the fact that the workers are so desperate that they accept whatever they are offered. The workers are accepting about 2,000 pesos (about $275) as severance, but afterwards they can't work and don't find employment anywhere else.

Those of us who are injured but who haven't quit are forced to work as if there were nothing wrong with us. Only those workers who have a medical excuse signed by a doctor are given any lighter treatment. These are the workers who are most severely injured, and shouldn't even be working at all. The company has sent me to the union twice, asking that the union fire me for lack of production, but so far they haven't been able to get rid of me. The union hasn't done anything to help us, and has allowed the company to fire a lot of people. No one believes in the union.

The personnel director of the company said that we can do whatever we want, but we aren't going to beat them. They say that they are ready to pay in legal fees whatever they have to make sure they don't have to give us pay for the damage done to our hands. They say all this to make us give up. The doctors are also turning against us, not giving any of us a medical pension or even sick leave. They say that if they help us, they will have problems with the company and could lose their jobs.

We also work in close contact with dangerous chemicals. We use glues to stick the leather onto the steering wheel, and we use solvents to clean them. Some of the substances that we use are: Varsol, Butanol, trichloroethylene, Baltol, Locktite, "Cicomet" white glue, yellow glue No. 260 and No. 230. These are the names that we see everyday, but really we have no idea what kind of chemicals they are and what they contain. The company has never given us information or training on this.

Sometimes they give us latex gloves, but not always. We use masks, but these only protect us from dust, and not from vapors, and they don't even want to give them to us all the time. The toxics that we use are stored in open containers and they have very strong odors. We have to put our hands straight in them when we wet the towels to wipe the steering wheels. The solvents and the glues are kept in the chemical room, and only authorized persons can enter there. We have wanted to find out more about the chemicals that we use, but we don't understand anything because all of the labels are in English.

I feel very poor of health, and my blood pressure gets low. I often get dizzy, my neck and my head hurt, and at night I have trouble sleeping. Every morning when I enter the factory, my nose hurts, and I can smell the solvents very clearly. After a while of working, I get used to the smell and I don't notice it anymore. About halfway through the shift though, I feel like I can't think straight, my hands feel numb, my breathing gets short and I get pains in my chest. Sometimes I feel like quitting this job, I get so frustrated. But I know that I can't get a job in any other maquiladora, because the other factories don't accept people that have worked at Autotrim.

Reprinted from the newsletter of the Coalition for Justice in the Maquiladoras, San Antonio, TX. Originally published in *La Chamba de Cada Dia* (The Daily Grind), a newsletter for young workers published in Matamoros by the Pastoral Juvenil Obrera, a church group. Reprinted by permission.

I go to the company infirmary, and all they do is give me Naproxen and Lonol for the pain in my hands. The majority of coworkers complain of the chemicals, and they have all of the same problems I do. In 1993, the company was closed for a day by SEDESOL [the Mexican equivalent to EPA at the time]. Before this happened, the company had us hide all glue and toxic substances. It must have been that the company bought off the SEDESOL inspectors, because the plant began to work again and there were no changes at all. The company was working for more than six years without any kind of exhaust system, and only two years ago did they put one in place. But it's not sufficient.

Before, I wasn't so aware of what is happening in the factory. But about a year ago, my second son was born with anencephaly and he died. I really got angry, and I asked myself, what is going on here? Two weeks later, another baby girl was born to a woman at the plant, and she too died of anencephaly. Over the last year, there have been two babies born with anencephaly, one with hydrocephaly, and three with respiratory problems. Also, there have been more than ten miscarriages suffered to women at the plant.

Ever since all of this, I have been talking with my coworkers about what is going on. Just two months ago, I began to study the Federal Labor Law to learn my rights, participating in meeting of the Comité Fronterizo de Obreras. I have learned a lot, and my coworkers believe what I am saying.

I get really angry when I think of the injustices that they commit against me and my coworkers. I want to do something to prevent them from messing up more of us....

Someone has to stop this! Even though not all of my coworkers respond, there are many that do want to fight, and this motivates me to keep working hard. There have been a lot of difficulties, they don't offer any overnight hours any more and they have taken away the right to ask for permission to leave the plant. They keep their eyes on me all the times, and they've looked for excuses to fire me. But they aren't going to stop me. I am going to carry this through to the end.

Free Trade: The Politics of Toxic Waste
By Mary E. Kelly

The border town of Matamoros, located in northeastern Mexico across the river from Brownsville, Texas, was once a quiet ranching and agricultural community. Over the last decade, however, it has undergone a startling transformation. Under Mexico's border industrialization program, which provides incentives to U.S.-based companies to set up manufacturing operations along Mexico's northern border, Matamoros now has over ninety maquiladora factories, many of which are owned by U.S. corporate giants such as General Motors, AT&T, and Zenith. Mexico's woefully underfunded and politically weak environmental regulatory program has not kept up with the rapid industrialization. Maquiladora plants in Matamoros operate without the scrutiny and environmental controls they would have faced had they stayed in the United States.

The town's residents are now feeling the consequences of this neglect. Behind the Stepan Chemical plant, and just yards from the small, broken-down dwellings of Colonia Chorizo, environmental tests revealed the presence of xylene at levels more than 50,000 time the U.S. standard for safe drinking water. About half a mile away, in a canal near General Motors' Rimir plant, investigators discovered xylene at levels more than 6,000 times the U.S. standard.

The pollution is visible to the naked eye—orange and purple slime pours out of discharge pipes and flows down open canals, eventually discharging into a sensitive coastal lagoon south of Matamoros on the Gulf of Mexico. One can often see dead animals in these ditches. Children, oblivious to the contamination, play at the edge of the murky water. When the Matamoros city dump is on fire, as it often is, the billowing black smoke can be seen from the north side of the river in nearby Brownsville. A visit to the dump itself is like stepping into a nightmare of industrial society run amok. People scavenge among the acres of municipal trash and industrial waste, slogging through pools of black-gray water to find the most sought-after prize—a used industrial chemical barrel in which to collect water at their homes on the edge of the dump.

In the face of these horrendous environmental conditions, some residents of Matamoros have begun to mount a campaign for stronger environmental protection. Working with religious, environmental, and political groups in the United States, neighborhood leaders have developed a "toxic tour" of Matamoros. "We have had visits from countless major Mexican, U.S., and foreign media organizations, environmental activists, and U.S. congressional delegations," said María Teresa Méndez, one of the organizers. "No visitor goes away unmoved."

Efforts to call attention to the border's environmental problems have begun to bear fruit. U.S. House Majority Leader Richard Gephardt took the toxic tour of Matamoros in the fall of 1991. He met with colonia and *ejido** leaders while officials of the Mexican, U.S., and Canadian governments were negotiating the North American Free Trade Agreement (NAFTA). In a major trade policy speech to the Institute for International Economics in Washington in July, Gephardt spoke about the environmental devastation he had witnessed. "In Matamoros, some of America's biggest corporations dump toxic waste directly into the water supply— water that turns the colors of the rainbow," he said. "When I stood outside the homes of families living near Mexican factories owned by U.S. chemical corporations, the emissions made my skin burn." Gephardt went on to outline specific initiatives he argues should be enacted before Congress can approve NAFTA (see "Gephardt's Proposals," page 48).

Environmental issues have moved to the center of the public and congressional debates over NAFTA, with much of the focus on the U.S.-Mexico border region. Critics of NAFTA in both the United States and Mexico are concerned that the trade negotiations have been put on a fast track to bolster the political fortunes of President Bush and Mexico's President Carlos Salinas de Gortari. In the rush to complete NAFTA, these critics argue, the governments have failed to develop meaningful proposals to address the border's current environmental and health problems, or to provide the necessary resources and infrastructure to handle what is expected to be a significant increase in U.S. industrial investment in Mexico under a free-trade accord....

* *Ejidos* are cooperative peasant farms established through Mexico's agrarian reform program, which was launched in 1917 and further extended in the 1930s. They were privatized beginning in 1992.

Losing Control

Industrialization of the border has greatly increased the amount of hazardous waste being generated in the region, but tracking is woefully inadequate. Mexico does not keep an inventory of hazardous waste and, unlike the United States, Mexico does not have a law requiring industries to publicize basic environmental data on their operations.

Many of the plants use large amounts of toxic solvents, acids, metal-plating solutions, and other chemicals that result in hazardous by-products. The U.S. General Accounting Office (GAO), using information compiled by Mexico's environmental agency, reports that about half of the approximately 2000 maquiladoras in Mexico may generate hazardous waste. The limited environmental testing that has been done near maquiladora parks in the border region also shows the presence of high levels of toxic contaminants associated with hazardous waste.

Mexico's ground-breaking 1988 environmental law requires that most hazardous waste generated by U.S.-owned maquiladoras be returned to the United States. But Mexican and U.S. environmental officials acknowledge that they cannot account for most of the waste. According to data from the U.S. Environmental Protection Agency (EPA),

only 91 of the 600 maquiladoras along the Texas-Mexico border have returned waste from Mexico through U.S. Customs ports in Texas since 1987. The GAO concludes that, although Mexico is trying to create a stronger waste-management program, the Mexican government does not know how many maquiladoras are generating hazardous waste, the amount of waste generated, or the final disposition of that waste.

Hindering efforts to legally dispose of toxic waste is the lack of approved final disposal facilities in Mexico for toxic waste. According to law, the waste must be sealed in barrels and transported to landfills. There are currently only two authorized sites in Mexico—one in San Luis Potosí, and the other in Monterrey in the border state of Nuevo León. Rene Franco, an environmental consultant in Juárez, Mexico, says "the geographic location of these facilities, as well as their installed capacity, are far from satisfactory for existing industry, much less for the industry that will result from a free-trade agreement." The Mexican border had a toxic-waste incinerator in Tijuana, but its permit was revoked this June after neighboring residents protested. Proposals for two large waste dumps in Texas have generated vocal opposition from communities on both sides of the

Gephardt's Proposals

As the U.S. Congress prepares for hearings and debates about whether to approve NAFTA, environmental and public-health conditions in the U.S.-Mexico border region are in the spotlight.

In late July [1992], House Majority Leader Richard Gephardt laid down what many consider to be "bottom-line" conditions for Democratic support of NAFTA in Congress. The following are among his proposals concerning the border region's environment:

- Allow shareholders of U.S. companies that do business in Mexico to sue the company for failure to abide by Mexico's environmental laws.
- Treat the failure of Mexico-located companies to abide by environmental regulations as an unfair trade subsidy, entitling U.S. companies in the same industry to request protective customs duties.
- Expand the budget of the EPA's border and international operations.

- Expand U.S. "community right-to-know" statutes so that U.S. companies doing business in Mexico within 100 kilometers of the U.S.-Mexico border must inform the public of basic toxic-pollution emissions from their plants.
- Establish a binational commission along the border with the power and resources to address environmental enforcement, and basic water and waste water issues.
- Require U.S.-owned maquiladora plants to follow a "Code of Conduct," which addresses basic health, safety, and fair-wage issues.
- Enact a "cross-border transaction tax" on movement of goods between the United States and Mexico, with each country's revenues used to fund necessary programs in worker training, infrastructure development, and environmental protection.

border (see "Proposed Waste Dumps Spark Protest," page 50).

Much of the hazardous waste generated by maquiladoras and other border industries is being disposed of illegally. This January, in a public environmental forum in Monterrey, Mexico, then–Subsecretary of Ecology Sergio Reyes Luján said only 10 percent of the toxic waste generated by industry in Mexico goes to authorized disposal facilities.

The vast desert region of northeastern Mexico is a favorite location for clandestine dumps. In May, for example, environmental officials discovered a dump of over 600 barrels of toxic waste located about 20 miles south of Juárez, across from El Paso, Texas. Investigators have begun to trace many of the barrels back to U.S.-owned maquiladora plants.

Health Risks

Exposure to illegally disposed hazardous waste can occur in a variety of ways. In the border region, children play in open sewage canals which contain waste from industrial parks, and people fish in contaminated streams or use old hazardous-chemical barrels for storing drinking water. Exposure to such waste can have serious health ramifications, including various forms of cancer and birth defects. Recent investigations have begun to bring potential problems to light.

Health-care workers in Brownsville, Texas have documented a sky-rocketing rate of birth defects, particularly in the number of babies born with undeveloped brains, a condition known as anencephaly. Researchers have found that anencephaly rates in Brownsville are over three times the U.S. national average. In Matamoros, across the river, researchers have documented at least forty-two cases of anencephaly over the last year and a half.

"To date," says Gregoria Rodríguez, a health-care doctoral student and a volunteer at the Brownsville Community Health Clinic, "our research indicates that environmental toxins which are emitted by many of the maquiladoras operating in Matamoros may indeed be one possible cause of this tragedy." After the Brownsville/Matamoros anencephaly investigation received national attention in both the United States and Mexico, health-care workers in other border cities such as Ciudad Acuña and Juárez began reviewing their limited records and discovered similar anomalies.

Observers say the border's toxic waste crisis stems from two basic problems. First, Mexico lacks sufficient financial resources for a strong environmental enforcement and oversight program. Burdened by a foreign debt of over $100 billion, Mexico spent much less on environmental programs per capita in 1991 than the United States did, even though funding levels in Mexico increased 100 percent over 1990. The disparity between the amount that each country budgeted for hazardous waste management is striking. In the United States, the EPA had a 1991 hazardous-waste budget of over $300 million, supplemented by significant state spending on hazardous-waste regulation. Mexico, by contrast, had a 1991 hazardous-waste budget of only $2.3 million.

Limited resources also impede Mexico's ability to clean up illegal disposal sites. For example, at the recently discovered 600-barrel dump outside of Juárez, Mexican environmental investigators have been severely hampered by the lack of money needed for testing the ground water and soil samples for contamination. Moreover, Mexico does not have an equivalent to the U.S. Superfund Law, which requires those responsible for generating the waste to pay for the clean-up of abandoned disposal sites. Therefore, "it is not clear whether the land will ever be fully cleaned up," says Texas Water Commission Border Director Héctor Villa, whose agency has helped Mexico's environmental authorities transfer the barrels to an authorized disposal site.

Agreements Lack Teeth

Another basic problem is that the United States and Mexico have relied strictly on informal cooperation to deal with toxic waste in the borderlands. Under the La Paz Agreement, signed in 1983 by then-presidents Ronald Reagan and Miguel de la Madrid, the two countries agreed to work with each other to address a range of environmental problems in the region. Yet neither country devoted sufficient resources to set up an adequate binational system that would track the generation and disposal of toxic waste in the region.

This year, after the border's environmental woes were spotlighted during the debate over NAFTA, the two countries' environmental agencies agreed to deal with pollution with a new "Integrated Plan for the Mexico-U.S. Border." Included among the plan's goals for the next few years are improved surveillance and tracking of cross-border movements of toxic waste, as well as the ability to determine the amount of waste being generated by the maquiladora plants. However, the plan remains strictly an informal agreement.

The integrated plan is the centerpiece of efforts by presidents Bush and Salinas to convince the public in both countries that they are addressing border environmental issues. The Bush Administration also argues that NAFTA will improve Mexico's ability to deal with environmental problems because Mexico's revenues from foreign investment and trade with the United States will increase as a result of the agreement.

Proposed Waste Dumps Spark Protest

Proposals for two large toxic-waste dumps in Texas, both of which would be located within twenty miles of the Rio Grande/Rio Bravo, have spurred unprecedented binational concern among governmental and nongovernmental organizations alike. Chemical Waste Management, Inc. is proposing to build what would be one of the United States' largest toxic-waste landfills in Terrell County, about 100 miles upriver from Del Rio, Texas. A newly formed company called Texcor, Inc. wants to create a landfill for uranium mining and other radioactive waste in Kinney County, near Eagle Pass, Texas. These sites must receive a license from the Texas Water Commission, the state's primary environmental agency, before beginning operation.

The two proposals have garnered strong opposition, both in Texas and Mexico, prompting at one point a brief binational citizens' blockade of the international bridge between Eagle Pass and Piedras Negras, Coahuila. The proposals have also sparked formal diplomatic protests by Mexico to Washington, DC, and were a prominent issue at the U.S.-Mexico Border Governors' Conference in San Diego, California this April. In an unprecedented move, the state of Coahuila, the *municipio* of Ciudad Acuña, and Mexican environmentalists intervened in the Texas state proceedings to oppose the granting of permits for either site.

At first glance, the proposed Chem Waste site looks like an ideal spot for disposal of toxic waste, but appearances can be deceptive. Although the landfill would be located in somewhat isolated desert territory, the area's steep side canyons, giant underground caves, sink holes and limestone formations contain several potential pathways by which contamination from toxic waste could reach the ground water supply, says Robert Kier, an expert hydrogeologist hired by the City of Del Rio to evaluate the proposed site. The aquifer below the proposed site, known as the Trinity Plateau of the Edwards aquifer, supplies several fresh-water springs, among them San Felipe Springs, the City of Del Rio's sole water source. The aquifer also crosses the border into Mexico, although less is known about its exact configuration there. "If pollution escaped from the proposed landfill," says Kier, "there is little doubt that it could reach the San Felipe Springs and other important fresh-water springs in the area."

Opponents of the Chem Waste site are also concerned about the company's history of environmental violations at its other facilities. Says Del Rio City Attorney Jim Bayne: "This company has been assessed some of the largest penalties of violations of hazardous waste laws in the United States." A report by the environmental group Greenpeace, USA brands Chemical Waste Management's parent company, Waste Management, Inc., as "one of the world's biggest polluters." Greenpeace based its assessment on the company's record-setting payment of over $45 million in penalties and settlements in environmental cases of the last decade.

Opponents of Texcor, on the other hand, are concerned that the company does not have a track record to show it can safely operate its proposed radioactive-waste dump. According to Madge Belcher, a long-time Kinney County rancher and president of Communities Against Radioactive Environment (CARE), Texcor has never operated any waste-management site or any other type of industrial facility.

But what seems to most frustrate opponents on both sides of the border is the contradiction between the current governmental efforts to clean up the Rio Grande—spurred on by the desire to eliminate environmental objections to NAFTA—and the thought of major toxic-waste facilities being located nearby.

"It is incredible for the United States, on the one hand, to expect the government of Mexico to spend over $400 million to clean up the Rio Grande," says Belcher, "and, on the other hand, to sanction radioactive and hazardous waste dumps close to that same river."

Some critics claim both countries should permit greater cross-border cooperation among state and local governments. "It is the border communities that are feeling the impact of this rapid industrialization on a day-to-day basis," says Helen Ingram, director of the Udall Center for Public Policy at the University of Arizona. "It is those communities that can best make concrete progress in protecting their shared environment. But they can't do that if Washington, DC and Mexico City continue to insist on tight federal control over U.S.-Mexico environmental relations."

Calls for change are also being heard in Mexico. Alberto Székely, one of Mexico's leading environmental law experts who helped negotiate the agreement on behalf of Mexico, argues that although U.S. and Mexican environmental agencies have opened lines of communication since 1983, a new agreement is needed that would deal more forcefully with border environmental issues, particularly toxic waste.

Roberto Sánchez, the director of Urban Studies at the Colegio de la Frontera Norte in Tijuana, recommends creating a new binational environmental agency. Sánchez says this new agency could be given oversight authority for environmental and worker-health issues in the borderlands, and could help to coordinate the efforts of various federal, state, and local authorities.

Many observers feel that without a strong new agreement or treaty on border environmental issues to accompany NAFTA, problems such as the illegal disposal of toxic waste and battles over new disposal sites will continue. Those concerned with the welfare of border communities acknowledge that the NAFTA negotiations provide a golden opportunity to grab the attention of federal officials in both countries. Says Ingram: "We have not had this much attention to the border in years—and now is the chance for us to get some fundamental changes in the way we try to protect our shared environment. We just hope Washington and Mexico City are taking us seriously."

Workers' Health Is on the Line:
Occupational Health and Safety in the Maquiladoras
By George Kourous

In today's global climate of free market economics and de-regulation, workplace occupational health-and-safety (OHS) issues are anything but a priority for policymakers worldwide. The relocation of industry from "developed" nations to "developing" ones with regulatory structures attractive to foreign investors not only creates risks to the working populations of those countries but also fosters a dynamic in which safety-conscious corporations and nations with effective OHS enforcement become uncompetitive. Mexico's maquiladora sector provides an example of how free market pressures discourage effective OHS enforcement by national governments and transnational corporations alike. During the heyday of Mexican economic nationalism, the maquiladora program was regarded as an unfortunate necessity, required to earn foreign exchange, generate employment, and speed the process of industrialization. Since then, las maquilas *have become a linchpin in Mexico's development strategy. Sectoral growth rates of 10.5 percent in 1995 and 18 percent in 1996 indicate that this will remain true for some time to come, making close examination of the hazards threatening the health and safety of maquila workers more important than ever.*

… Working conditions in the maquilas vary from plant to plant. Some maquiladoras are well-run factories with enforced safety codes and adequate engineering controls, while others—too many—seem sprung straight from a Dickensian nightmare. Their activities range from sorting coupons for U.S. chain stores to automobile assembly to manufacturing complex electronics. A maquila worker may spend her or his days sewing steering wheel covers for new cars, varnishing furniture, or making batteries.

Wages are extremely low by U.S. standards (between $3-$4/day on the border) but, coupled with bonuses given for high production rates, provide a constant magnet for low-skilled workers from the economically stressed interior. Yet employee turnover in the maquilas is high—reach-ing 80 percent in some cities—in large part because of the stress and health-threats common to maquiladora work. A study published in the *International Journal of Occupational and Environmental Health* last year found that between 15 and 20 percent of female maquiladora workers in Tijuana had left their previous job due to concerns over OHS issues. Sexual harassment of female workers is another cause for high turnover. Because jobs are so readily available along the border, women who experience problems at one plant can easily quit and find similar work in another facility.

One hazard endemic to the maquiladoras is inadequate or nonexistent safety controls. Burns and cuts are common because heated or moving parts on production machinery are not guarded. Additionally, precautions for dealing with dangerous materials are inadequate. In late 1996, for example, PROFEPA (Mexico's environmental enforcement authority) closed a Juárez-based maquila owned by Bobinas del Sur after an explosion involving toxic substances left eight workers with third-degree burns. The facility was found to own neither protective clothing nor fire-fighting equipment, despite the fact that flammable and hazardous substances were regularly handled there.

Because safety controls are frequently lacking, exposure to a wide array of chemicals is a common health threat facing maquila workers. One study, whose results appeared last year in the *American Journal of Industrial Medicine* (*AJIM*), found that many maquila employees reported exposure to toxic materials in one form or another: 43 percent of those interviewed reported being exposed to dust-borne chemicals during at least part of their shift, while 45 percent reported gas or vapor exposure. The study also established a correlation between a number of neurotoxic symptoms and inhalation exposure to solvents, glues, and gums. Similarly, in a 1996 survey of maquiladora employees in Tijuana, the Comité de Apoyo Fronterizo Obrero Regional (CAFOR) found that 70 percent of workers reported excessive mucus formation when working in fume-ridden areas; 58.55 percent suffered from upper airway irritation; 57.65 percent complained of sore throats; and 76.5 percent experienced chest pain. These workers also endured rashes (62.5 percent) and hair loss (66.7 percent).

Originally published in *borderlines* 47 (Vol. 6, No. 6, Aug. 1998). Reprinted by permission of the Interhemispheric Resource Center, PO Box 2178, Silver City, NM 88062.

Skin contact with toxics is another threat to the safety of maquila workers: 41 percent of employees surveyed in the *AJIM* study reported that their day's work regularly involved handling chemicals. These workers experienced frequent problems with headaches, fatigue, depression, chest pain, insomnia, memory loss, stomach ailments, dizziness, and lack of sensation in their extremities. This type of numbness, known as peripheral neuropathy, has been associated with exposure to certain chemicals. A similar study, conducted in Tijuana, found that 35 percent of those surveyed handled chemicals on a daily basis, and according to CAFOR's 1996 survey, 21 percent of respondents reported illnesses they believed to have been caused by work conditions, with the lion's share attributed to chemical exposure.

Repetitious manual work and ergonomic stresses are, perhaps, the most common occupational health threat found in maquiladoras. Repetitive manual labor, especially if combined with additional stresses such as intense machine vibration or the repeated use of physical force, frequently leads to cumulative trauma disorders. Indeed, 21 percent of workers surveyed for the *AJIM* study reported pain, numbness, or tingling in one or both hands; others indicated they experienced chronic elbow, forearm, or shoulder pain.

A number of additional risks not directly linked to work can affect maquila employees. For instance, though most maquiladoras have on-site medical clinics, as mandated in Mexican OHS laws, these facilities are frequently underfunded, or the quality of the care they provide is compromised by the profit incentive. In early 1998, for example, *El Mañana* newspaper learned from workers at Ararat, a Wal-Mart subcontractor located in Nuevo Laredo, that the company doctor was giving them "vitamin pills" of an uncertain nature. Activists suspect the pills were probably amphetamines.

Food served by company cafeterias has been a source of worker illness as well. In a 1995 incident, 105 workers at a Philips maquiladora and 180 workers at an RCA maquila (both in Ciudad Juárez) suffered severe gastrointestinal pain and diarrhea after dining in the company eatery. And according to the *AJIM* study, 12 percent of workers surveyed in Reynosa reported that a toilet was not available in their workplace and that showers were rarely provided, even when there was an obvious occupational health rationale for having them.

Conditions in the smaller, boom/bust machine shops that operate on the fringes of the formal economy (Mexi-

can workers call them *golondrinas*—or swallows—because they can close up and fly away overnight) are even more untenable.

Management Often Forgoes Precautions, Neglects Training

There is a hierarchy of causal forces shaping the work environment of Mexico's border maquilas. Problems at the plant level related to an inadequate allocation of attention and resources to precautionary measures are reinforced at higher levels by insufficiently funded government OHS programs; budget allotments to oversight agencies, in turn, are constrained by development policies attuned to the needs of foreign investment and a social agenda profoundly influenced by the current global climate of austerity and free market reform.

Frequently, individual maquila facilities fail to implement legally mandated safety education programs. For example, 53 percent of the Tijuana/Tecate maquila workers surveyed by CAFOR had not received Material Safety Data Sheets (MSDSs) from their employers, as required by Mexican law. MSDSs explain hazards involved with substances used on-site and provide guidelines for treatment in case of exposure. Of the 27 percent who could identify the sort of chemicals they used at work, the responses were frequently generic terms such as "solvent," "acid," or "thinner." Compliance with the MSDS requirement in the electronics industry, in particular, was poor: 60 percent of workers employed in electronics plants indicated that they had never received any MSDSs from management. And 40 percent of all workers surveyed had not received any training from employers regarding on-site hazards or recommended protective practices.

A similar survey of maquiladora workers in Reynosa, Tamaulipas, conducted by the Centro de Estudios Fronterizos y de Promoción de los Derechos Humanos (CEFPRODHAC), yielded similar results: 72 percent of respondents had not received any training in handling toxic substances, 53 percent had no training in general health risks related to their work, and 50 percent hadn't been taught the proper execution of plant emergency response plans. (The same survey revealed that 75.8 percent of workers surveyed were interested in getting information and training in OHS, emergency response procedures, and labor rights.) Another study of employees at Reynosa/ Matamoros maquiladoras revealed that only 45 percent of surveyed workers reported that containers of chemical substances in their places of employment were labeled, and less than 20 percent reported that the labeling was complete and included information such as the name of the substance and how to treat adverse health effects. In fact, workers told researchers that the most credible health-and-safety information available was provided by unions or community-based organizations, not employers.

Failure of management to implement adequate worker protection controls is another frequent factory-level problem. For instance, "lock-out/tag-out" protocols and controls intended to cut off power to machinery during servicing are ignored, either to quicken repairs or to keep a jury-rigged, unfixed piece of equipment running. Indeed, such lockout failures are responsible for 27 percent of injury deaths in Mexico's automobile industry—the largest cause of occupational fatalities. Similarly, failure to guard (cover) moving parts is common. The CAFOR survey found that 26 percent of interviewed workers reported that points of operation, pinch points, and other potentially dangerous moving parts on the equipment in their places of employment were unguarded. A related problem involves noncompliance with legally required hazard-monitoring activities such as measuring for noise levels or airborne contaminants.

Adequate and appropriate protective equipment is oftentimes not made available to personnel. The CAFOR survey reveals that management failure to provide electronics workers with appropriate equipment and protective clothing is quite common: for instance, only 33 percent of electronics workers with exposure to airborne toxins reported being given filter respirators. And according to a 1997 CAFOR follow-up interview with a line supervisor at one Japanese electronics maquila, although management had given workers respirators, it had neglected to fit-test them to insure a protective seal and had not trained employees in their use. The supervisor added that workers frequently did not use the respirators, either because they were not aware of the need to or because they found the respirators uncomfortable due to the high temperatures common in the facility.

Plant-level problems are aggravated by an industry tendency to employ engineers as health-and-safety managers even if they have no formal OHS training. Additionally, effective training of employees is difficult due to high turnover rates, and parent companies are often unwilling to assume the added expense that ongoing, proactive, and context-sensitive training strategies in tune with worker's educational backgrounds require.

Plant Problems Aggravated by Global Economic Paradigm

Given the larger context surrounding the evolution of the maquiladora industry, these sort of plant-level problems are unsurprising. In addition to low wages, minimal or nonexistent taxes, and cheap supplies, an infrequently discussed but important reason behind the spread of foreign-owned maquilas in Mexico is lax enforcement of health-and-safety regulations. In a cycle of codependence, Mexico has come to rely on the benefits generated by the maquiladora sector (primarily foreign exchange and investment, employment, and technology transfer) while transnational corporations assess that they cannot profitably operate in the global economy unless they site their manufacturing facilities within the shelter of the developing world's export processing enclaves.

Some parent companies claim to enforce one global standard in all their workplaces, but maquila inspection visits by representatives from the corporate headquarters (usually between one and four times/year) are frequently announced ahead of time and conducted by non–Spanish speakers who are guided through the plant by management. According to Garrett Brown of the Maquiladora Health and Safety Support Network, "Impending corporate inspection visits are well-known in advance and site preparation happens often. Assuming you have a conscientious corporate rep coming in, he or she will have a difficult time getting an accurate picture of normal, day-to-day working conditions."

On the Mexican side, the incentive for policymakers to avoid taking too close a look at the ugly side of the maquila industry has a certain logic—over the last decade, the maquiladora sector has become a driving force of the country's economy. Indeed, in 1981 Mexican exports totaled $20.1 billion, with about 70 percent consisting of oil; today manufactures account for roughly 85 percent of all Mexican exports. Nineteen ninety-seven alone saw maquila-generated revenue climb 25 percent, while the amount of foreign exchange earmarked for servicing foreign debt rather than social spending generated by the sector (currently $6 billion/year) grew by 20 percent. And although only roughly eighteen cents of every dollar of maquila-generated export earnings is earned by someone in Mexico, the industry is the country's second largest employer. Unsurprisingly then, plant-level management problems are reflected by a general failure by Mexican authorities to monitor compliance with OHS regulations and to punish rule-breakers.

Primary responsibility for the enforcement of Mexican OHS laws falls to federal and state officials of the Secretariat of Labor and Social Welfare (Secretaría del Trabajo y Previsión Social—STPS). The STPS enforces the Federal Labor Law (Ley Federal del Trabajo—LFT), the Federal Regulation on Workplace Safety and Health, and more than 100 Official Mexican Norms (NOMs) covering specific hazards and activities. But the agency's inspections are infrequent and oftentimes cursory: most STPS activity involves office review of documents regarding injury and illness rates provided by plant management. Workers do have the right to initiate complaints with the STPS, but the agency is not obligated to undertake inspections as a result, and penalties against employers are issued only if companies fail to abate identified violations. Additionally, Mexican law places a great deal of responsibility for workplace health and safety in the hands of employers, and accident and illness investigations are frequently conducted by a single, employer-appointed engineer or safety officer, despite the fact that the law requires that workers be involved.

The agency is also charged with facilitating workplace OHS training sessions, but CEFPRODHAC's survey of Reynosa-based maquilas revealed that only 52 percent of interviewed workers reported having observed STPS participation in or oversight of training at their workplaces. In fact, only 47 percent could report ever having seen government inspections of workplace safety, and many indicated that inspections were either very intermittent or otherwise "extremely inadequate."

Unfortunately, because access to the maquiladoras is usually restricted, independent assessments of workplace safety are rare. Workers don't report violations for fear of reprisal—despite the fact that Mexican law calls for worker participation in plant safety management. Article 509 of the Ley Federal de Trabajo mandates the creation of workplace Comisiones de Higiene y Seguridad (Joint Management-Worker Hygiene and Safety Commissions —HSCs) whose role is "to investigate causes of accidents and diseases, propose measures for their prevention," report accidents, and check on compliance with safety laws. The commissions, however, only play a consultative role and do not have the ability to enforce their recommendations.

In theory, the HSCs offer workers the opportunity to play a participatory role in monitoring and ensuring workplace safety. Among their duties are monthly OHS reports presented to STPS, and all STPS inspection reports must by certified by the commissions. But fully active HSCs are few and far between. According to the CAFOR survey, 40 percent of respondents indicated that their workplaces had no functioning joint management-worker hygiene and safety commission.

Numerous flaws in the Mexican system of OHS enforcement were highlighted in February 1998 during hearings regarding a citizen's complaint—initiated under NAFTA's North American Agreement on Labor Cooperation (NAALC)—against the Korean-owned, Tijuana-based Han Young maquiladora, which makes chassis for Hyundai [see page 82 for excerpts from the official response to this complaint]. In June 1997, for example, an STPS inspection of Han Young produced forty-one separate health-and-safety violations, but no corrective action was mandated for eighteen of these infractions. Among these were the failure to provide workers with OHS training, a lack of on-site medical personnel, missing fire safety plans, and a lack of protective equipment. The STPS did require that the remaining twenty-three violations be abated within twenty-five days, but the agency's follow-up visit didn't occur until September 1997, at which point, despite the fact that management had been informed a week ahead of time of the impending inspection, the STPS found that six of the pre-existing violations remained uncorrected. Instead of imposing a fine, STPS officials gave Han Young another ten working days to correct the situation. The agency didn't return until January 1998, however, at which point it found new hazards in addition to thirty-six uncorrected older ones.

To a great extent, STPS effectiveness and credibility have been undermined by Mexico's recent economic crises and the reduced social spending imposed by the neoliberal remedies applied to those crises. Before the 1994 peso crisis, the STPS employed 800 inspectors, or one inspector for every 750 workplaces in Mexico. Today, the agency employs 333 inspectors, in spite of the explosive growth of maquila facilities in recent years.

The workload facing this small pool of inspectors is daunting. In addition to on-site inspection duties, their work involves reviewing numerous documents as well as miscellaneous administrative tasks in the office. A standard inspector's schedule only allows him or her one hour to inspect businesses with under 50 employees, two hours for businesses with 50–500 employees, and three hours for businesses with 500–1,000 employees. This includes travel time to and from the inspection site. (The handicaps restricting STPS activity are less an indictment of the Mexican government than of the current global climate of profit-driven social agendas: while Mexico had one inspector per

750 workplaces in 1990, the United States had one inspector per 2,500 workplaces.)

A study conducted by the International Labor Organization (ILO) in 1993 highlighted additional problems with STPS inspections. The ILO found that officials consistently failed to consult with either the HSCs or workers at inspection sites and tended to make only visual assessments of safety conditions. The ILO also reported that bribes were a common strategy used by management to solve inspection problems—unsurprising, given the small STPS budget and the low salaries paid inspectors. A similar pre–peso crisis study found that labor inspectors in Mexico did not have access to basic inspection equipment, such as sound meters and devices to measure airborne vapors, dust, and gases.

Finally, for many workers, employment is essential. For working-class families, the necessities of day-to-day life demand compromise, making organizing difficult despite labor's long history in Mexico. The anti-union climate in the maquiladoras (workers are ostensibly represented by "self-appointed" safety committees and by government-affiliated unions) simply means that workers, faced with blacklisting and unemployment, often accept work-related health-and-safety risks as a necessary trade-off.

Hazardous Waste Management on the Border: Problems with Practices and Oversight Continue

by Cyrus Reed, Texas Center for Policy Studies

The creation of Mexico's Border Industrialization Program (BIP) in 1965 sparked a period of rapid industrialization in the U.S.-Mexico border area that today continues apace as NAFTA takes hemispheric economic integration to new levels. One predictable by-product of the border's shift to a manufacturing-based economy has been a striking increase in the amounts of hazardous wastes being generated and disposed of in the region. The explosive growth of Mexico's in-bond manufacturing industry (maquiladoras), however, has not been matched by a concomitant expansion of the sort of infrastructure needed to deal with toxic by-products. Of the twenty-seven hazardous industrial solid waste facilities in Mexico, only two (both located in border states) are capable of handling the most dangerous of these substances. Current law mandates that maquiladoras return all hazardous wastes to their country of origin. Early next century, however, NAFTA will nullify this requirement, exposing a Mexican environmental services industry incapable of handling even domestically generated waste to a massive increase of incoming traffic.... Cyrus Reed of the Texas Center for Policy Studies takes a critical look at the state of hazardous waste management in the borderlands today, with an eye to that impending change.

Hazardous waste is defined in both Mexico and the United States as waste that is toxic, corrosive, ignitable, or reactive. In the United States, the Environmental Protection Agency (EPA) reports that about 279 million tons of hazardous waste were generated in 1995. In Mexico, on the other hand, the Instituto Nacional de Ecología (INE) can only estimate that about 10.5 million tons of hazardous waste were generated by manufacturing plants in 1997 (up from 8 million tons in 1996). Unfortunately, that year domestic and foreign-owned industry in Mexico only reported generating 1.4 million tons of waste, or about 13 percent of INE's estimate. This dearth of information regarding the generation and disposal of hazard-

ous wastes in Mexico is particularly problematic in the border region, where maquiladora industry compliance with hazardous substance reporting laws remains poor.

One of the highlights of 1992's U.S.-Mexico Integrated Border Environmental Plan was a computer database, called HAZTRAKS, that would track the movement of hazardous waste back and forth across the border. The binational system, it was hoped, would address troubling data gaps and permit effective management of hazardous wastes in the region. Six years later, HAZTRAKS provides on-line data for hazardous waste flows (at least from Mexico to the United States) and has even been used in a few high-profile cases to catch generators and shippers who weren't playing by the rules. Yet HAZTRAKS can hardly be labeled a success: the United States and Mexico can't agree on whether the numbers are correct, information on the flow of hazardous waste from the United States to Mexico is limited, and the input of hazardous waste manifest information from Mexico to HAZTRAKS has often been sporadic.

According to one study, by 1995 the border's maquilas were generating an estimated 164 tons of hazardous waste per day—nearly 60 thousand tons per year. Today, there are roughly 3,600 maquilas in Mexico, 2,000 of which are located in the 100-kilometer zone along the U.S.-Mexico border. Whatever the exact numbers are, the amount of hazardous waste reported in HAZTRAKS—7,796 tons in 1996—as flowing from Mexico to the United States is minuscule, a tiny proportion of the waste that foreign-owned maquiladoras in Mexico are likely generating.

Both Annex III of the 1983 U.S.-Mexico La Paz agreements and Mexican law require maquilas to return hazardous waste to the country from which their raw materials originated—usually the United States. The small numbers reported in HAZTRAKS fly in the face of this requirement. Clearly, hazardous waste is being improperly disposed of in Mexico, is entering the United States without being properly reported, and is being stored on-site by industries.

Indeed, even though Mexico currently has only two fully operational hazardous waste Treatment, Storage, and Disposal facilities (TSDs), requires maquilas to return haz-

Originally published in *borderlines* 46 (Vol. 6, No. 5, July 1998). Reprinted by permission of the Interhemispheric Resource Center, PO Box 2178, Silver City, NM 88062.

ardous by-products to countries of origin, and prohibits the import of nonrecyclable waste, INE reports that the amount of waste flowing from the United States to Mexico is twenty to thirty times greater than the amount shipped from Mexico to the United States. In 1996, according to INE, only 29.3 percent of U.S.-owned maquilas reported returning hazardous waste to the United States, while 5.4 percent disposed of waste legally within Mexico—leaving some 65.3 percent unaccounted for. Estimates from official Mexican sources regarding the amount of hazardous waste disposed of improperly throughout Mexico range from 75 percent (SEMARNAP, 1997) to 88 percent (INE, 1996). Borderlands environmentalists guess that illegal dumping in Mexico occurs even more frequently than these figures indicate.

Improper Management, Transportation, and Disposal a Major Problem in Mexico

The vast majority of hazardous waste in the United States is treated on-site. For example, Texas industries, which generate more than 50 percent of all hazardous waste in the United States, treat some 99 percent of their waste on-site, usually utilizing wastewater plants or underground injection.

But because hazardous waste generation is not adequately reported and monitored in Mexico, it is more difficult to assess how wastes are managed there. It is clear, however, that most waste generated in Mexico is not exported to the United States. In fact, the majority of hazardous waste generated in Mexico's border states is not reported to the government at all, according to INE's own estimates. For example, the agency reports that in the State of Chihuahua in 1997 an estimated 512,241 tons of hazardous waste were generated, but only 81,496 tons were reported and registered by participating companies.

Where does the rest of the waste go? Let's look at Ciudad Juárez. According to PROFEPA, Mexico's environmental enforcement division, there are 352 industries in Juárez that produce hazardous waste, and all but seventy of these return their wastes to the United States or send them to RIMSA, the hazardous waste landfill located near Monterrey, Nuevo León. PROFEPA also alleges that the wastes at the other seventy companies do not cause a problem because they are stored on-site.

But PROFEPA bases its analysis only on hazardous wastes that are reported in its internal tracking system and does not take into account hazardous waste that is never reported. A 1995 analysis of Annex III compliance completed under the World Bank's Northern Border Environmental Project Loan estimated that only half of the maquiladora firms in the Ciudad Juárez area were found in the HAZTRAKS database; of these, only one in ten shipped the expected quantity of hazardous waste back to the United States. In fact, only 20 percent of the total quantity of hazardous waste estimated to be generated by these companies was in fact shipped back.

There is abundant and ever-increasing evidence that large quantities of hazardous waste are simply being dumped in the desert around Ciudad Juárez. For example, in a series of stunning developments reported in the local press in 1995 and 1996, a number of industrial dump sites were discovered in the desert outside of Juárez. One of these sites, El Sauzel, was located a stone's throw from an industrial park and led to enforcement actions against Polímeros de México. Such unlicensed dump sites are common on both sides of the nearly 2,000-mile-long border, although in the United States they are usually limited to household waste and construction debris, not industrial waste.

In addition to illegal dumping, abandoned factories that closed or went bankrupt without adequately disposing of their hazardous wastes are also a problem. A well-known example in the Ciudad Juárez area is Condados Presto, closed through enforcement action by PROFEPA. Canisters of hazardous waste still litter the grounds of the New Jersey–owned company, and despite the existence of warning signs, children and vandals frequently visit the abandoned factory and some canisters have been stolen.

Transportation spills and accidents involving hazardous waste are also common. In 1995, for example, there were three consecutive accidents involving firms contracted by PEMEX—the national Mexican petroleum company—along the "Ecological Route," which (despite its name) passes through residential neighborhoods. Hazardous cargo transport routes are frequently established with an eye to minimizing costs rather than avoiding population centers.

Finally, an additional cause for concern is lax safety standards at facilities where waste is stored prior to cross-border transport. Fires are frequent at paper warehouses, cardboard plants, paint shops, and bulk gasoline stations as reactive or incendiary hazardous wastes are handled without proper controls. In July 1997, for instance, a Tijuana storage facility used to house toxic maquila waste prior to shipment to the United States caught fire for unknown reasons. Nearby neighborhoods were exposed to the smoke, and 500,000 gallons of water used to douse the fire escaped untreated into the city's sewer tunnels and, eventually, to the Pacific Ocean. The company that owns the facility, Pacific Waste Treatment, had previously operated a hazardous waste treatment facility in San Diego's Barrio Logan cited sixteen times for violations of safety regulations. Tijuana civil protection chief, Antonio Rosquillas, noted afterward that stricter building and construction codes are needed for hazardous waste facilities in Mexico, and a PROFEPA official observed that emergency response infrastructure is all too often lacking at such sites.

Pollution Haven Industrialization?

Many of the problems associated with hazardous waste management along the border are attributable to the economic development strategies Mexico has pursued in order to increase employment and exports. Mexico's industrialization in the 1960s and 1970s was based on the development of PEMEX and the border's maquiladora program. PEMEX, viewed for decades as the engine that would drive the Mexican economy toward first-world industrialization, was allowed to evolve with very few environmental controls and relative impunity from enforcement. Once regarded as a necessary evil needed to increase foreign investment and speed technology transfers, today maquiladoras occupy a central role in the Mexican economy. In addition to Mexico's cheaper labor market and the privileged tax status granted these facilities, lax enforcement of environmental law is tacitly understood to be one reason behind the maquila sector's ongoing expansion.

The industrialization of recent years, moreover, occurred without the development of basic infrastructure—wastewater treatment plants, hazardous waste management facilities, water treatment, and safe roads. Because maquilas pay few (if any) taxes, local governments have simply not been able to provide such basic services. Most of the taxes generated from maquila production have flowed to Mexico City and have not been redistributed equitably to the border region. During the debate on NAFTA, the estimated cost to provide the border with environmental infrastructure ranged from $8 to $20 billion.

This lack of infrastructure provides an economic incentive to dump illegally. As a study by the Tucson-based National Law Center for Inter-American Free Trade (NLCIFT) points out, because there are only two fully operational TSDs in all of Mexico, "companies are unwilling

to pay the costs of legal dumping in a market of few suppliers, often at large geographic distances from the site of generation." In Mexico, cash-strapped environmental enforcement agencies and a government determined to attract foreign investors do not provide an effective counterbalance to such market forces. In turn, though U.S. law does not prohibit the importation of hazardous waste from nonmaquila facilities, given transportation costs and U.S. EPA/Customs Service requirements, illicit dumping south of the border is by far the cheaper option.

The EPA does not track shipments of production materials to Mexico, nor would it have authority to force U.S. firms to return their hazardous by-products even if it were in possession of hazardous material import-export data. And Mexico's proximity, the relative ease with which southbound cargo passes through customs, and a higher standard of environmental enforcement in the United States contribute to illegal dumping south of the line. As NLCIFT's David Eaton observes, "the more costly it becomes to comply with the laws in the United States, the more incentives there are to export and illegally dump hazardous waste in other countries," which, he adds, leads to "the movement of hazardous waste along a path of least resistance to countries which have lower costs, reduced regulatory requirements, and fewer organized citizen groups."

Another pertinent factor is the effect that Mexico's episodic economic instability has on the effective enforcement of environmental laws. Every time the country suffers through a peso devaluation—as in 1982, 1987, and most recently, 1994—maquila employment and production have jumped. While peso devaluations help keep wages low and thus attract more investment, they also add an incentive to dump illegally, because the costs of proper management of hazardous wastes in the United States remain high—paid in dollars. Moreover, peso devaluations and the resulting economic crises have shrunk the funds available for spending on basic environmental infrastructure and enforcement of environmental rules.

Those environmental rules, including basic regulations on managing hazardous waste, weren't established until Mexico's 1988 General Law of Ecological Equilibrium was passed. Patterns of industrial activity in the maquiladora section were well-established long before then. (Part of the rationale for the 1983 La Paz agreement requiring that hazardous waste be returned to the United States was precisely that Mexico had neither the regulations nor the facilities to deal with hazardous waste.)

Even after passage of the 1988 law, Mexico has continued to attract industrial development and foreign investment by minimizing both labor costs—through pacts with government-controlled labor groups—and environmental costs—by not enforcing rules.

Where the political will to adequately oversee hazardous waste management in Mexico's border zone does exist, other barriers impair effective waste management—for example, the fact that Mexican law differentiates between imports of recyclable (permitted) and nonrecyclable (ostensibly not permitted) wastes. Additionally, since NAFTA's passage cross-border commerce has increased dramatically and is projected to continue to grow. As a result, Mexican customs officials not only have a larger volume of cargo to inspect but are also subject to intensified pressure to facilitate trade by keeping traffic moving. And, as a PROFEPA official admitted in a 1995 interview with NLCIFT researchers, "if waste clears Mexican customs as recyclable, there is little possibility of detection should the importer choose to dump the waste illegally rather than transport it to the designated recycling center."

As long as there isn't adequate enforcement, the incentive to dispose of waste properly doesn't exist. In addition, though state and local environmental officials may more closely monitor the day-to-day operations of industries in their areas, enforcement of maquiladora regulations and hazardous waste statutes is a federal responsibility in Mexico. Local officials must depend on PROFEPA and INE to inspect sites and enforce these regulations, usually with a meager staff to monitor more than 3,000 plants.

Another factor in the improper management of wastes is the lack of community participation in the policymaking process, particularly in Mexico. This situation is largely a result of the dearth of information available to the public about the types of waste being generated and handled by local industry.

U.S. law requires an opportunity for citizen review and comment on drafts of environmental impact statements (EIS) for proposed hazardous waste disposal sites, allowing community input in the process before the final EIS is issued. In general, community pressure on the U.S. side of the border has made it difficult to site new hazardous waste facilities—forcing companies to look for ways to reduce waste at the source.

In Mexico, however, public participation does not begin until the final EIS has been promulgated. Nonetheless, community pressure against proposed hazardous

waste facilities in Mexico has become more widespread in recent years (see *borderlines* Vol. 6, No. 4). Industry and government complain that such community-level resistance scares off foreign-based investors seeking to establish themselves in Mexico's environmental services market and prevents the development of an adequate hazardous waste disposal infrastructure. If the siting process were more transparent and involved community education at an earlier stage, however, this dynamic might change. Additionally, public attention generally focuses on disposal sites, and there is not a corresponding pressure on generators of waste to reduce dangerous by-products in the first place.

Current Management Options: 'End-of-Pipe' Technology Versus Pollution Prevention

A 1995 World Bank study concluded that excess treatment capacity exists in the United States for recovery, treatment, and disposal of hazardous wastes generated in Mexico, while the capacity to construct large, fixed-site, capital-intensive waste treatment and disposal facilities on the Mexican side is limited. Be that as it may, Mexico has opted to try to attract foreign investment in the building of capital-intensive waste treatment and disposal facilities, with some success.

For example, the Spanish firm TECMED recently began operation of a hazardous waste landfill roughly six kilometers outside of Hermosillo, Sonora, amid much controversy (see *borderlines* Vol. 6, No. 4). Last year, the facility began receiving shipments of hazardous waste from the Alco Pacifico waste site, an abandoned lead smelter and battery recycling plant just outside of Tijuana. Community groups in Hermosillo have protested the removal of the waste from Tijuana to Hermosillo, believing the CYTRAR landfill should only receive waste from industries within Sonora itself and not become a national dumping site for highly contaminated waste streams. They also point out that the municipality has never granted a land use permit for the site. Despite blockades by citizen groups and other public protests, the site remains in operation.

Mexico has also encouraged the practice of blending used oils, solvents, and other hazardous wastes to be burned in cement kilns. This practice has been advocated by both the cement industries themselves, which are attempting to save money on fuels, and by major hazardous waste management companies in the United States, including Waste Management, BFI, and Mobley Environmental Services. Currently, two cement plants in Mexico—Cementos Apasco in Ramos Arizpe, near Saltillo, Coahuila, and Cementos de México (CEMEX) in Torreón, Coahuila—have permits to burn "alternative fuels" while nineteen other plants in Mexico have received temporary permits to test-drive the technology (see *borderlines* Vol. 5, No. 6, June 1997).

The practice of burning alternative fuels in cement kilns has a long and complicated history in the United States. Currently, for example, more hazardous waste is burned in cement kilns in the United States than in incinerators, which must meet tougher air emission standards. Activists opposed to such facilities cite the dangers of the chemicals emitted (including dioxin and furans, persistent carcinogenic substances) and evidence of health impacts to area residents.

Although fuel blending and cement kiln burning in Mexico have so far been limited to Mexican wastes, under article 142 of Mexico's General Environmental Law, importing hazardous waste is permitted for recycling. If burning hazardous wastes for energy recovery is considered to be a form of recycling—as it is in the United States—then Mexico could import hazardous wastes for incineration as the number of cement plants seeking alternative fuel increases. Not surprisingly, environmental groups in both countries are opposed to the practice of burning hazardous wastes.

Finally, Mexico has been promoting the establishment of a series of Integral Industrial Waste Management Centers (CIMARIs) having waste disposal, fuel blending, recycling, and treatment components to alleviate the country's lack of disposal facilities and to increase its market share of the waste disposal industry. Currently, eight Mexican companies (most of whom have a U.S. partner) have been approved by INE as meeting the technological requirements to establish a CIMARI.

One of those companies, Servicios Ambientales de Coahuila, has proposed building a CIMARI just north of the town of General Cepada, Coahuila, between Saltillo and Torreón near an important water reservoir and migratory bird sanctuary called Presa de Tulillo....A $70 million joint venture between RACT, a Utah-based management company, and CleanMex, a Tamaulipas company, the landfill and recycling facility now appears stalled due to opposition from farmers, ranchers, residents of Saltillo and Torreón, and Mexico's political opposition parties.

As with Hermosillo's CYTRAR facility, the proposed General Cepada site was supported and approved in virtual secrecy by the local municipality. And before the plans

were made public, INE gave the green light to a "preventative study." Unsurprisingly, when the plans became public, community concern was both passionate and widespread. INE then backpedaled, declaring that a more rigorous environmental impact statement would be necessary.

Although production techniques that reduce the amount of hazardous by-product produced in the first place are preferable to "end-of-the-pipe" technology that deals with waste only after it has been created, the fact remains that Mexico is indeed in dire need of adequate, safe, and professionally managed disposal sites. Both noncompliance with the law requiring an official EIS and exclusion of nearby communities from the planning process make this task unnecessarily more difficult and expensive than it already is.

Government and Market Responses to the Problem

The United States and Mexico have both adopted similar waste management hierarchies. At the top of their list are source reduction and waste minimization—in other words, either not producing the waste in the first place or minimizing the waste stream through better pollution control or internal recycling. Under the binational Border XXI Program, Mexico and the United States have formed both a Solid and Hazardous Waste Workgroup and a Pollution Prevention Workgroup.

North of the border, the EPA and the Texas Natural Resource Conservation Commission (TNRCC) have voluntary programs in which major industries pledge to reduce hazardous wastes or emissions of toxics by a significant percentage. The Border XXI Program has attempted to extend this effort to Mexico through a series of workshops and conferences. The TNRCC has even conducted plant visits at maquiladoras in Mexico to help companies locate opportunities for source reduction.

In Mexico, the government has promoted a voluntary auditing program in which (in return for enforcement leniency) companies inspect their own plants for opportunities to reduce waste generation and emissions and to improve worker safety and compliance. Many companies such as Cementos de México have conducted environmental audits and signed agreements with PROFEPA to implement plans based on those audits.

But voluntary pollution prevention programs in Mexico and the United States, while potentially valuable, often ignore the important role that enforcement—as well as input from citizens and workers—must play if the process is to be successful. Part of the reason voluntary source reduction programs work in the United States is that the cost of managing hazardous wastes is so high—it is cheaper for companies to reduce wastes than to dispose of them. The market only works this way, however, where enforcement is stringent.

If most of the waste in Mexico cannot be tracked by enforcement agencies, it is not in a company's best interest to account for it through auditing procedures—and then be obligated to manage it. In the United States, right-to-know laws such as the Emergency Planning and Contingency Response Act (EPCRA) force manufacturers to report the toxics they emit and transfer to the government. That information—by law—is then accessible to the public. In Mexico, on the other hand, toxics and hazardous waste information remains a private matter. Without citizen oversight of how much companies generate and whether they are actually reducing waste, effective community pressure is absent, and volunteer auditing and reduction programs will fall well short of the mark.

Nongovernmental organizations in Mexico have been struggling for years to force both government and industry to adopt right-to-know regulations, but with only limited success. Mexico has officially adopted a Pollutant Release and Transfer Register and has begun inventorying industries, but this information has remained in government hands. Local citizen and environmental groups that have tried to negotiate directly with companies in Mexico about source reduction and emergency planning issues have had limited success, due in part to the lack of basic environmental information.

INE is currently creating a "vulnerability atlas" for the entire length of the U.S.-Mexico border. The idea is to determine the most appropriate sites for the management, treatment, storage, and disposal of hazardous waste. According to INE's Luis Wolf, one of the Border XXI Solid and Hazardous Waste Workgroup coordinators, Mexico will use the atlas to conduct meetings in each state to determine appropriate locations for facilities. In this way, Mexico hopes to prepare for changes in the year 2000 when few companies will be required to return waste to the United States and avoid public opposition to hazardous waste sites, as has occurred in Saltillo and Hermosillo. The EPA has offered $10,000 to Mexico to help conduct public meetings, but Mexico has refused the money.

Despite these more proactive government responses, it is clear that the hazardous waste management agenda on the U.S.-Mexico border is and will continue to be set largely by the free market and in the boardrooms of major U.S. hazardous waste management companies like Waste Management and Brown Ferris Industries. Already, these industries have promoted the blending of hazardous wastes into the fuels burned in Mexican cement plants as an acceptable management option. As the amount of hazardous waste generated in the border region increases, these firms will play an influential role in determining how this waste is managed. And as long as government oversight remains lax, grassroots opposition to waste disposal practices will remain the only force prompting industry to explore more responsible alternatives.

FOUR
CROSS-BORDER
INITIATIVES

Margarita del Angel, a worker from Reynosa, Tamaulipas who assembles car parts and air conditioners for a subsidiary of General Motors (GM), had a chance to discuss workers' concerns with company executives when she attended the firm's annual shareholders meeting in May 1997. Del Angel traveled by plane to Wilmington, Delaware, where she discussed the problem of abysmal wages in the maquiladoras with GM's president and chief executive officer, John F. Smith.

Del Angel, who earns less than $45 a week for forty-two hours of work, also challenged GM's failure to make legally mandated profit-sharing payments in 1996. According to the Mexican constitution, as well as the country's labor code, all firms operating in Mexico must distribute 10 percent of their annual profits to their workers. In order to maximize the benefits of moving across the border, however, most U.S.-based firms categorize their maquiladora operations as "cost centers," in which parts are "assembled" but not "manufactured." The corporations arrange their accounting systems so that the maquilas reflect the lowest possible profits. GM thus argued it was justified in paying its Reynosa workers only 200 pesos ($26.67 U.S. dollars in 1996) for profit sharing in 1995, even though the company grossed nearly $7 billion and enjoyed the most profitable year in its history.[1]

Del Angel's trip to Wilmington was sponsored by AFSC and the Interfaith Center for Corporate Responsibility (ICCR), a New York-based group that utilizes the stock holdings of major religious bodies to raise issues of corporate accountability at strategically selected shareholders' meetings. Also sponsoring the trip was the Mercy Consolidated Asset Management Program, another church-based investment group that owns GM stock.

Two other GM workers from Reynosa who had planned to attend the meeting decided to cancel their trip, after Human Resource personnel in their plant called them in and began asking them about their parents' names and other personal information.

In response to her comments at the shareholders' meeting, GM's president suggested to Del Angel that she apply to participate in the company's housing program, which aims to help build 7000 houses for GM's Mexican workers, and has provided materials for the construction of fifty homes in Matamoros. Nonetheless, notes Margarita, "the housing program will only help one in 200 workers in Matamoros. We all need money to improve our housing. It would be better to have a just wage than a housing program."[2]

GM's housing program resulted from another ICCR initiative—a 1995 tour of workers' neighborhoods in Reynosa by GM executives from Detroit, as well as some of the company's local managers. There they saw firsthand how workers live in shacks built of sheets of corrugated metal, with no running water or electricity. While ICCR members commend GM's efforts to ease their workers' misery, they have criticized the program as "unaffordable to most maquiladora workers."[3]

Behind the trip to Delaware was an ongoing campaign by Mexican GM workers and their allies protesting the company's failure to distribute profit sharing payments. In mid-1997, two weeks of organized *paros*, or work stoppages, resulted in a mixed victory for GM workers in Reynosa. The company ended the *paros* by offering workers 600 pesos each (about $77). While most workers seemed pleased with the amount, some were dissatisfied with GM's response to their grievances.

"The company thinks with 600 pesos they can buy

us," commented Celia, a GM worker, "but we still have not gotten what we wanted." She said the workers will not stop until they win fair treatment, a good salary, and share of the profits. "This isn't profit sharing," according to Celia. "This is only some money to make us shut up."[4]

A Growing Trend

At the border and beyond, the adoption of the North American Free Trade Agreement (NAFTA) has underscored the importance of international alliances to defend the interests of working people in the face of global economic integration. As revealed in the example given above, such alliances can be highly effective in increasing the visibility of maquiladora issues. While concrete gains for maquiladora workers have been more modest, current cross-border campaigns lay an indispensable foundation for longer-term struggles.

One key grouping for cross-border initiatives has been the Coalition for Justice in the Maquiladoras (CJM), which defines itself a "trinational coalition of religious, environmental, labor, Latino, and women's organizations that seek to pressure U.S. transnational corporations to adopt socially responsible practices within the maquiladora industry, to ensure a safe environment along the U.S.-Mexico border, safe working conditions inside the maquila plants, and a fair standard of living for the industry's workers."[5]

The CJM has developed the "Maquiladora Standards of Conduct" (included in the readings at the end of this chapter). Individual corporations are pressured through various means to pledge their adherence to these standards, which are based on widely held ethical principles that are embodied in Mexican and U.S. labor law, as well as in standards established by the International Labor Organization, an agency of the United Nations.

In recent years, the CJM has moved to deepen its commitment to binational cooperation on maquiladora issues. As a result of the organization's efforts to increase the voice and participation of Mexican individuals and groups, since 1997 more than 50 percent of its board members have been representatives of Mexican organizations. CJM's executive director, Marta Ojeda, is a former maquiladora worker who became involved in activism through a 1994 campaign to form an independent union at a Sony Electronics plant in Nuevo Laredo, Nuevo León. Ojeda was one of numerous workers who were fired for their organizing activities, in an incident that led to the first major complaint filed under NAFTA's labor side accord (see chapter 6 for additional details).

Strategic Tensions

Ojeda's story highlights some of the conflicts and tensions that underlie maquiladora activism. On the Mexican side of the border, union activity has long been dominated by groups affiliated with the Confederación de Trabajadores Mexicanos (CTM—Federation of Mexican Workers), a body that forms an integral element of Mexico's ruling Partido de Revolución Institucional (PRI—Institutional Revolutionary Party). CTM unions have often been unresponsive to the needs of the rank and file, a problem that is aggravated in the border region. In extreme cases, they have exhibited the worst traits of business unionism, signing "protection contracts" without the knowledge of their members and using political muscle and, sometimes, violence to keep workers in line. In other cases, CTM unions have represented the interests of their members, while nonetheless discouraging the active participation of the rank and file.

Mexican organizations and social movements have differed widely in their response to the CTM. Some groups, including the Comité Fronterizo de Obreras (CFO), have tended to work inside CTM structures, seeking to make official unions more responsive to women's leadership and rank-and-file participation. Others have worked to build unions that are independent or affiliated with smaller and more militant federations.

The maquiladora industry has been particularly ferocious in its opposition to independent unions, as evinced by the ongoing struggle of workers at the Han Young maquiladora in Tijuana, a contractor that manufactures truck chassis for the Hyundai Corp. In 1997, Han Young workers voted to affiliate with the independent Union of Workers in the Metal, Steel, Iron, and Connected Industries (STIHMACS). Subsequently, the company, the CTM, and local labor authorities sought to prevent recognition of the independent union, through a combination of legal challenges, stonewalling, and outright violence. Han Young workers have nonetheless persisted in their efforts, garnering extensive support and publicity from U.S.-based groups.

When STIHMACS was finally recognized by the local labor board, after winning two successive elections at the plant, the company refused to negotiate. Health-and-safety conditions in the plant have been a particular focus of the Han Young campaign, and the U.S. National Administrative Office (NAO), the body charged with administering NAFTA's labor side accord, issued blistering criticisms of Han Young in an August 1998 report. Most recently, in September of 1998, the company closed down the plant and moved to another area of Tijuana, where it was operating with a skeleton crew of replacement workers.*

For some U.S.-based unions, the divisions between independent and official unions in Mexico have restricted their participation in cross-border alliances. In international union structures, the CTM is the official counterpart to the AFL-CIO, the major U.S. labor federation, and AFL-CIO unions have traditionally worked exclusively through union-to-union contacts. Some union activists have sought to sidestep the issue by working in cooperation with coalitions like the CJM, echoing the trend inside the United States toward greater reliance on working in coalition with religious and community groups. Others have forged direct ties with Mexico's independent labor movement.

A notable example of the latter approach is the United Electrical, Radio, and Machine Workers of America (UE), which has long emphasized the importance of international solidarity. UE, which parted ways with the AFL-CIO in 1950, has not hesitated to look beyond the CTM for cross-border partnerships. In 1992, it formed a "Strategic Organizing Alliance" with the Frente Auténtico del Trabajo (FAT—Authentic Labor Front), an autonomous Mexican federation uniting independent unions, cooperatives, peasant groups, and neighborhood organizations. STIHMACS, the union chosen by workers at Han Young, is a FAT affiliate.

As a result of the UE/FAT alliance, the CETLAC Workers' Center was opened in 1996 in Mexico's second largest border city, Ciudad Juárez in the state of Chihuahua. CETLAC offers maquiladora workers education on labor issues, legal assistance, and a progressive vision of what labor unions can and should do. UE supported the establishment of the center because "it is our belief that this workers' center is a good step toward helping the people who work in the maquiladoras become educated about their rights on the job and their right to join the union of their choice," according to UE President John Hovis.[6]

As noted in chapter 1, a major realignment is currently underway in Mexico's labor movement, in the wake of the 1997 death of Fidel Velázquez, head of the CTM since 1940, as well as other political changes. These changes are already having an impact on cross-border initiatives, as Mexico City–based organizations forge stronger ties with groups in the traditionally isolated border region. Meanwhile, the increased legislative clout of the Partido de Revolución Democrática (PRD—Democratic Revolutionary Party) has given greater legitimacy and support to labor militancy.

A Living Wage

ICCR, the group that funded Margarita del Angel's trip to Delaware, has a long history of support for worker solidarity. In the words of David Schilling, director of the group's Global Corporate Accountability Programs, "ICCR members have raised their voices in corporate boardrooms and shareholder annual meetings since 1971, when the Episcopal Church filed the first religious shareholder resolution calling on General Motors to divest of its operation in apartheid South Africa."[7]

In 1995, ICCR launched a living wage campaign, with the cooperation of CJM and maquiladora workers. According to Schilling, "U.S. companies rationalize paying poverty-level wages in two ways. They point out that wages paid to workers are competitive with what other companies are paying in a specific area and that the wages paid to workers are above the minimum wage set by governments. But workers in Mexico and elsewhere can be paid a competitive wage well above the minimum required by law and still not be able to feed themselves and their families."[8]

The living wage campaign was undertaken in response to the loss of purchasing power of the Mexican peso, a trend that began in the 1980s and took an especially precipitous drop after the December 1994 devaluation. Citing research showing that maquiladora salaries are not adequate to meet workers' basic survival needs,[9] the campaign calls on companies to pay a "sustainable living wage" to their workforce. Shareholder resolutions were filed by religious investors at twelve maquiladora firms, calling on the companies to review and adjust wages and benefits in their Mexican operations. The resolutions came to the floor in nine cases and received votes ranging from 4.4 to 8.5 percent, "expressing serious shareholder concern with these issues."[10]

Workers like Margarita del Angel hope that such efforts will convince companies of the injustice of their low wages. When Margarita met with GM CEO John F. Smith, she urged the businessman to consider another side of company operations. "It's very important that you treat us like human beings," she said.[11]

---

* Excerpts from the NAO report on health-and-safety violations are included among the readings at the end of this chapter. The report on freedom of association (Public Report of Review of NAO Submission No. 9702) is available from the U.S. NAO in the Department of Labor.

Notes

1 "Message from the U.S./Mexico Border to GM's Board of Directors and Shareholders," Interfaith Center for Corporate Responsibility, New York, May 23, 1997.

2 "'Pay Us a Living Wage!' Mexican General Motors Workers Tell GM Chairman Jack Smith in Historic Face-to-Face Meeting," Interfaith Center on Corporate Responsibility, New York, May 23, 1997.

3 Ibid.

4 Interview with Anya Hoffman, Reynosa, June 1997.

5 Coalition for Justice in the Maquiladoras, 1996 Annual Report, CJM, San Antonio, p. 2.

6 Judy Ancel, "Exploring Workers' Rights on a New Frontier," United Electrical Workers, Washington (reprinted from *UE News*), n.d.

7 David M. Schilling, "Sneakers and Sweatshops: Holding Corporations Accountable," *Christian Century*, October 9, 1996.

8 Ibid.

9 Rev. David Schilling, "Maquiladora Workers Deserve a Sustainable Living Wage," *ICCR Brief,* Vol. 23, No. 10, 1995.

10 Ibid.

11 Jeanne Russell, "Maquila laborer talks issues with GM brass," *The Monitor,* McAllen, Texas, June 23, 1997, p.8.

READINGS

Since the late 1980s, U.S. labor unions have become increasingly involved in maquiladora activism. Two staff members of the United Electrical Workers, Robin Alexander and Peter Gilmore, offer an overview of labor initiatives in "The Emergence of Cross-Border Labor Solidarity." Their article also offers a deeper discussion of the tensions between official and independent unions in Mexico and the response by trade unions in the United States. Alexander is UE's director of international labor affairs, while Gilmore is editor of the UE News.

Since Alexander and Gilmore published their analysis in 1994, further changes have occurred in the volatile scene of Mexican labor. Perhaps most significantly, in November 1997, a new labor confederation, the Unión Nacional de Trabajadores (UNT—National Workers Union) was formed to advance the cause of independent unionism in Mexico. The move followed the collapse of traditional union power structures after the death of Fidel Velázquez earlier that year. In forming the UNT, three major unions—the Mexican Telephone Workers Union (STRM), the Union of Workers of the National Autonomous University (STUNAM), and the Union of Social Security Workers (SNTSS)—joined together to challenge the dominance of the two major federations linked to Mexico's ruling party, the Confederation of Mexican Workers (CTM, the organization headed by Velázquez for nearly six decades), and the Congress of Labor (CT).

According to the UNT, its affiliates soon included nearly 150 unions, representing 1.5 million workers. A year later, however, UNT leadership conceded that the new federation had so far failed to fulfill the vision of forging a militant new front to fight for the overall demands of Mexican workers. The new federation has not engendered significant organizing efforts, and at times has even allied itself with the CT and CTM to form a "workers' bloc" to jointly negotiate changes

in the Federal Labor Law with the government and employers.

Nonetheless, the UNT continues to offer a space where independent voices can demand a clear responses from the government to the new federation's platform of union democracy, political independence, and an alternative framework for economic policy. Further, its very existence has legitimized the right of debate and dissent in the unions. (For ongoing updates, consult Mexican Labor News and Analysis, *available through UE's website at http://www.igc.apc.org/unitedelect/alert.html.)*

A second reading, "Reaching Across the Rio," originally published in the now-defunct periodical Beyond Borders, *chronicles a worker-to-worker interchange cosponsored by the Tennessee Industrial Renewal Network and the CFO.*

Illustrating a different type of cross-border strategy, two excerpts from "Double Standards: Notes for a Border Screenplay," recount the case of Mendoza v. Contico, *in which a Texas court agreed to hear a case charging a St. Louis manufacturer with criminal negligence in the horrific death of one of its Mexican employees. While the case was settled before it could go to the jury, it marks a significant moment in the ongoing struggle to hold parent firms legally accountable for the behavior of their maquiladora subsidiaries.*

Next, excerpts are presented from the National Administrative Office's report on working conditions at the Han Young plant in Tijuana (see page 64 for a discussion of efforts to organize an independent union at Han Young). The report offers another example of the use of NAFTA's labor side accord as a mechanism for cross-border organizing, and represents an unusually strong confirmation of activists' concerns in an official government document.

The final selection for this chapter is the Maquiladora Standards of Conduct, developed as an organizing tool by the Coalition for Justice in the Maquiladoras.

The Emergence of Cross-Border Labor Solidarity

By Robin Alexander and Peter Gilmore

For six years Fernando Castro had responsibility for the management of chemicals at a motor plant owned by General Electric (GE) in the Mexican border city of Juárez. Last November he was fired for union organizing, a relatively common occurrence in Mexico. But this time, things were different. In the shadow of the NAFTA debate, a spotlight was cast on the dismissals at this GE plant. By early February, the soft-spoken technician was on tour in the United States, stressing to North American audiences the importance of the assistance that the Mexican workers and their union had received from trade unionists north of the border.

"I want to tell workers here," Castro said, "that some of us who have been fired are continuing to organize from the outside, together with workers on the inside. I am here to make a commitment to those who are supporting our efforts that we will not stop until we have succeeded in organizing the plant."

The GE motor plant, Compañía Armadora or CASA, employs approximately 950 workers and 100 supervisory staff. It produced 35,000 small motors in 1993—up from 24,000 the previous year. Work at the plant largely came here from a Decatur, Indiana plant closed in 1989, which had been represented by the United Electric, Radio & Machine Workers of America (UE). The hourly wage of GE workers in Decatur—approximately $13.50—was more than twice the daily wage of their Mexican counterparts in Juárez.

"Workers in the United States and Canada share a common interest in ensuring that Mexico workers are successful in organizing democratic unions and improving wages and benefits," says UE Secretary-Treasurer Amy Newell. "If they fail, we share a future of common misery. I prefer to think of a future where we sit together at the bargaining table with trade unionists from Mexico and Canada, and together take on transnational corporations such as General Electric and Honeywell."

For these reasons, explains Newell, UE and Mexico's only independent labor federation, the Authentic Labor Front (FAT), created a Strategic Organizing Alliance two years ago. "We believe it is imperative that we develop a new kind of international solidarity—one which is focused on organizing."

In this alliance, FAT agreed to target transnational companies in the maquiladora zone that have a bargaining relationship with UE in the United States. Since last summer, UE and STIMAHCS, the metal workers' union affiliated with FAT, have targeted the Juárez plant. UE has also established a solidarity fund, and recently launched a sponsor-an-organizer campaign to encourage unions, individuals, and other concerned organizations to contribute a fixed amount each month for a year. This will enable FAT to finance its budget and to put some of the fired workers back to work as organizers.

From November 4 to 7, 1993, a delegation composed of General Electric workers from UE Locals 506, 731, and 1010 met with workers from Compañía Armadora engaged in organizing. The U.S. delegation toured the neighborhood where the majority of Mexican GE workers live, and discussed ways in which GE workers in the United States could support the efforts of the Mexican workers to organize a union. A MacNeil/Lehrer news team filming a story on cross-border organizing accompanied the delegation during part of its trip.

Revelations that GE management had actively obstructed union-organizing efforts outraged (but did not surprise) the UE members. They learned, for example, that the company now requires buses to drop workers off inside company property, so as to prevent them from receiving union literature. In other instances, managers snatched union literature out of workers' hands.

More serious, last fall GE terminated or pressured into "voluntary" resignations more than 100 Mexican workers, including a woman who attended the UE convention last August in Cleveland. This was widely perceived as an effort by GE to rid itself of senior workers, of workers who speak up or complain about shop conditions, and of union activists. Because the economic pressure on workers to accept indemnification (legally mandated severance pay) is so extreme, most of them leave quietly and do not challenge the company's actions.

The Mexican GE workers revealed that the company uses chemicals which have been banned at U.S. GE facilities. They described a variety of other violations, including failure to pay overtime properly, give light work to pregnant women, provide adequate protective equipment and properly ventilated work areas, comply with the health-and-safety requirements, and properly test workers who may have been exposed to chemicals or inform them of the results of these exams. The U.S. and Mexican workers also discovered that they were subject to the same unacceptable company practices—such as providing pizza, in lieu of compensation, to workers who meet major production goals. Out of these conversations, the workers began to develop plans for future communication and support.

Upon their return to the United States, two UE locals immediately shipped a typewriter and health-and-safety information to STIMAHCS in Juárez. On November 22, UE leader Amy Newelll wrote to the U.S headquarters of General Electric outlining the types of labor-law violations described by the Mexican GE workers, and requested a company investigation and corrective action. An article about the trip was published in the November 19 edition of the *UE News*.

Then the reprisals began. Over the course of the next two weeks, GE fired ten Mexican workers, all for spurious reasons related to union activity and what the company called "insubordination." Most had attended the meeting with the UE delegation. Among those fired were the man who hosted the gathering with UE and a worker interviewed on MacNeil/Lehrer.

As news reached UE's Pittsburgh headquarters, Newell wrote a series of letters to General Electric. She gave the company until December 10, the date of a previously scheduled Conference Board meeting of UE leaders from GE plants, to correct the situation. When the board convened, delegates instructed Newell to inform President Clinton about the firings. They stressed the need for prompt action in light of the promises to protect labor rights made during the NAFTA debate.

On December 22, General Electric advised UE that it had offered to reinstate six of the ten fired workers. GE sent form letters to those people who inquired about the Juárez firings, declaring that all of the workers in question had accepted statutory severance pay. In fact several of the fired workers—one of them Fernando Castro—have refused all deals, and are demanding their jobs back.

Meanwhile, at Honeywell's Chihuahua plant—a sec-
ond factory targeted by the Strategic Organizing Alliance—low pay, lack of protective equipment and poor treatment by management had convinced workers to organize as a local of STIMAHCS, the metal workers' union. The company responded viciously, coercing twenty women into signing statements that said they were voluntarily resigning. Management interrogated the women individually for up to four hours, in some cases offering them money if they revealed the names of those responsible for the organizing effort.

The Honeywell management offered in-shop organizer Ofelia Medrano a deal: if she signed a statement assuming responsibility for the organizing campaign and pledging to abandon the campaign, the company would guarantee her continued employment at the plant. After hours of harassment, Medrano eventually signed the statement, but was fired anyway. The Teamsters Union, which represents many organized Honeywell workers in the United States, took the initiative in developing the U.S. support effort for the Mexican workers. The Teamsters encouraged concerned trade unionists to write protest letters to the company and President Clinton.

Dissatisfied with the responses of GE and Honeywell, and with the failure of President Clinton to even answer their correspondence, UE and the Teamsters took further action. On February 14, the two U.S. unions—with the full support of FAT—filed the first two complaints under the labor side agreement of NAFTA, with the U.S. National Administrative Office (U.S. NAO), a small agency housed in the U.S. Department of Labor. The unions requested that the U.S. NAO initiate an investigation and hold hearings on the mass firings and numerous labor-rights violations committed by GE and Honeywell in response to organizing campaigns at their Juárez and Chihuahua plants. UE and the Teamsters also asked the U.S. NAO to examine the failure of the Mexican authorities to enforce Mexican and international laws protecting organizational and labor rights.

The two unions also organized a thirteen-city tour by fired GE worker Fernando Castro, fired Honeywell worker Ofelia Medrano Sánchez, and STIMAHCS General Secretary Benedicto Martínez, to publicize the violation of workers' rights in Mexico. The tour included rallies, press conferences, and meetings with members of Congress and a wide variety of groups. The tour was supported at the local level by various unions, Jobs with Justice chapters, and fair-trade campaigns.

The efforts of UE, the Teamsters, and FAT, through

STIMAHCS, to organize GE's Juárez plant and Honeywell's Chihuahua plant are two examples of what has become known as cross-border labor organizing. The global reach of this type of organizing mirrors the rapid globalization of the world economy and the increasing mobility of international capital.

The Mexican government under President Carlos Salinas has enthusiastically implemented a neoliberal "modernization" program which has decimated real wages, cut social services, privatized much of the state, and opened the country to foreign investment. In the fire sale of state companies to private business overseen by Salinas, the government savaged collective-bargaining agreements, slashed wages, laid off thousands of workers, and destroyed job-security guarantees. The PRI's development strategy culminated with the implementation of NAFTA on New Year's Day.

A centerpiece of the drive to attract foreign investment is the maquiladora program. The maquiladoras, with foreign ownership, produce goods for export, largely to the United States. Today, half a million workers toil in some 2,000 maquiladora factories. While once restricted to Mexico's northern border, maquiladoras are now appearing in the interior as well. The maquiladora work force is overwhelmingly women and poorly paid.

Over eight million Mexican workers are unionized. The vast majority, however, belong to unions tied directly to the "official" or government-dominated federations. (See "Official and Independent Unions Angle for Power in Mexico," page 70.) It is extremely difficult to organize independent, democratic unions. "When we begin an organizing campaign," says Benedicto Martínez, one of FAT's national officers, "it is with the knowledge that we are taking on not only the company, but the government and official unions as well."

In general, unions with the AFL-CIO have been both reluctant and unable to establish meaningful relationships with independent unionists in Mexico. In part this is because the AFL-CIO has a historic relationship with the corrupt, government-dominated Confederation of Mexican Workers (CTM). The reluctance is also, in part, a consequence of protectionist and xenophobic cultural traditions within the United States and the trade-union movement. The changing economic reality—reflected in the loss of thousands of high-wage jobs in the United States as U.S. corporations move to Mexico to take advantage of low-wage labor and slack environmental controls—is prompting U.S.

unions to change their tune. The debate around NAFTA has caused many in the U.S. union movement to question the AFL-CIO's exclusive relationship with the CTM and to explore the meaning of international labor solidarity.

Some U.S. unionists have begun to envision a future that includes not only cross-border organizing, but coordinated bargaining, strikes, and political action. Progressives see similarities in the struggles that U.S. and Mexican workers face. The labor laws in Mexico are, ironically, much better than those in the United States, but enforcement of these laws is a major problem in both countries. Organizing is tough in Mexico, but is hardly easy in the United States. Trade unionists generally agree that U.S. unions should not organize in Mexico; rather, they argue, U.S. unions should help provide resources and create the conditions—through pressure on the U.S. government and U.S.-based transnationals—to enable Mexican trade unionists to organize in Mexico.

"We need an organizing response, not a political response," says Baldemar Velasquez, the president of the U.S. Farm Labor Organizing Committee. "We must fashion a union with workers in alliance, state by state, country by country. We must insist that workers' rights to wages and benefits such as health, education, and environmental safety be protected everywhere. As Americans and Mexicans alike, we are now less citizens of the nation in which we are born, and more citizens of the company for whom we work. This makes us equal. We must insist that this equality be reflected in our paychecks, our work conditions, our living conditions, our environmental conditions—for which the common company is responsible. This should impact the security of our jobs here and in Mexico."

U.S. progressives within the labor movement have responded to the crisis of labor rights in Mexico with a wide range of solidarity actions. These efforts have taken four forms: worker-to-worker interchanges, ranging from exchanges of information to financial or other kinds of aid; general support for independent organizing efforts; relationships between unions, ranging from exchanges of information to joint organizing projects; and efforts to spotlight poor environmental and working conditions, especially in the maquiladora sector.

One of the most interesting relationships was spearheaded by members of the United Auto Workers (UAW) Local 879, where Ford workers from Minneapolis joined with Canadian Auto Workers (CAW) members to provide support for Ford workers in Cuaútitlan. Unionists from all three countries have met on several occasions. In a symbolic gesture of solidarity, they have worn black arm bands to commemorate the death of Cleto Nigmo, a Ford worker killed by CTM goons. The UAW local has also initiated several innovative campaigns to provide financial assistance, among them an adopt-an-organizer campaign in which the local has pledged $300 a month for the Ford Democratic Movement. Workers who contribute receive an international organizers' jacket patch.

Other efforts have focused on unorganized workers. Mujer a Mujer is an organization based in San Antonio, Mexico City, and Toronto which facilitates contacts among women workers in Mexico, the United States, and Canada. It has organized tours, enabling rank-and-file and unorganized women—especially garment workers from Mexico and the southern United States—to begin a dialogue.

Official and Independent Unions Angle for Power in Mexico

Mexican workers, whose newly developed labor movement had radical socialist and anarchist leadership, played a major role in the Mexican revolution of 1910. The pact between the Constitutionalist forces of Venustiano Carranza and the anarchist House of the Workers of the World was the beginning of what is rhetorically known in Mexico as the "historic relationship between the working class and the State."

Article 123 of the new post-revolution Constitution enumerated a series of labor rights and protections: it guaranteed the right to organize unions and strikes; it established the eight-hour workday and minimum-wage and overtime standards; it protected the rights of women and children; it mandated health-and-safety protections; and it declared that workers must share in industry's profits.

The Confederation of Mexico Workers (CTM) was founded in the 1930s. With the backing of President Lázaro Cárdenas, it quickly became the dominant labor federation in Mexico. Fidel Velázquez was the first organizational secretary of the CTM; in 1940, he become general secretary, a post he has held ever since. To limit the power of the CTM and strengthen government control over the unions, Cárdenas oversaw the creation of—apart from the CTM—a mixed organization of farmworkers and small property owners called the National Confederation of Cooperatives (CNC), and an organization of public-sector workers, the Federation of Unions of Workers at the Service of the State (FSTSE).

He made the CTM, CNC, and FSTSE official affiliates of the Mexican ruling party, the PRI. As a result, most union members were until very recently required to join the PRI. In many cases, dues were automatically deducted from workers' pay for both the union and the party.

Unions of this type have become known as "official" unions, because of their direct relationship with the PRI.

The PRI-CTM links are especially tight. Many CTM leaders are important PRI politicians, often controlling the PRI machine at the local level. These politicians/union bureaucrats control vast amounts of patronage and have the police at their disposal. The official unions lack democratic procedures such as membership meetings and secret-ballot elections.

In addition to the official unions, there are the *sindicatos blancos* (white unions), which are company unions that are not independent in any real sense. These unions are particularly prevalent in Monterrey, the base for two *sindicato blanco* federations. Even more pernicious is the practice of "protection contracts," whereby official unions sell companies a contract which remains in a drawer until such time as a real union appears on the scene. Thus, workers may go for years without any knowledge that they are "represented"—with no knowledge of their officers, no meetings, and no actual representation.

During the 1970s, movements for independent, democratic unions developed in many different sectors. These were met with a combination of violent repression and co-optation.

As part of its modernization effort, and to improve Mexico's image abroad, the Salinas government has attempted to distance itself somewhat from the official unions. Salinas has attacked many of the old-line, corrupt CTM bureaucrats, often replacing them with "modernizers" who support his program. The government has, however, continued to viciously attack all efforts by workers to assert their rights, or to organize independent or democratic unions outside of state control.

Labor Notes, a monthly publication of the Labor Education and Research Project, and the Transnational Information Exchange (TIE) have also organized conferences and delegations in an effort to foster a dialogue between both unionized and rank-and-file workers, generally on an industry-wide basis. TIE has helped organize several trinational auto workers' conferences in Mexico, which were attended by both union leaders and rank-and-file members. It also helped coordinate a telecommunication workers' conference in Mexico in February, which was attended by members of CAW, the Canadian Communication, Energy, and Paperworkers Union, and three Mexican telephone workers' unions. This conference focused on changes in technology in the telecommunications industry and the unions' response. Participants agreed to exchange information on a continuing basis via electronic mail, to summa-

---

Government hostility is the major reason that independent unions are such a small part of the Mexican labor movement. Mexican labor law requires that unions obtain "juridical personality" (a charter granting legal recognition) from the government. The government has enormous power to intervene in the labor movement, to arbitrarily dismiss union leaders, to declare strikes "illegal," to militarily seize workplaces, to grant or withhold legal recognition and to delay the proceedings by which workers can change union representation.

Despite these enormous obstacles, a small genuinely independent militant wing outside the PRI-controlled Congress of Labor has emerged. The Authentic Labor Front (FAT) is a federation of independent unions, cooperatives, and farmworker and community organizations, comprising some 50,000 members. Formed in 1960, FAT now represents workers in a wide variety of industries in over half the states of Mexico. Over the years, FAT has provided crucial organizational and political support to many parts of the independent union movement which were not formally connected to it, as well as to democratic currents within the official unions.

Although relatively small, FAT has influence disproportional to its size, due to its principled determination to create independent, democratic unions under extremely adverse conditions. For example, FAT was a key founder and active participant in the Mexican Action Network on Free Trade (RMALC), the coalition of over 100 Mexican organizations which opposed NAFTA. FAT national officers were, moreover, quoted extensively in the international press. Bertha Luján, one of FAT's three national officers, has announced that she will run as an independent women's candidate in the upcoming congressional elections.

Democratic currents are present within the official unions, reflected in the attempts of some unionists to establish independent locals. In the late 1980s, for example, the PRI-affiliated Revolutionary Workers Confederation (COR) opposed the government's wage-control program and participated in the founding of a progressive labor coalition, the United Workers Front. In response to requests for assistance and affiliation from locals, including the Ford Workers from Cuaútitlan, COR agreed to submit to the government requests for certification. The actions of the COR leadership did not go unpunished. In July 1990, the government replaced the top leadership of the COR with its own loyalists.

The Federation of Goods and Services Unions (FESEBES), formed in early 1990 by unions of telephone workers, electrical workers, pilots, flight attendants, and trolley drivers, is yet another example of the new unionism. Breaking with tradition, FESEBES did not require that union locals be members of the PRI. The Electrical Workers Union (SME), which is a member of FESEBES, also has a militant history, and its democratic traditions are greatly respected within the union movement. These unions present themselves as alternatives to the outmoded CTM. Believing that modernization is inevitable, they push for as large a role as possible in controlling how change affects their members. FESEBES is, however, criticized by many progressives for supporting Salinas' neoliberal policies, including NAFTA. Moreover, recently the head of FESEBES, telephone workers' union president Hernandez Juárez, served as chief negotiator during the Volkswagen strike in 1992, which resulted in a devastating agreement.

rize collective bargaining agreements, and to create a bilingual compilation of telecommunications terms.

The North American Worker-to-Worker Network (NAWWN), a newer coalition based in North Carolina, serves as an informational clearinghouse. It sponsors tours of activists, and is developing an emergency-response network for labor-rights violations in Mexico.

The American Friends Service Committee (AFSC) has also brought workers and union officials together in a variety of forums. It places greater emphasis on dealing with representatives of Mexico's official unions. AFSC also provides financial and other support to the Border Committee of Workers (CFO), an independent organization of women workers in the maquiladora industry. CFO is composed of women workers from a variety of plants, who meet together in their neighborhoods to learn about their rights under Mexican labor law and to develop tactics to enable them to assert these rights without jeopardizing their jobs. CFO representatives have attended two annual Zenith shareholders' meetings to talk about low wages, long shifts, and exposure to hazardous substances at the Reynosa plant.

Cooperative efforts have also been made to provide training and technical assistance to Mexican workers, especially in the areas of health and safety. Last October, AFSC and the American Public Health Association sponsored the creation of a binational network of health-and-safety experts to provide free counsel for maquiladora workers. In a more problematic example, given this union's reputation and top-down organizing approach, the Laborers' International Union of North America recently announced that it intends to begin training Mexican workers in environmental clean-up; the union hopes to receive funding earmarked by the EPA and U.S. AID for this purpose. *Labor Notes* also recently conducted a cross-border organizers' school which focused on the nuts and bolts of "successful mutual solidarity efforts."

Other efforts have focused on highlighting labor and environmental problems, especially in the maquiladora sector. During the anti-NAFTA campaign, the International Labor Rights Education and Research Fund submitted a petition to the U.S. government seeking to expel Mexico from the Generalized System of Preferences (GSP). The petition, drawn up with the assistance of the Mexican National Democratic Lawyers' Association, detailed systematic labor-rights violations in Mexico.

The Coalition for Justice in the Maquiladoras (CJM), a coalition of labor, religious, and community groups, ini-

tially focused on environmental contamination by U.S.-based transnational corporations. CJM was responsible for much of the media attention during the NAFTA debate on environmental pollution along the Mexican-U.S. border, including reports of the high rate of anencephalic births in the Brownsville/Matamoros area. In coordination with community leaders, CJM targeted specific polluters on "chemical row" in Matamoros. These campaigns led to the closure of two plants, which significantly reduced pollution in the neighboring colonias. More recently, CJM has supported community and worker organizing efforts, both directly and through activity by shareholders. It has begun an initiative to draw attention to the problem of the inadequate translation of warning labels on chemical containers, and has been instrumental in publicizing the recent firings of and police brutality against Sony workers in Nuevo Laredo.

Relationships between unions—generally either industry or company specific—also have been developing for some time. One of the first company-specific relationships was developed by the Farm Labor Organizing Committee (FLOC) with its counterpart SNTOAC, an official farmworkers' union which represents Campbell's workers in Mexico. FLOC president Baldemar Velasquez credits the exchange of information and mutual support with helping SNTOAC get a 17 percent increase in wages and benefits in its contract at a time when a 10 percent ceiling was in place.

The International Ladies' Garment Workers Union (ILGWU) also views work with Mexican workers and unions as a "key strategic front for the American labor movement," according to Jeff Hermanson, the union's director of organizing. It meets with Mexican unionists to provide them with encouragement and assistance in organizing.

Others, such as Eduardo Diaz of the U.S. Postal, Telegraph, and Telephone International views the international secretariats of trade union federations as promising vehicles for furthering international solidarity efforts. Historically, the international labor secretariats functioned primarily to promote their respective capitalist or socialist political programs. With the end of the Cold War, however, some trade secretariats are turning their attention to supporting organizing work by member unions. "It is important to refocus the secretariats away from meetings and resolutions," says Diaz, "and to provide concrete assistance to those who are trying to organize.

The Mexican trade unionists who toured the United States in February received a warm welcome at various union meetings, clearly signaling a greater openness on the part of the AFL-CIO and affiliated unions to expand their support beyond the CTM. This is an important and welcome change which has been developing over time.

"I give credit to UE for being in the vanguard of efforts to raise living standards in both Mexico and United States," says Rosemary Trump, international vice-president of the Service Employees International Union (SEIU). "We are working through our international department to encourage the AFL-CIO to follow UE's lead in supporting independent trade unions in Mexico."

With respect to internationalization, multinationals have been way ahead of the unions. The debate over NAFTA had one silver lining: it forced U.S. unions to reconsider international solidarity. Unionists will encounter innumerable obstacles in their efforts to forge linkages with their counterparts in Mexico, among them differences in language and culture, limited resources, the historical relationship between the AFL-CIO and the CTM, and a strongly ingrained sense of rivalry between U.S. and Mexican workers. It is imperative, however, that unions move forward to establish strategic international alliances. Ultimate success, of course, will require political change, not only in Mexico, but in the United States and Canada as well. But nothing will happen unless workers begin taking what at this point appears to be impossibly small steps.

Reaching Across the Rio
by Mary E. Tong

They had been workers, and women, a world away, who had "stolen our jobs," somehow partly to blame for the ever more desperate circumstances so many of their listeners faced.

But when they rose to speak in eastern Tennessee's union halls, churches, and public forums, when they told of their fight for a decent life and what it cost them, barriers of language and border began to weaken, animosity gave ground to admiration, resentment to respect, suspicion to solidarity.

They said their typical sister worker began work as early as thirteen, supports her family, earns seventy-five cents an hour, and works forty-eight hours a week. She is routinely exposed to toxic chemicals and other hazardous conditions, they said, until she is replaced at twenty-four or twenty-five when she falls prey to severe headaches or skin disease, or her eyesight or lungs fail due to the strain and constant exposure to soldering fumes, solvents, and other chemicals. She is most often from a rural area and the first person in her family to hold an industrial job.

One of the speakers had herself worked for seventy-five cents an hour assisting the production supervisor at a Reynosa GM plant where she was responsible for seeing supplies were provided to work stations and the assembly line kept moving. She was fired for asking too many questions. The other had threaded wire used for auto flasher assembly at a Matamoros maquila, earning $1.10 an hour, with $6 deducted weekly for transportation.

What follows is their story, the story of the worker exchanges they helped inspire, of the organizations that help make them possible, and of the promise of what they have done and continue to do to build the cross border alliances so long in coming, so long overdue.

A decade ago, when the Maquiladora Project of the American Friends Service Committee (AFSC) took up the challenge of teaching maquiladora workers their rights and how to demand their enforcement, workers who participated in the consciousness-raising sessions formed the Comité Fronterizo de Obreras (CFO), the Border Women Workers Committee. By holding weekly meetings and con-

ducting training sessions for workers, says AFSC's Ed Krueger, CFO generated volunteers for action inside the factories.

Mexican law is far more favorable to workers than the United States', guaranteeing a minimum wage, an eight-hour day, the right to strike (except for public employees), severance pay, overtime pay, workers' compensation, and liberal maternity-leave benefits.

Armed with this law, CFO organizers taught workers how, in a quiet, low-profile, but firm way, to defend themselves—a method supervisors found extremely difficult to react negatively to. For thousands of CFO members in over 100 chapters, the complacent, easily victimized workers became a relic of the past.

CFO came to work closely with the Coalition for Justice in the Maquiladoras (CJM), an alliance of labor, religious, environmental, and community groups devoted to publicizing and improving conditions in maquila areas. The coalition developed standards of conduct, a document calling all U.S. corporations operating subsidiaries, having affiliates or using contractors or shelter plants in Mexico to standards of a safe workplace, environmental protection, human rights, and economic justice on both sides of the border. To date, industry trade journals have responded defensively, claiming the industry is "clean" and a blessing for Mexican workers. The coalition hopes trade talks will nevertheless provide an opportunity to develop binational policies incorporating the standards as part of an enforceable social charter.

It was two CFO organizers, Teresa Hernández and Olga Jiménez, who came to Tennessee in February 1991 at the request of Frances Lee Ansley, an associate professor at University of Tennessee Collage of Law with a research interest in plant closings and maquiladoras.

As board member of the Tennessee Industrial Renewal Network (TIRN), Ansley's interest was more than academic. TIRN, a coalition of workers, unions, community organizations, church groups, and concerned citizens—formed in 1989 to organize and participate in finding solutions to plant closings—teaches workers to take action to prevent closings and lessen their impact. TIRN is a local affiliate of Federation for Industrial Renewal and Retention (FIRR), a nationwide grouping of grassroots or-

Originally published in *Beyond Borders,* Spring 1993.

ganizations that oppose plant closings and runaway shops. Affiliates engage in solidarity activities addressing such concerns as the effects of the North American Free Trade Agreement (NAFTA), and FIRR advises them on organizational methods and resources. FIRR also assists organizations with worker exchanges.

Susan Williams of the Highlander Center, a member organization of TIRN, coordinated funding and preparation for the exchange. For sixty years, Highlander has made grassroots leadership development its objective. One of the most important training groups for union organizers in the 1930s, its focus shifted in the 1950s to civil rights, influencing such Highlander participants as Rev. Dr. Martin Luther King, Jr., and Rosa Parks, and inspiring Septima Clark's "citizenship schools" that taught thousands of African Americans to read and write so they could vote. Center workshops bring together grassroots organizers dealing with labor, community, and environmental concerns to share their experiences and visions with other leaders, analyze their work, and determine ways to help each other. Highlander also works with local organizations to conduct schools in communities across the country.

In addition to sending two organizers to Tennessee, CFO agreed to host a worker delegation from Tennessee. Many more Tennessee workers signed up to go than could be accommodated, so those most directly hurt by the emerging changes in the global economy were chosen. All had been involved in efforts around plant closures and were committed to take action in the interest of workers on both sides of the border upon their return. Besides Frances Ansley and Susan Williams, the delegation included a Palm Beach Company garment worker and six workers who lost jobs to Mexico: two from Magnavox, two from GE, one from Allied-Bendix Safety Restraints Division, and one from North American Phillips.

TIRN member Shirley Reinhardt participated because she lost her job when a GE plant moved to Mexico. Despite many months of looking for work, she only found temporary jobs, doing the same tasks as full-time workers for a fraction of the pay, with no benefits. (An article on her efforts to organize the Committee Against Temporary Services [CATS] appeared in *Beyond Borders* Winter '92 issue.) She reported to other TIRN members that a GE supervisor sent to Nogales, Mexico to train employees to replace their U.S. counterparts returned horrified that the plant was working children at incredibly low wages and using candy as a bonus rather than money.

At another Tennessee plant, the manager came to production workers after most of their work was transferred to Mexico and told them they had one year to convince management the Tennessee plant was important to the company's future. Workers called it "economic blackmail" but didn't know how to resist and found themselves discussing concessions rather than gains. One of the trip's objectives was to use the lessons they gained to turn the situation around.

Before the trip, participants learned how the U.S. established its maquiladora policy in the 1960s when the bracero program, which encouraged Mexicans to migrate to work in U.S. agriculture, ended. Touted as a remedy for massive unemployment, rapid maquiladora emergence provoked a sudden migration to the border area. With no housing available, shantytowns, known as colonias, sprang up—often without running water and public services.

When the nine women arrived in Matamoros, they saw not only what attracts U.S. plants to Mexico, but what Mexican border workers are doing about it. Workers in Matamoros—the most advanced area of CFO organizing—know enough about labor law that if they are laid off or fired, they are most often able to get the indemnity funds or severance pay to which they are entitled. When unjustly fired, workers can now get before an arbitration and conciliation panel to place their *demanda* or lawsuit.

CFO members have consistently pressed their unions. Almost all maquiladora workers are members of unions belonging to the Confederación de Trabajadores de Mexico (CTM), which is generally considered to be government run. Matamoros is known by many as a "labor town" with 35,000 maquiladora worker members of Sindicato de Jornaleros y Obreros Industriales (SJOI), the Union of [Day Laborers] and Industrial Workers. Founded by Agapito González Cavazos over 50 years ago, SJOI is known for its tough, nationalistic stance. Local sources credit González's personal aggressiveness in confronting the maquiladora owners as the reason Matamoros workers boast wages 50 percent above their counterparts in other areas of Mexico.

But last fall, with Mexico's election and contract negotiations coming up, government and corporate forces seemed determined to reduce Matamoros' wages by one-half to four fifths to match Reynosa or Rio Bravos.

After settling with GM, and with twenty-five plants yet to negotiate, seventy-four-year-old Agapito was arrested last winter by a truckload of government troops and held for two weeks before any charges were made known. Then he was charged with tax evasion and kept in prison without a hearing for the eight-month period of build-up to the local elections in which the Institutional Revolutionary Party (PRI) wanted SJOI members' votes.

González had to pay a bond for his release and could still be reimprisoned at any time. At the time of this writing, contracts are being negotiated without González. Meanwhile, in an attempt to reduce the average wage, plants have been laying off workers and directing them to go to another factory where they will start over. CFO has responded with stepped-up training.

The Tennessee contingent attended CFO's semiannual meeting. They heard delegates from CFO chapters in many border cities report on their success and plans. Said María Guadalupe Torres, Regional Coordinator of CFO, "We discussed why here in Matamoros we have influenced many unions to bring change. We have the highest wages and least hours per week—forty instead of forty-eight. In other places they tell workers that if they don't work overtime, they won't work at all. This is a way of oppressing us, making us work two, three, four double shifts each week."

Through CFO, workers have their own counselors to provide protection against attorneys too eager to settle with the company. Workers threatened with firing know they are entitled to demand a written letter of dismissal. Such a request is usually enough to force rescindment of the firing. In many plants the supervisor or manager must now fear the law rather than intimidate workers by breaking it. Members discussed how hundreds of these workers have avoided firing, having shifts changed or other corporate impositions regarding their work and defended themselves against sexual harassment by abusive supervisors through using their skills. They know how to run work stoppages if goggles are not provided when needed, or if an extractor or exhaust fan is not working.

Since the Tennessee workers did not speak Spanish and few CFO members spoke English, a skit was chosen as the best way to convey the Tennessee delegation's objectives. After drawing on each other's experiences and knowledge of the maquiladoras, the travelers rehearsed their collaborative effort at overnight hotel stops on the way to Mexico. Their play, depicting U.S. worker concerns on and off the job and why they chose to make the trip, was well received by the gathering, who joined in singing a rousing "Solidarity Forever" in Spanish.

Mexican workers responded with their own ad-libbed, impromptu play about maquiladora workers who protest unsafe working conditions. CFO often uses such "sociodramas" as a skills training exercise. Workers are assigned roles, a situation is defined, they act it out, and discuss it.

The exchange of performances and real-life concerns, fears, and hopes for the future forged a resolve toward action that all worker participants agree would have been impossible without the trip.

CFO and CJM organizers took the delegation through a neighborhood between two chemical plants with a chain link fence on one side and a concrete wall on the other. Behind the wall was an open chemical vat. After experiencing chemical contamination following a 1983 plant explosion, community residents here organized to protest the constant, unbearable stench and publicized their fear of another explosion at Retzloff, Petrolite, or Stepan Chemical. In 1987 they presented a petition with their concerns to the Matamoros mayor, explaining they had faced chemical intoxication and had to flee their homes many times.

"In 1990 they had a spill where people had to leave their homes for days," says Barbara Bishop, a member of the delegation. "Any of the animals that didn't die had to be killed."

Recalls Jiménez, "There was a very serious accident which was a big leak at the Retzloff plant. A pipe exploded. A big cloud came out of the plant and drifted away in the wind downtown to another maquiladora plant. Through the ventilation system, workers inside this plant started breathing poisonous air. More than eighty-three workers got sick and starting having headaches, but the manager wouldn't allow the paramedic team in. They would only allow workers into the backyard. It was only when workers started passing out that they would allow doctors in to assist them." Local newspapers reported the poisonous gas was pentachlorophenol—a wood preservative linked to cancer, birth defects, weakening of the immune system, and blood, liver, and skin disease.

Since the worker exchange, reports Torres, twenty workers became ill from exposure to another chemical accident involving pentachlorophenol in December 1992.

Retzloff Chemical recently closed as the result of a campaign by the Texas Center on Policy Studies which has, together with CJM and CFO, focused attention in the past few months on the Illinois-based Stepan Chemical Company dumping solvents and other chemicals into the canals and grounds of the colonias.

While the Mexican workers welcomed the visitors, management was less friendly. At General Motors' Deltrónicos maquiladora in Matamoros, the manager, who said he would arrange their entrance, never returned. Tired of waiting, the workers marched into the lobby and began taking pictures of this plant known locally for its refusal to allow emergency equipment to come in during a large fire in May 1990. Local papers reported ninety women workers suffered intoxication from fumes while Deltrónicos denied paramedics entry, claiming the situation was under control. The manager, who reappeared and ushered the crew into a conference room, claimed he could not tell the delegation what the average hourly wage at his plant is.

June Hargis reports this factory moved from Kokomo, Indiana. Workers make auto stereos and are paid $35 for a forty-five-hour week. Seeing the stark reality of these wages amid prices for goods like those in the United States, says Hargis, is when she fully realized NAFTA was solely for the interest of the corporations moving to Mexico to increase their profits. "It's a one-way street. There's no way at the wages these companies pay Mexican workers that they can afford to buy anything we'd make in the United States. I believe we'll never get those jobs back, but, if we insist the Mexican people are treated right, the U.S. government and corporations will not be so ready to move, because they won't be able to get by with paying slave wages." The Coalition for Justice in the Maquiladoras says GM is in clear violation of environmental laws because of its release of xylene, a toxic chemical.

"The Mexican workers thought the first thing we would say was we were mad because of all the lost jobs, but we had to realize it's not their fault. The U.S. government and the corporations have made slaves out of them, and they face the same threats we do of plants fleeing to other countries if they demand better conditions," said Hargis.

This understanding spawned another worker exchange between Guatemalan maquila workers and CFO members in the summer of '92. Guatemala, where labor law is also quite favorable to workers but its enforcement weak to nonexistent, has become not only a primary maquila growth area, but one of the most dangerous places in the world for labor organizers. CFO organizers compared Guatemalan labor laws with their own to determine ways Guatemalan workers could apply CFO methods to their own defense. They showed the Guatemalans their own approach to skills training through role playing and discussed ways Guatemalans could take low-key but effective action in their plants. Since then, CFO organizers have kept in regular contact with their sister workers in Guatemala's garment in-

dustry. The workers at Phillips–Van Heusen's subcontractors who visited CFO went on to win union recognition by the Guatemalan government last fall.

These workers have forged the beginnings of a relationship of international solidarity they believe is crucial to their future in the global economy. Remarked Torres, "These workers from Guatemala suffer such oppression, yet they continue. We've been building this movement for ten years through very slow, very discreet, very quiet organizing. In Guatemala they face so much repression that I'm unsure our methods will work, but it is important they try. We gave them the materials we could and will keep in contact."

While concern about job loss and Tennessee's future propelled the U.S women to take two rented vans to the Mexican border to visit CFO members, it was a newfound solidarity with the women they befriended that compelled them to make their exchange the launching-off point for continuing solidarity efforts. The excursion had changed their lives forever, building relationships and understandings that would reach far beyond themselves and the individuals they met.

After their return, the Tennessee workers presented a slide show of their journey to labor organizations, peace groups, church groups, and community organizations throughout the region. "Every time I show it, it's like I go back there. It will always be with me.... Those people will be in my heart and mind hours a day," says Hargis. A pitch for funds for a CFO van accompanies each presentation.

Exchange participants wrote letters in support of the workers and the surrounding community to companies they saw. Hargis gives an example: "In Matamoros we met with farmers next to a chemical plant. They were told it would be making cosmetics, but when it moved in they found it produces insecticides. Now their crops are half what they had been before the plant came. The company told them, 'if you don't like it, you must move.' The farmers said, 'We have been here twenty years. You move!' We wrote letters to the company about the farmers' situation."

According to Austin, Texas news reports, farmers believe the chemical hydrofluoric acid causes fruit to drop off trees, leaves never to become green, and their children to cough and gasp. An analysis of sorghum and other plants in the area by Dr. Maria de Lourdes de Bauer of the Autonomous University of Chapingo, Mexico confirmed the farmers' belief, showing fluoride content of 40 parts per million in the leaves. This plant is partly owned by Dupont Chemical Company and 85 percent of its production is sold to a Dupont subsidiary.

Three delegation members testified about maquilas and the ill effect of the proposed free trade agreement at the Bush administration's interagency hearings on NAFTA organized by the Office of the U.S. Trade Representative in Washington, DC and the Trade Staff Policy Committee.

Two exchange participants made presentations to INFACT, the international corporate accountability group that won reforms in infant formula marketing through its Nestlé boycott and recently succeeded in moving GE, the most influential nuclear weapons contractor in the United States, out of that business. They stayed on in Washington, DC to lobby Tennessee Congressional people about NAFTA. They also helped to organize a rally last fall against the agreement, joining union, environmental, community, and international human rights organizers from throughout Tennessee.

The exchange was featured on the PBS Nova series hosted by Robert Reich in an episode entitled "Made in America—Winners and Losers." TIRN plans to make a video for use in education and organizing from the leftover footage.

The exchange demonstrates the tremendous impetus meeting and sharing among workers north and south of the border can be to organizing cross-border solidarity. It provides other unions and activities concerned with globalization an excellent example of how to cement international understandings and pave the way for change.

Luvernel Clark, shop steward and head of ACTWU's Allied-Bendix health-and-safety committee, remarked, "We were not prepared for what we saw or heard. It was strange, because I had looked at pictures that other people brought back. And I had seen slides and even some video.

"One person on our trip said that they should put up a sign by those neighborhoods 'American made.' As long as I live, I'll never forget seeing the conditions our own corporations are willing for their Mexican workers to live under.

"We are not against increased trade with Mexico. And we are certainly not against Mexican workers having jobs. But we are against blackmail. We are against any kind of system that pits workers against each other on the basis of which one can be forced to take the lowest wage. We are against any system that encourages corporations to go shopping for the lowest wages or the most lax law enforcement or the biggest tax break. But our government seems like it wants a system like that. Its reaction to the global economy is that corporations need more freedom! A visit to the maquiladoras will show you what freedoms without responsibility can mean.

"Going to Mexico made me realize what a huge gap there is—in wages, and conditions, and law enforcement. Our fight is not about taking jobs from Mexican or U.S. workers. It is not about trying to keep that gap. It is about unity and human dignity."

Says Torres, "I believe the only way of solving the problems is to continue organizing workers throughout the world, wherever they work. Oppression is the same in different industrial areas, and we must strategize together to confront the problems affecting our lives and culture. . . . that are making us like machines. Together we can organize more each day for respect of human rights, the protection of life, health of women, and an end to violations of women's rights."

Double Standards: Notes for a Border Screenplay

By Debbie Nathan

PART 1: Negative Hallucinations

The case had been settled only minutes ago, and now jurors for *Mendoza v. Contico* were seated in a room outfitted with movie theater chairs and plugs for devices like VCRs. They were in the "Ceremonial Court" in El Paso, where victorious lawyers often hold post-trial press conferences. In any other place, at any other time, what happened next would have been bad *Geraldo*. But here it wasn't—not after the horror that had come out during the past two weeks at trial. "Ladies and gentlemen, some of you may have weak stomachs," lawyer Jim Scherr intoned as reporters poised their pens and tried to look cynical. "If so, close your eyes or leave the room." He popped a videotape into a TV with an outsized screen.

Mexican police had recorded the tape. It opened with nighttime shots of the desert outside Ciudad Juárez—jumpy, silvery, and spooky, like NASA footage of landings on the moon. Suddenly a wrecked car loomed out of the dark, its chassis blackened by fire and the body work torched to bubbles. The muffled soundtrack was policemen's Spanish: monotonous and forensically throwaway until the tape showed a cop's hand prying the trunk open with a screw-driver. Then you could hear the policemen gasping.

Inside the burned-out trunk was plaintiff Mendoza. Lorena Mendoza—and an enlarged portrait propped near the TV showed what she had looked like before she ended up in the car. She'd been twenty-seven years old, petite and wiry, fair-skinned for a Mexican, partial to bright red lipstick, possessed of an insouciant smile, and not shy about angling her body to the camera and tossing her hair. That was in life. Now, in the video, a man wearing surgical gloves gingerly lifted a rib-cage from the trunk, and a skull. They were charred and compacted like logs on a cold campfire, and when the man picked them up, chunks of Lorena Mendoza thudded to the ground.

Jurors began weeping. The press looked tearful too, even reporters from local papers and stations whose editors had ignored the two-week trial proceedings, perhaps

so as not to ruffle local industries like Contico International, the defendant.

Contico is based in St. Louis, but it is also owner of Continental Sprayers of El Paso, which has as its subsidiary Continental Sprayers de México. The last is in Ciudad Juárez, right across the border from El Paso. Look under your sink at your bottle of window cleaner, or in your garage at the bug killer, and there is a good chance that the trigger gizmo you push to dispense the liquid says "Continental Mfg. Co.–Mexico." Sprayers are what the company makes, and they do it in Juárez because the wages there are $24 a week for forty-eight hours of work.

Up and down the border, more than 2,500 mostly American-owned manufacturers have been taking advantage of similar low wages for a generation. The companies are called maquiladoras, and in the United States lately, much has been written about their effects on the economy and workers of this country. Less has been said about how they affect standards of living in Mexico, and still less about how that country's 800,000 maquiladora laborers are impacted by working conditions and safety standards—which are often inferior to those in U.S. factories owned by the same companies.

While the $24 weekly wage is technically no secret, Americans confronted with the figure often react with what psychologists call a "negative hallucination"—they blot it from consciousness or mentally reconfigure it to $24 a *day*. Safety conditions are more deeply occluded in the U.S. mind. On the border, one constantly hears accounts from poor Mexicans about relatives and friends injured and killed in maquiladoras. But the stories virtually never make the U.S. media or the Mexican press—in part because negligence suits in Mexico are practically unheard of, and when they are filed, plaintiffs seldom prevail. Meanwhile, international labor rights activists have a hard time monitoring maquila safety conditions because plant managers are notoriously unwilling to open their plants to careful inspection.

On the few occasions they have, gringos like Martha Mimms have spotted egregious double standards. Mimms is a glass worker, at a Ford Motor Company plant in Nashville that makes automotive windshields and windows. In 1994, while on a transborder workers' solidarity tour with the Tennessee Industrial Renewal Network she visited

---

Excerpts from an article originally printed in the *Texas Observer*, June 6, 1997. Reprinted by permission.

Autovidrios, a Ford maquiladora in Juárez that manufactures the same products that her Nashville plant does, and at the time even employed American supervisors who once had given orders at Mimms' workplace. At Autovidrios, Mimms saw conditions that are thoroughly outlawed in U.S. factories: conveyor belts with no guard pieces; tables, where workers were eating snacks and lunch, covered with toxic lead paint waste; workers laboring next to robots slinging sharp glass and which, in U.S. factories, are always separated from humans with bars and gates. Autovidrios is the same factory in which—four years before Mimms' visit—a sixteen-year-old worker named Julio César Macias died after getting caught in a dangerous conveyor belt. In Nashville, the type of area he was assigned to is deemed so risky that two workers must be present at all times to monitor each other. Julio was by himself at the Autovidrios conveyer belt when he was crushed to death.

The fate of Lorena Mendoza—the protagonist of *Mendoza v. Contico*—was even worse. As a bookkeeper for Continental Sprayers de México, she was charged with transporting cash wages for seventy workers down an eighty-mile, two-lane highway to Palomas, an abject border pueblo where the company had opened yet another plant. The route is desolate and infamous for drug trafficking and vehicle hijackings. In its U.S. operations Contico uses Brink's trucks to transport payroll. Such services are readily available in Mexico. Yet Lorena Mendoza and other bookkeepers and unarmed security guards carried money from Juárez to Palomas in a private car every other Friday, always at the same hour. Under such circumstances, Mendoza's survivors and their attorneys said, it was a foregone conclusion that eventually she would be attacked.

Her death, the lawyers said, was an American company's fault, and therefore the company should be subject to U.S. tort laws. The principle might sound elementary, but when El Paso Judge Jack Ferguson ruled three years ago that Mendoza's family could have its day in a Texas court, he helped set a national and international precedent. Since 1993, when the Legislature closed the door on foreign plaintiffs after a group of Costa Rican farmworkers sued a Texas chemical company whose product had rendered them sterile, it has been extremely rare for foreign plaintiffs to be allowed standing in Texas courts. When the case against Contico opened in El Paso in late March of this year, it was the first time a maquiladora had ever been put on trial in America for negligence in Mexico. That made it the first time that the day-to-day details of maquiladora

exploitation were described in sworn, on-the-record testimony that anyone could hear, simply by going down to the courthouse and walking past the shoeshine boys....

What We're Not Talking About

After days of such testimony, anti-Contico sentiment is starting to show on the jury's faces. It gets more intense when Mendoza family members take the stand. A sister, San Juana (who once invited Lorena to the movies), is a doctor, and she sends shivers through the courtroom as she talks of visiting the morgue—she wanted to examine the body to prove that it wasn't really Lorena's. On arriving, she was petrified to find that there was no body, only a plastic bag of bones and ashes, from which she extracted a womb, an ovary, and some molars whose fillings she ascertained were her sister's. Afterwards she closed the bag, returned home and assured her mother that yes, she combed Lorena's hair, and yes, bought a lovely dress to bury her in.

The mother is sworn in, downcast; and her old husband, half deaf, with a hearing aid like a wad of bubble gum in his ear. After seven years both clearly are still in mourning for their youngest daughter's cheery disposition, her beauty, her dreams of life in the United States; and they stolidly describe how they haven't eaten right since she died, or slept, or been able to maintain normal blood pressure. When they finish, the jury glares at everybody and everything related to Contico. The panel's growing animus is obvious to the company's lawyers, and just before closing arguments, they offer the Mendozas $1.75 million to settle out of court. The family's lawyers approve the deal, because although the jury will later tell the judge that they unanimously wanted to convict Contico and award the Mendozas up to $27 million, Contico has vowed to appeal. The Mendoza attorneys know that higher Texas courts have turned markedly pro-business since the early 1990s. Not only would they probably overturn an anti-Contico verdict, they would also nullify local Judge Ferguson's 1994 ruling allowing a Texas company's wrongdoing in Mexico to be tried in this state. If they were to make that ruling, no international cases like *Mendoza v. Contico* would ever get into court in Texas.

So the Mendozas take Contico's offer, along with the company's promise to build a statue of Lorena in Juárez dedicated to employee safety, and to establish a maquiladora worker scholarship fund her name. Then everyone troops to Ceremonial Court for the press conference and its chilling videotape. Lawyer Scherr tells the jurors to teach their friends and family the lesson of *Mendoza v. Contico:* that when it comes to workers' safety, double standards between the United States and Mexico are intolerable.

"Of course, we're not talking about wages," Scherr repeated, which is ironic given the post-trial comments of jurors. Donna Ricci is one; she is middle-aged and a long-time El Pasoan. Yet Ricci tells me, until she sat through *Mendoza v. Contico,* she had no idea how meager maquiladora pay is (and the figures used for trial were from seven years ago: since the 1994 peso devaluation, they're down from $35 to $25 per week). Twenty-year-old Vanessa Rodarte has lived here all her life but until the trial she had never heard of maquiladoras—period—much less what they pay. When she and the other jurors went out for lunch, Rodarte says, they would talk about "how we were getting paid $6 a day for jury duty—a total joke—and we'd go to a restaurant and blow it all on a meal, and maquiladora workers don't make $6 in a whole day!"

Wages *are* what *Mendoza v. Contico* was about. These days it hardly takes Karl Marx to understand that the global stampede to bargain-basement Third World labor is what leads to discounted safety standards and the kind of fire-sale ethics that put Lorena Mendoza on a highway to her death. Susan Mika, the San Antonio–based coordinator of the Coalition for Justice in the Maquiladoras, refuses to concede the question of wages, as she makes a short but eloquent speech at the Ceremonial Court press conference. When she finishes, the audience breaks into applause.

Mika has just spent the past two weeks in court, furiously typing testimony into a laptop. Now she prepares to leave the border with her hard drive, but, because the case was settled, without the official transcripts she'd hoped to distribute to the world. The Mendozas return to Juárez and are immediately terrorized by unknown men who torch a family car. On the front seat they leave a burned coin— apparently part of the evidence collected seven years ago when Lorena's body was retrieved. The family goes to the Juárez police station for help. When they arrive, they see the same men who burned their car—walking around the office as though they work there. Afraid for their lives, the Mendozas petition the U.S. government for refugee status.

It remains to be seen whether they will win asylum, and if they do, whether they will ever see a statue of their daughter in Juárez. As for their case, perhaps it will go down as a footnote to later trials that raise the same issues of maquiladora double standards, by succeeding in producing a verdict and a written record.

For now, *Mendoza v. Contico* is nothing more than potential: notes for a screenplay; a sheaf of grim scenes; glimmerings of worker consciousness; a primer on maquiladoras for *norteamericanos.* Modest hope for the future.

NAO Findings on Working Conditions at Han Young Plant

Below is the text of the "Findings" and "Recommendations" sections of the Final Report of the U.S. Department of Labor's National Administrative Office (U.S. NAO) on working conditions and Mexican government inspections at the Han Young de México truck chassis assembly plant in Tijuana. The NAO report was issued on August 11, 1998, in response to the health-and-safety complaint filed under the provisions of the NAFTA labor side agreement by [The Maquila Health and Safety Support Network] and others in February 1998.

V. Findings

The information from expert witnesses, workers, and inspection reports is consistent and credible in describing a workplace polluted with toxic airborne contaminants, strewn with electric cables running through puddles of water, operating with poorly maintained and unsafe machinery, and with numerous other violations and omissions of minimum safety and health standards. This workplace was severely lacking in adequate sanitation facilities for workers to relieve themselves and bathe in minimally acceptable hygienic conditions or even get a drink of water.

These problems and shortcomings had been identified since at least June 1997, and serious issues as to their abatement remain. Corrective action to remedy some of the major problems was undertaken only at the initiative of Hyundai Precision America, and there are no assurances that these will be maintained with any consistency, if at all.

The information available indicates that Han Young was subjected to eleven safety and health inspections over the years since it began operations in 1993. At least four inspections took place since June 16, 1997. This date follows shortly after the enactment of the new health-and-safety regulations in April 1997. Four inspections in the space of one year is substantial.

Notwithstanding repeat inspections, however, serious unabated violations were allowed to continue over this entire period. These hazards undoubtedly existed before June 16 and pose imminent short-term as well as long-term dangers to health and safety of workers in the plant. Though

Reprinted by permission from *Border/Line,* the newsletter of the Maquila Health and Safety Support Network, Vol. 2, No. 3, Sept. 1998.

fines in the amount of $9,400 were assessed against the company, there is no information as to whether the fines were actually collected or if the cases were otherwise disposed of. The NAO has been unable to ascertain if financial penalties were assessed and collected for the violations identified in the subsequent inspections.

The health-and-safety conditions reviewed should be viewed in the context of the workers' efforts to organize an independent union at Han Young as reported by the NAO on March 28, 1998. Though a union at Han Young had been in existence since the plant began operations in 1993, there is nothing to indicate that it undertook any efforts to address the conditions that have been described. This failure to act on safety-and-health problems was one of several reasons that prompted workers at the plant to seek representation by a union that would more effectively represent their interests.

However, of immediate concern to the NAO is the effectiveness of the inspection and sanction process in Mexico to enforce compliance in regard to workplace health and safety. Inspections, in and of themselves, are not sufficient to deter an employer determined to violate or ignore the law. However, regular inspections combined with the certainty of the imposition of significant, incremental, and ongoing financial penalties, have a demonstrated record of promoting compliance.

The NAO makes the following findings:

1. By enacting a new Federal Regulation on Safety, Health, and the Workplace in April 1997, Mexico has undertaken a serious effort to improve the enforcement of safety and health in the workplace.

2. The company in question was subjected to thorough and repeated inspections by [Mexican] federal and state authorities. Nevertheless, a number of questions have been raised with regard to the efficiency of the inspections. Further, despite these efforts, serious hazards continue unabated at the plant.

3. The fines totaling approximately $9,400 that were assessed against Han Young were substantial, provided they were enforced. The doubling of these fines, as provided for by the law, for unabated violations would arguably have had a significant deterrent effect, even more so if they were again doubled and enforced as appropri-

ate. The NAO, however, has been unable to ascertain if these sanctions were applied in the case of Han Young, in accordance with Mexican law, and what, if any, further action is contemplated by the Mexican authorities to seek compliance in the case.

4. A major instrument to ensure compliance with workplace health-and-safety regulations is the deterrent effect afforded by the conduct of comprehensive periodic inspections combined with the certainty of the assessment of significant financial penalties against violators. This deterrent effect is lost if penalties are not enforced. Additional information on the process for conducting inspections and assessing, increasing, and collecting financial penalties would enable a more thorough valuation of the matter.

Given these considerations, including consultations at the ministerial level on these safety and health issues would further the objectives of the NAALC [North American Agreement on Labor Cooperation, the labor side agreement]. Consultations should discuss (1) the final disposition and/or current status of the health-and-safety cases involving Han Young de Mexico, S.A. de C.V.; (2) the status of the efforts by the government of Mexico to enforce compliance with that country's health-and-safety laws and regulations through implementation of the Federal Regulation on Safety, Health, and the Workplace; and (3) discussion of the process by which workplace inspections are conducted and the process by which financial penalties are imposed, escalated, and collected.

VI. Recommendation

Accordingly, the NAO recommends that pursuant to Article 22 of the NAALC, ministerial consultations [between the US and Mexican Secretaries of Labor] on NAO Submission No. 9702 include the safety and health issues raised.

Complete copies of the forty-three-page report are available from the U.S. NAO, Department of Labor, Bureau of International Labor Affairs, 200 Constitution Avenue NW, Room C-4327, Washington, DC 20210, (202) 501-6653.

Maquiladora Standards of Conduct

INTRODUCTION: Purpose and Scope of the Standards of Conduct

The Maquiladora Standards of Conduct are addressed to all U.S. corporations, which operate subsidiaries, have affiliates, or utilize contractors or shelter plants in Mexico. The objective of these Standards is to promote socially responsible practices, which ensure a safe environment on both sides of the border, safe work conditions inside maquiladora plants and an adequate standard of living for maquiladora employees.

U.S. citizens who urge U.S. transnational corporations to adhere to these standards recognize that both Mexico and the United States have the inherent right to regulate commerce within their own boundaries. These Standards are designed to help promote binational efforts to secure a safe workplace for maquiladora employees, the protection of the environment, and the promotion of human rights and economic justice on both sides of the border.

All company disclosures associated with these Standards should be provided in Spanish and English.

SECTION I: Responsible Practices for Handling Hazardous Wastes and Protecting the Environment

Pollution from the maquiladora industry is a binational problem which threatens the health of citizens in both Mexico and the United States. Illegal dumping of hazardous wastes pollutes rivers and aquifers and contaminates drinking water on both sides of the border. In addition, accidental chemical leaks from plants or transportation vehicles carrying hazardous materials impact both sides of the border.

In general, corporations operating maquiladoras will be guided by the principle that they will follow SEDUE (Secretaría de Desarrollo Urbano y Ecología)[1] and EPA (Environmental Protection Agency) regulations and will exercise good faith to secure the best possible protection of the environment. Corporations operating maquiladoras will:[2]

Developed by the Coalition for Justice in the Maquiladoras. Reprinted by permission.

1. Act promptly to comply with Mexican environmental laws (Ley General del Equilibrio Ecológico y la Protección al Ambiente), by submitting environmental impact statements to SEDUE, obtaining proper permits from SEDUE, and adhering to all ecological technical standards. Twice a year, corporations will publish a list of all notices of violations received from government agencies with notations as to the status of efforts to come into compliance on such violations.[3]

2. Annually provide full public disclosure of toxic chemical discharges and releases into the air, water, and land and amounts of hazardous materials stored and utilized. In addition, annually companies will disclose the movements of hazardous materials and wastes between facilities in the United States and Mexico, and the movement of hazardous materials from storage to usage.[4]

3. Provide full public disclosure of hazardous waste disposal methods, including the final location of waste disposal. If a maquiladora contracts with a Mexican company to dispose or recycle hazardous waste, it will publicly disclose the name of the company and provide documentation that the company has required SEDUE authorization.[5]

4. Use state-of-the-art toxics use reduction, chemical accident prevention, and pollution control technologies to reduce hazardous discharges and releases and ensure compliance with SEDUE's ecological technical standards.[6]

5. Ensure safe and responsible transportation of all hazardous materials in Mexico and the United States. As required by Mexican law, prior to transporting hazardous waste, the companies will obtain SEDUE authorization. Vehicles used for transporting hazardous waste will be properly inspected and operated by qualified drivers.[7]

6. Provide public verification of all hazardous materials being returned to the country of origin, as required by international treaty and Mexican law, including disclosure of the method and location of final disposal.[8]

7. Ensure proper disposal of all spent containers used for chemicals and take necessary initiatives to assure that these containers are not used for the storage of drinking water.

8. Take remedial action to clean up any past dumping which threatens to release hazardous materials into the environment.

9. Provide fair damage compensation to any community or individual which has been harmed by pollution caused by the corporation or its subsidiary.

10. Discuss environmental concerns with the community. Enter into "good neighbor" agreements with the neighbors of facilities in Mexico to allow verification of compliance with all of these environmental provisions and to foster further dialogue with the community on environmental protection issues.

SECTION II: Health and Safety Practices

In general, corporations operating maquiladoras will be guided by the principle that they will follow regulations established by the Secretaría del Trabajo y Previsión Social and the Occupational Safety and Health Administration (OSHA).[9]

Corporations operating maquiladoras will:

1. Disclose to employees, their designated representatives, and the public the chemical identity of all chemicals used, as well as amounts of chemical materials and wastes stored on premises. Ensure that all chemical containers will have appropriate warning labels in Spanish as well as English.[10]

2. In accordance with Mexican law, provide employees with written explanation of risks associated with the use of toxic materials, including information currently required for Material Safety Data Sheets under U.S. law. This information will be conveyed with illustrations in simply understood Spanish.[11]

3. Use chemicals that are the safest and least toxic for employees, especially from the standpoint of their reproductive and other functional capacity.[12]

4. Design work operations and tasks to limit repetitive strain injuries and other ergonomic problems.[13]

5. As required by Mexican law, each plant will establish worker/management health-and-safety commissions, allowing workers to elect their representatives to these commissions. These commissions will be trained in health and safety and charged with making monthly plant inspections and recommendations for improving plant safety.[14]

6. Provide all employees with health-and-safety training using a qualified instructor approved by the Joint Health and Safety Commission. Training will include identification of and protection against health-and-safety hazards, including those which negatively affect human reproductive health and function. Training and drills will be conducted on evacuation procedures for facility emergencies including fire and chemical leaks.[15]

7. Provide an adequate ventilation system including local exhaust for all point sources of air contamination, as well as provide employees with appropriate protective equipment and clothing to minimize risk of toxic exposure and as a backup (not a replacement) for ventilation. The corporations will keep sources of clean water for washing and showering and fire fighting equipment in areas where hazardous materials are used.[16]

8. Arrange health-and-safety inspections by qualified outside consultants (approved by the Joint Health and Safety Commission) at least once every six months and provide public disclosure of inspection reports.[17]

9. Provide fair damage compensation to any worker who suffers an occupational injury or illness.[18]

10. In accordance with Mexican law and the OSHA Medical Records Rule, provide all employees and their designated representatives access to medical records, including medical and employment questionnaires and histories, results of medical examinations and lab tests, medical opinions and diagnoses, and descriptions of treatments. U.S. corporations will be responsible for providing maquiladora employees and their representatives access to both in-house and contractual medical records.[19]

SECTION III: Fair Employment Practices and Standard of Living

U.S. corporations will respect basic workers' rights and human dignity.

1. U.S. corporations will not engage in employment discrimination based on sex, age, race, religious creed, or political beliefs. Equal pay will be provided for equal work, regardless of sex, age, race, religious creed, or political beliefs.[20]

2. In general, workers will be provided with a fair and just wage, reasonable hours of work, and decent working conditions.[21]

3. U.S. corporations will not interfere with workers' rights to organize and to reach collective bargaining agreements, including grievance procedures. Workers who seek to organize will not be harassed in present or future work endeavors.[22]

4. U.S. corporations will not employ or utilize child labor and will exercise good faith in ensuring that employees are of legal working age.[23]

5. U.S. corporations will distribute profit sharing to employees as required by Mexican law. For accounting purposes and calculating fair distribution of profit sharing, U.S. corporations will consider maquiladoras as profit centers, provide full financial disclosure in an annual report for maquiladora facilities (or entire Mexican subsidiary), and make public formula and calculations used for determining profit sharing distribution.[24]

6. U.S. corporations will print and distribute a written handbook on company employment policies to all employees as required by Mexican law. This handbook will include a description of basic employee rights under Mexican labor laws and information on government-mandated benefits such as severance pay and medical treatment. When a union contract exists, it will be posted in the plant.[25]

7. In the workplace, U.S. corporations will take positive steps to prevent sexual harassment. Policies will be developed to ensure strict disciplinary measures against sexual harassment. To support these policies, programs will be established to educate employees about what constitutes sexual harassment. Finally, a supportive environment will be created, giving workers the confidence needed to report incidents of sexual harassment.[26]

SECTION IV: Community Impact

U.S. transnational corporations recognize that they have social responsibilities to the local communities in Mexico and the United States where they locate facilities. These responsibilities include a commitment to community economic development and improvements in the quality of life. Facilities will not be abandoned to avoid these responsibilities.

1. U.S. corporations will not promote barracks-style living arrangements for employees. Where these living arrangements already exist, U.S. corporations will take immediate action to improve living conditions and ensure that workers are provided with basic human rights. U.S. corporations will also schedule biannual inspections of the barracks by representatives of an internationally recognized human rights organization. Finally, U.S. corporations will seek positive housing alternatives to present barracks living arrangements.

2. Corporations operating maquiladoras will work to es-

tablish special trust funds to finance infrastructure improvements in colonias near maquiladora plants. All area maquiladora operations will be asked to contribute to these trust funds. The funds will be managed by trustees representing the corporations, employees, and community leaders. Educational institutions on both sides of the border are possible resources for directing appropriate allocations of these funds. Trust fund contributions, investments, assets, and expenditures will be publicly disclosed.

Notes

1 Agency of Urban Development and Ecology.

2 All references to "corporations operating maquiladoras" include corporations which utilize contractors or shelter plants.

3 The *Mexican General Law of Ecology and Equilibrium and Protection of Environment.*

4 *U.S. Emergency Preparedness and Community Right to Know Act,* P.L. 99-499, Title 111. The *Mexican General Law of Ecology and Equilibrium and Protection of Environment* obligates a generator to file a monthly record on hazardous waste generated. Generators are required to report, every six months, a detailed record of movements of hazardous materials from storage.

5 Present environmental regulations in Mexico do not include the concept of "from cradle to grave," applicable under U.S. environmental law *(RCRA [The Resource Control and Recovery Act]).* Therefore, under Mexican law, in some cases, there may be loopholes which would allow U.S. companies to avoid disclosure of final location for disposing hazardous waste. However, in the case where hazardous wastes are shipped back to the United States, a company must disclose the final location for disposal under EPA regulations. If a U.S. company is contracting with a Mexican firm for the disposal or recycling of waste in Mexico, the Mexican firm contracted must have authorization by *SEDUE.*

6 *The Mexican General Law of Ecology and Equilibrium and Protection of Environment,* Title 1, Chapter VII, Ecological Technical Standards.

7 *The Mexican General Law of Ecology and Equilibrium and Protection of Environment* requires that a maquiladora file an Ecological Clearance Certificate *(Guia Ecológica)* with *SEDUE* to obtain authorization for transporting hazardous waste. U.S. corporations that are trucking materials into the United States should be using trucks which meet federal and state transportation regulations including inspection, proper placarding, and weight restrictions.

8 Both Annex 3 of the *Agreement Between the United States of America and the United Mexican States on Cooperation for the Protection and Improvement of the Environment in the Border Area* and the *General Law of Ecology and Equilibrium and Protection of Environment* require that hazardous waste generated during maquiladora production operations be returned to the country of their origin. Certification of final disposal location is required under *RCRA.*

9 The Mexican Secretary of Labor and Social Provision is responsible for issuing occupational health-and-safety regulations in Mexico. The U.S. *Occupational Safety and Health Standards* are codified in 29 CFR 1900–1910.

10 Refer to *Ley Federal de Trabajo,* Art. 132, XVII and *Reglamento General de*

Seguridad e Higiene en el Trabajo 138, 123, 128, 134, 189, 190, 203–205, 209, 218, 221, 222, 225. U.S. law: 29 CFR 1910.1200 (the *Hazard Communication Standard)* requires that employers must disclose to employees and their designated representatives information about the identity and use of chemicals used on the premises (29 CFR 1910.1200 (e)). It also requires labeling of chemicals (29 CFR 1910.1200 (f) (5)). See also *International Labor Organization Convention* No. 170. (The ILO has developed internationally recognized standards for many health-and-safety and fair employment practices. ILO standards, referred to as Conventions, are ratifiable by and, when ratified, binding on countries sending union, management, and government representatives to the ILO. ILO Recommendations are nonmandatory guidelines for national action, legislation, and collective negotiations.)

11 Refer to *Ley Federal de Trabajo,* Art. 132, XVII and *Reglamento General de Seguridad e Higiene en el Trabajo,* Reg. 138, 123, 128, 134, 189, 190, 203–205, 209, 218, 221, 222, 225. U.S. *Information and Material Safety Data Sheets* are required by 29 CFR 1910.2000 (h). See also, 29 CFR 1910.1200 (g); ILO *Convention* No. 170.

12 Refer to *Reglamento General de Seguridad e Higiene en el Trabajo,* Reg. 136-I(a); Reg. 136-I(c); ILO Recommendations Nos. 97 and 42.

13 Refer to *Ley Federal de Trabajo,* Art.138.

14 Refer to *Ley Federal de Trabajo,* Art.509; 133 XXVII, 391 1X and *Reglamento General de Seguridad e Higiene en el Trabajo,* Reg. 193-212; ILO *Convention* No. 155 and Recommendation No. 164.

15 Refer to *Ley Federal de Trabajo,* Art. 153-F (111) and *Reglamento General de Seguridad e Higiene en el Trabajo* Reg. 30. ILO *Convention* No. 155 and Recommendation No. 164.

16 Refer to *Ley Federal de Trabajo,* Art. 132 XVI, XVII and *Reglamento General de Seguridad e Higiene en el Trabajo,* ventilation Reg. 146, 154, 168, 210; clothing Reg. 136, 170–174; water Reg. 132, 179, 180; fire 15, 16, 136, 161. U.S.

29 CFR Section 1910.1000 (*Toxic and Hazardous Substances)* covers maximum air levels for specific chemical substances. 29 CFR 1910.1000 (e) requires engineering and administrative controls (e.g. ventilation) to take precedence over personal protective equipment; requires personal protective equipment where necessary. ILO *Conventions* Nos. 148, 155, and 156 and Recommendation No. 164.

17 Refer to *Ley Federal de Trabajo,* Art. 511, 512, 527, 529, 992, 1008; *Mexican Constitution XXI,* and *Reglamento General de Seguridad e Higiene en el Trabajo,* Reg. 202, 213, 214. ILO *Conventions* Nos. 148, 155, and 156.

18 ILO *Conventions* Nos. 17, 18, 19, 25, 42, and 121.

19 Refer to *Reglamento General de Seguridad e Higiene en el Trabajo,* Art. 215, 224. U.S. law: 29 CFR 1910.20.

20 Refer to *Ley Federal de Trabajo,* Art. 3, 133-1, VIII. ILO *Conventions* Nos. 90, 100, 111; for women, see *Conventions* Nos. 89 and 103.

21 ILO *Convention* Nos. 82, 110, 131; cf. also *Conventions* Nos. 1, 14, 47, and 116; and for women, Nos. 89 and 103.

22 *Ley Federal de Trabajo,* Art. 5, 111 and *Mexican Constitution,* Art. 123, XXVII(a). ILO *Convention* No. 87.

23 *Ley Federal de Trabajo,* Art. 175. Mexican law prohibits utilization of workers under the age of sixteen years. Industrial night work (after 8 p.m.) is prohibited for workers under the age of eighteen. ILO *Conventions* 5, 10, 59, 60, 123, 124, 138 and 146.

24 Profit sharing or "Reparto de Utilidades" is required under *Ley Federal de Trabajo,* Art. 117–131, 1334V, V, 354, 357, 359, *Mex.Constitution* Article 123-XVI–XXII.

25 Required under *Ley Federal de Trabajo,* Art. 425, 422, 423, 424, 1001, 1003 and *Reglamento Interior del Trabajo,* Art. 192.

26 *Ley Federal de Trabajo,* Art. 56, 3, 132, refers to fair treatment and prohibits sexual discrimination.

FIVE

A BORDER PARTNERSHIP: THE CFO AND THE AFSC

After three months with General Electric (GE), a young man named Eduardo was laid off. His friend Alicia, a member of the Comité Fronterizo de Obreras (CFO—Border Committee of Women Workers), warned him against signing resignation papers and informed him of his right to substantial severance benefits under Mexican labor law. GE offered him 800 pesos, but Eduardo knew he was entitled to more and refused to sign. The next day, on Alicia's recommendation, he came back to work as usual. After a while he was escorted out by company security guards. When he came back the following day, management offered him 2200 pesos. He accepted.

About a month later he saw Alicia in the street. "Thanks to you I was able to put a roof over my children's heads," Eduardo told her excitedly. "Now we have three rooms to our house instead of two. I used to feel ignorant, but I've been sharing what you taught me with other workers."[1]

At Carrizo, a garment company in Piedras Negras, Coahuila, operators were plagued by lint and dust accumulation. It settled on them while they worked, covering their skin, hair, and clothing. The workers tried petitioning for better ventilation, but management did not respond to their pleas. CFO members who worked in the plant realized they had to demonstrate their need more creatively. Instead of constantly brushing themselves off, the workers allowed the lint to collect one morning when they knew the general manager would be in their area. The sight of workers coated in lint and dust shocked the manager, and he immediately stopped to talk to them. The workers, who had prepared themselves through role plays and discussions in CFO meetings, took advantage of the situation to voice their complaints.

Conditions changed rapidly. Extractors were adapted to old machines to carry the lint away, and new air pres-

sure extractors were attached directly to the cutting machines to keep the lint from escaping into the air. At their next meeting, the CFO workers laughed as they shared the strategy behind this victory.[2]

Such shopfloor actions have formed the lifeblood of the CFO. Women begin by meeting in small groups to discuss their problems at work. Most are surprised to learn of their rights under Mexico's labor law, one of the strongest labor codes in the world. "For me to learn the labor law was like opening a window," says María Guadalupe Torres, one of the founders of the CFO and coordinator of the group's eastern region until her retirement in 1998.[3]

Through brainstorming and role plays, participants in these groups develop tactics to address their immediate complaints. When they are ready, they begin asserting their rights at work. The CFO helps workers develop knowledge, confidence, and leadership ability to carry with them inside and outside the factory. Perhaps most important, CFO members develop a sense of solidarity: they come to understand that through mutual support, they can be instrumental in bringing about change in the workplace, in their unions, and at home. In hundreds, perhaps thousands, of cases, maquiladora workers have won victories like those described above.

Increasingly, the CFO is building on this base of shopfloor activism to strengthen organizing efforts in the maquiladora industry. An important step forward came in 1998, when the group filed for legal status as a nonprof t organization (asociación civil) in Mexico and opened i s own office in Piedras Negras, Coahuila. This move h. s strengthened communication among CFO groups in different cities, as well as relationships with other organizations. Not long after, a group of maquiladora activists in

Agua Prieta, Sonora (on the Arizona border) joined the CFO, extending the group's reach beyond its traditional base at the Texas-Mexico border. AFSC's Tucson, Arizona office has been supportive of the new CFO branch in Sonora.

The CFO grew out of outreach efforts by AFSC that date back to the early years of the maquiladora industry in the late 1970s. Although today the CFO is an autonomous Mexican grassroots organization, the two groups continue to maintain a close partnership, collaborating on a variety of projects.

One such effort is the Maquiladora Health Initiative, launched in 1997. This project will provide advanced training in occupational and environmental health to CFO activists. A key goal is to develop more integrated strategies to protect worker and community health, rather than responding to problems on a case-by-case basis.

The CFO is also working to strengthen its ties with Mexico City–based groups, in an effort to overcome the isolation of border towns from the significant political changes underway throughout the country. In 1998, CFO collaborated with the Red Mexicana de Accion Frente al Libre Comercio (RMALC—Mexican Free Trade Action Network) to research the impact of NAFTA on the maquiladora industry. As part of this initiative, RMALC activists provided training on NAFTA and the global economy to the CFO membership.

The CFO has long provided a crucial link for U.S. groups seeking to understand the reality of the maquiladoras, as well as individual researchers, reporters, and policy makers. The fieldwork for numerous studies and reports has been carried out with the group's assistance. As labor unions and women's groups in Central America seek to respond to the growth of the maquiladora industry

in their countries, many of them have also received help from the CFO.

In 1995, the CFO brought its experience to the global arena through nongovernmental fora held in conjunction with two United Nations summits: the Social Summit in Copenhagen in March, and the Beijing Women's Conference in September. At both meetings, CFO coordinator Julia Quiñonez participated in international tribunals highlighting violations of women's human rights, which were organized by the Center for Women's Global Leadership at Rutgers University.

In Beijing, Julia spoke to an audience of over 2000 women from around the world. "Women's participation in the world is growing," she said. "I'm proud to be a woman, to feel anger and the thirst for justice … Through the Comité Fronterizo de Obreras, maquiladora workers are joining our strength, our ideas and our hearts into a movement of solidarity. We are asking, who is benefiting from this system? How is it possible to speak of justice when there exist international agreements which do not mention the rights of women workers? We are waiting patiently for the answers to these questions."[4]

Notes

1 Ed Krueger, Report on CFO Activities, Comité de Apoyo, Edinburg, Texas, Jan. 1996, p. 2.

1 Ed Krueger, Report on CFO Activities, Comité de Apoyo, Edinburg, Texas, Jan. 1996, p. 6.

3 "Knowledge is power for workers," *AFSC Community Relations Division Bulletin,* Summer 1994, p.2.

4 Testimony of Julia Quinoñes de Gonzalez to Global Tribunal on Accountability for Women's Rights, Nongevernmental Forum, Fourth World Conference on Women, Beijing, China, 1995.

READINGS

The selections in this chapter illustrate various aspects of the long-term collaboration between the CFO and AFSC.

In "Taking Flight," Ricardo Hernández, director of AFSC's Mexico-U.S. Border Program, introduces the group to the broad Mexican readership of La Jornada, *a prominent progressive daily published in Mexico City.*

In "We Are Not Machines," CFO founder María

Guadalupe Torres shares her story of personal transformation, interwoven with the texture of the group's grassroots organizing.

In the final selection, "Building Fairness in the Maquiladoras," Phoebe McKinney, director of AFSC's Maquiladora Project from 1991 to 1996, recounts her experiences as a maquiladora activist.

Taking Flight

By Ricardo Hernández

When I look at Julia Quiñonez it makes me think of director Wim Wenders and his film about the angels who come down to earth and get themselves mixed up with humans—real angels, not their cheap imitations in *Touched by an Angel*. A little while ago we drove across the border between Reynosa and McAllen, and the gringo immigration agents didn't ask her anything. They didn't even ask to see her papers. "It's because she's an angel," says a sixtyish compañero who is traveling with us. He meant it. And I believe it, because when I'm with the Comité Fronterizo de Obreras (CFO), worn-out metaphors mean something again, and trite remarks become inexplicably convincing.

Esperanza, who works for General Electric in Ciudad Acuña, Coahuila, is not being melodramatic when she says that the opening of the CFO office in Piedras Negras (on April 3, 1998), was like a dam bursting. After seventeen years of grassroots work with hundreds and thousands of workers in five border cities, the CFO finally went public by opening its first office—complete with computer and CFO@comuni-k.com.

The Zapatistas of the Maquiladoras

Esteban walks out of a factory called Rassini's and heads over to the CFO office to check the e-mail. From a maquiladora production line to the information superhighway. It's hard not to compare these workers to the Zapatistas at the other end of Mexico. Not just because they're surfing the net, but because these workers, just like the Indians of Chiapas, draw their strength more from moral authority than from political savvy.

Members of the CFO voice a constant refrain: to stick with what the workers say. As a result, demagoguery is absent, and even oratory is scarce. They're not seeking political power and don't pay much attention to elections. Their decency, and the way they make everyone feel included, win them respect. It wasn't for nothing that at Carrizo Manufacturing, the workers themselves started calling the CFO members in their ranks "our Zapatistas."

Originally published in slightly different form in *La Jornada*, "Masiosare" (weekly review) No. 32, July 5, 1998. Reprinted by permission. Translation by Rachael Kamel.

Paty Leyva is one of them. She's been working in the maquiladoras since she was fourteen. Now she's twenty-seven, with three children. She has delicate ways and a certain air of distinction; I can imagine her running a non-profit in Mexico City, with sensitivity and good judgment.

Paty is with Armando; Norma with Esteban; "Dolly" with Rey; Julia with Oscar. Four young couples, like hundreds of thousands in these border towns, where there are by far fewer aunts and grandmothers to keep watch. I don't see many couples, or even single people, over thirty or thirty-five. Older people look out of place, as if we struck a sour note, at least in Piedras Negras and Ciudad Acuña.

Besides, career options here are limited; when you can't work in a factory any more, your only alternatives are to flip burgers or become a househusband (king of your own castle?), a small-time drug dealer, or perhaps a bouncer. Taxi drivers, that plague of Mexico City, don't even exist in these two cities.

Maritoña is with her boy, Isabel with her two kids, Mericia her three, and Esperanza, four. Single mothers, also young. They can talk to you about ergonomics and the Federal Labor Law. They also know that the 1996 salary of John F. Smith, the CEO of General Motors, was equivalent to the salaries of 3128$\frac{1}{2}$ Maritoñas.

The Wings of Many Desires

I'm trying to figure out whether it's their youth that allows the CFOs to smile so brightly when they leave the plants after a ten-hour shift with two short breaks. Like Paty smiles as she explores the computer in the CFO office and finds a picture of the orange-colored entrance to Carrizo, looking just like she saw it in person that morning, decorating the cyberpropaganda of the Piedras Negras industrial park, which announces in English its search for "a few good companies—seeking a large, low-cost, skillful labor force."

I think that Esperanza, at least, would like it if I said out loud that the CFOs wear their own wings of desire: the desire for justice. If I keep on like this, though, I'll only deserve to be washed away like toxic waste to the circle of hell reserved for sentimentality, there to burn myself up in about three more lines. I don't want to gush, either, about the other dimension of the CFO: their distance from political games, or the way that for years they maintained an otherworldly, almost virginal silence in public (just like angels). For good or ill, the CFO stood apart, uninvolved and unaware of the last fifteen years in the development of Mexican social movements—perhaps because its eyes were turned more toward the north.

Duet: Eddie Vedder with Julia Quiñonez

The comparison is anything but gratuitous: neither Subcomandante Marcos nor Julia Quiñonez likes to be identified as the leader of the organizations they belong to. Although both have a voice in important decisions, they are more interested in trying to interpret and serve what comes from the grassroots. Julia is ten years younger than Marcos, not as sophisticated, and—thank heaven!—she doesn't smoke. Among her many virtues she has cultivated a genuine modesty and an unstoppable way of doing things that place her in the ranks of those who really make a difference. Maybe that's why she appeared in an article in the inflight magazine of Continental Airlines, crossing the skies in a photo that shows her talking on the phone with a big smile. She's standing in her house, her twins and her little girl behind her, before the birth of her fourth child.

I loathe talking about people as personalities. Here in the CFO office, though, we're not fifty yards from the Rio Grande/Río Bravo, and so many things are done gringo style. So I allow myself to imagine writing something that would start by saying, *when I look at Julia Quiñonez it makes me think of director Wim Wenders,* and that kind of foolishness. Like someone else might write, *All one night I walked through the jungle until at last, near dawn, I reached Marcos* . . . Instead of talking about the workers, or the Indians, their starvation wages or their starvation without wages. Or about the environmental nightmare and urban disaster that is Ciudad Acuña. Or about the workers who cross every week from Piedras Negras to Eagle Pass, Texas, where they sell their blood to help cover their weekly expenses.

I could be talking about Maritoña, who's trying to figure out where to get $1000 for the dental work that her ten-year-old son needs so urgently, because he hardly ever eats without his mouth bleeding. About how heavily that $1000 debt will weigh on her, because she only earns $37 a week. Or even about how Julia breaks out in a sweat when she sets off in her aging van to scale the hills that hold the shantytowns of Acuña, where her infinite patience takes her often to explain to more women their rights under the labor code.

So it feels contradictory when we send out PR telling how Julia spoke about the maquiladoras at the Copenhagen Social Summit, in the Beijing Women's Conference, in Guatemala, in Mexico City, and in more places than she can remember in the United States. How she herself worked in a maquiladora owned by Johnson & Johnson, from the age of fifteen until she was twenty. How she studied social work at night—and how she was born in Torreón, where she lived until her parents took her northward when she was eight, never suspecting that the change would make their little girl's eyes grow even bigger and brighter. But the propaganda serves a purpose: in Julia, you can see the great dignity and courage of maquila women.

I'm not trying to make a difference, says Eddie Vedder—naturally, after he already has. But I believe Pearl Jam after I hear Julia insist, with her steady gaze: *it's not me but the workers, the women who decide.* And Vedder again: *Let's call an angel* . . .

The Forklift Operator and the Minority Whip

April 1998: four women from the border travel to Washington for two days of lobbying. From Piedras Negras come Paty Leyva and Julia. Esther from General Motors arrives from Reynosa. All three are with the CFO. The fourth is Bety from Factor X in Tijuana. "We want to have influence in Washington," says Julia in a public meeting organized by the Washington Office on Latin America and the Latin America Working Group. Then she adds, "but we haven't come to ask for your pity, but to say that we believe it is very important for us to be connected to you, because together we can make positive change." That's the idea she wants to linger in the minds of those who are listening, not just the horrific stories that Paty and Esther have told.

In the Capitol we visit the office of the minority whip, David Bonior, third most important in the Democratic Party in the U.S. Congress. The four Mexican women sit across from nine representatives and a dozen congressional staff. Bonior called the meeting, sending an invitation describing the Mexicans as honored guests. Each of them speaks, then Paty Leyva shows some of the "safety equipment" that the maquiladoras give out to their workers: a flimsy cotton mask, which is supposed to protect against the lint that also gets in your eyes, your nose, and your ears in the garment plants; plastic goggles like swimmers use, which are supposed to protect workers from the rivers of mud at the LABASA brick-making plant; plastic earplugs, which are supposed to protect against the intense, unending noise of the riveting operation at Carrizo; and a pair of workgloves, which are supposed to protect those who handle the recently cast components of automotive chassis. The key term here is "supposed to."

The representatives feel the gloves, which once were yellow and now are stained with grease, stinking, stiff, held together with homemade denim patches, and even so falling apart. They look like hands. As if one of the forklift operators from Rassini's were here in person, shaking the hand of a congressperson.

Paty goes on, because she still has to show the solder used in the maquiladora Lirifius (that's "Spanish" for Littelfuse), whose label indicates that it's banned in California because it can cause cancer. She also has a photograph of a woman who was sickened by this solder and then fired by the company when she fell ill. The last thing Paty shows are the one-sided scissors that she uses when she sews Dockers. They look just like the ones I bought at Strawbridge's in Center City Philadelphia.

Workers in Black, Going Back to the Future

We move in a posse, because that's how they all live, inside and outside the factory. At 11:00 one night, eight of us set out from Piedras Negras, heading for Acuña. Julia is driving the '98 Ford Expedition rented by one of our friends on the other side: a black van with polarized windshield, black like the outfits that many of the CFOs agreed to wear for the inauguration of their office. Just like the Men in Black, they said. No way we're not going.

In the darkness of the highway, we turn on the hi-beams that Esperanza makes, while we're cooled by an air conditioner just like the ones that Esther is assembling right now on the graveyard shift in Reynosa.

Forget about not turning up the radio, says Julia, because it's so much better than her tape player; that's why Maritoña has already begun to sing "Jefe de Jefes" from the Tigres del Norte, while Esperanza and Julia flow together and turn into Candelaria, Rosa Lupe, and Marina, the Malinches of the maquiladoras, who go back to the future from the third paragraph of page 147 of *The Crystal Frontier* by Carlos Fuentes, singing softly, *I'm sailing beneath the water, and I can fly up high . . .*

— *May 1998*

We Are Not Machines

by María Guadalupe Torres

I was sixteen when I came from my home in central Mexico to Matamoros, on the border. My dream was to get a good job, save money, and return to my hometown to set up a small business.

I worked in a maquiladora . . . for eighteen years. Every day I rose at 4:30 a.m. and was at my work station at 6:45, where I spent the entire day. I couldn't go to the bathroom without getting permission.

My job was to assemble electronic capacitors with epoxy. Many coworkers developed health problems because of the epoxy. I don't know if it is responsible for my current health problems or not.

I was paid $27 for a forty-eight-hour week. Twenty-two percent of that went for transportation. I worked three-and-a-half hours to buy a gallon of milk. My diet was a few potatoes, six eggs, a kilo each of tortillas and beans. Meat, vegetables, and fruit were unaffordable luxuries.

I lived in one room with an outdoor toilet. My colonia [neighborhood] had no potable water, no electricity, no sidewalks, no infrastructure. (Maquiladoras do not contribute to local taxes.)

Families build their homes themselves, buying cheap construction materials over time. Workers for Fortune 500 companies like General Motors, Zenith, and AT&T don't even have decent homes and can only afford used clothes and just enough food to keep them alive.

Usually only women are hired in the maquiladoras, creating conflicts because the men cannot find work. Back home in the countryside, men worked in the *milpa* [cornfield], harvesting, earning the family living. This role loss creates huge conflicts as men struggle to adapt to city life. Some become alcoholic.

While some maquila workers may work twenty years at the same job, many leave because of illness. Many workers have carpal tunnel syndrome from repetitive work. Children are born deformed or anencephalic. There are tremendous health problems—and it's getting worse.

I began organizing to improve working conditions in the maquiladoras nearly fifteen years ago. As I saw the conditions in which we were forced to work, I got very angry. I was used to poverty, but not such mistreatment.

I said to my coworker, "How is it possible that we continue to put up with this? We have to do something!"

A couple of days later, she told me someone was teaching workers in one of the neighborhoods about the rights of the people. "Why don't we go?" she said.

Fifteen of us went, out of curiosity. We were shocked to realize we *had* any rights. We didn't quite trust this gringo, but we began asking questions and discovering. It was tremendous—like someone opening a curtain!

We organized within the factory. Slowly, things were added to protect us—like adequate ventilation, air conditioning, gloves.

It changed my life. I left the maquiladora several years ago to work as a full-time organizer with the Comité Fronterizo de Obreras (Border Committee of Working Women).

We go from colonia to colonia, getting to know people, talking to folk who are out washing clothes or watering plants. We talk with the mothers—if the parents trust us, they will begin to talk with their children.

It's beautiful work. Girls who are very timid and embarrassed begin to take hold of their lives. They organize in order to get electricity or sewage for their communities.

It's wonderful to hear them say, "Look, I did this!" or "I became a supervisor!" or "Look! We didn't have gloves before, and now they've given them to us." They realize that they can accomplish something.

Earning the trust of women is sometimes a miraculous process. Yesterday, I met a woman who told me the story of her life—of her problems with her husband (whom she eventually had to throw out), of a child that she was forced to abandon, of her work in the factory. I thought to myself, "God is with us, that this woman would trust us so."

But the demands life puts on the workers leave very little space for organizing. We may have a meeting planned for 5:00 p.m., and the women will often be detained at work, and arrive at six or seven—bone-tired, wanting to wash up and tend to the family. We have to postpone the meeting to a day when they won't have to work so late.

Weather also affects us. Extreme heat and heavy rains can make it impossible to go into the colonias. We would

---

Originally published in *The Other Side* magazine, Jan.-Feb. 1997. Reprinted by permission.

like to reach out to more colonias, but we don't have money to hire more organizers.

I have never been threatened or afraid. We work peacefully. We don't incite violent confrontation. We are working with women to help them claim their rights, and what matters to us is that they do so in a way that is persistent but nonviolent.

Over the years, that persistence has paid off. Salaries in Matamoros are higher than in other border cities. We've won a forty-hour week. We have security teams.

More water-treatment equipment has been installed so that the chemicals don't go directly into the soil. (Of course the soil is already contaminated. But measures have been taken to improve this.) Many workers who were fired have received *indemnización* [severance pay], in compliance with Mexican law.

The conditions in the colonias have changed too—many neighborhoods have now been paved or have sewage service. But the changes can't keep up with the outpouring of people from the interior. More colonias spring up overnight with no services. This is a huge problem.

I believe deeply in God. My life is a testimony to how much God has done in and for me.

When I am tired and don't want to continue, I hear an answer—I must continue because there is great need.

I believe that it is because God is with us that we have never been threatened or harmed even though the severe unemployment, poor conditions, and drug addiction produce high crime rates in many colonias.

I want to express to my Christian brothers and sisters in North America gratitude for your concern. I welcome you to come visit firsthand.

This work fills our spirits. Our spirits are fed because we are doing something for justice. We are doing work that God calls us to do. As for the companies that come here—I am grateful that there is work. Times are difficult. But tell them that when they come they should bring justice with them. They should bring protection and concern for our health. We are human beings, not machines. We are persons who feel and cry. We need the work, yes. But let it be a just and good work. Let it be work that brings us life, not death.

Building Fairness in the Maquiladoras
by Phoebe McKinney

Sure we need jobs, but not at the price of our health, not if it means killing people on both sides of the border.

— Woman maquiladora worker

I am one in a long line of cars waiting to cross the international bridge from Brownsville, Texas into Matamoros, Mexico. Sharing the line with me are dozens of trucks bearing the names of major American companies. I once believed that these names—General Electric, General Motors, Zenith—symbolized good jobs, decent pay, and a better future. However, as I watch the names of corporate America disappear over the bridge into Mexico, I am reminded of how much the globalization of the economy has changed everything—in today's global economy, corporations are no longer bound by promises and obligations to anything or anyone. . . .

As the Director of the Maquiladora Project, I frequently travel to the border in order to better interpret the "human face" of the maquiladora industry to concerned U.S. groups and individuals. I work closely with the women organizers (*promotoras*) of the Comité Fronterizo de Obreras (CFO). An autonomous Mexican women's worker movement, CFO developed as the result of the decade-plus efforts of the AFSC's Maquiladora Project. CFO's underlying principle is that the people that globalization of the economy affects the most—workers—are the most qualified to make far-reaching changes which enhance their basic dignity and worth in the maquiladora industry.

One of the CFO's primary organizing tools is the study of the powerful but unenforced Mexican federal labor law. Many workers in the maquilas come from economically devastated communities in Mexico's interior, lured by the promise of "good jobs" working for giant U.S. corporations. Most are unaware that as Mexican citizens they are protected by some of the most stringent labor laws in the world. The maquiladora industry exploits this lack of awareness, violating workers' rights frequently and with impunity. Frequent abuses include illegal payroll deductions, harsh and arbitrary discipline, sexual harassment, and forbidding

workers to go to clinics when ill or injured on the job. CFO *promotoras*, all of whom who work, or have worked in the maquilas, bring small groups of workers together to study the law, gently encouraging self-expression and the participation of the workers themselves in the organizing process.

My essential task on this particular day is to accompany several CFO *promotoras* in Matamoros on their daily organizing work. Our first stop in Matamoros is at the house of a Zenith worker.

In Matamoros, the CFO has struggled long and hard for stronger, more effective union representation. Because of their efforts, workers in Matamoros receive higher wages and work a shorter week than in other border towns. The Zenith worker we are with today however, complains that despite a government-mandated wage increase, she is actually earning less money than before because she is only working four days a week. She adds this is part of an ongoing slowdown at Zenith, and that there are half as many workers in the plant as there were a year ago. She fears losing her job.

Generally, wages throughout the maquiladora industry are abysmal, and cuts in earnings can spell disaster for workers and their families. The average daily take home pay is $4.00 for a 48-hour week, almost half the daily wages in Asia's four major export processing zones (Hong Kong, Taiwan, Korea, and Singapore). Maquiladora workers complain bitterly that it is impossible to make ends meet, especially since prices for basic commodities on the Mexican side of the border are often higher than they are in the United States.

As we leave, the *promotoras* and I talk about how gains made by Matamoros workers are undercut as Zenith shifts its production to other border towns. The *promotoras* tell me they are frustrated because they have no way of knowing exactly how bad conditions are for workers in other Zenith plants. They have been busy here in Matamoros assisting laid-off Zenith workers to fight to secure their legally mandated severance pay.

Toxic Tour

Our next stop is the FINSA Industrial Park in Matamoros, home to a number of giant assembly plants, including Magnatek, GE, GM, and Trico, a windshield wiper

Originally published in *Listen Real Loud,* newsletter of the AFSC Nationwide Women's Program, Vol. 12, No. 1, 1993.

factory which moved its operations from Buffalo, New York several years ago.

From the outside of the plants, there is no hint of criminally low wages, inhumane treatment, and dangerous working conditions. They look more like community colleges, with trim grass and attractive landscaping.

We arrive in time to watch the shift change, and as usual I am amazed that the thousands of energetic, attractively dressed young people pouring out of the plants look more like students with promising futures than full-time industrial workers completing long workshifts. Their youthful demeanor belies the fact that the average productive life of a maquiladora worker is ten years. Few can endure the mental and physical strains of dangerous working conditions, escalating production quotas (when a plant moves to Mexico, production speed is increased an estimated 25 percent), and the constant fear of being fired. Despite the lack of alternatives, turnover in the industry can be as high as 180 percent a year.

One of the most critical issues raised by the maquiladora workers is the danger their work poses to their health. Workers are exposed to a variety of hazardous substances, including xylene, trichlorethylene, and lead. Despite working with dangerous substances, the workers are rarely given health and safety instructions or protective equipment.

These chemicals and other toxic substances are also dumped directly into the air, water, and ground in border communities. As part of their efforts to alert people in the United States to the multi-faceted impact of the industry on their lives, the CFO often takes visitors on a "toxic tour." The proposed Free Trade Agreement (NAFTA) has greatly increased the level of international interest in the border, and in the past two years the CFO ... has taken journalists, labor unions, politicians, environmentalists, religious groups, and researchers on the "toxic tour."

Our first stop on the "toxic tour" is to inspect three large cement pipes pouring effluent into a canal. Each time I visit, the effluent is a different color. Today, one pipe is spewing pitch black, and while the other two are clear, they emit a smell which is so powerful that I spend the next ten minutes attempting to clear my throat of a strong burning and choking sensation.

Further down the canal, we stop to inspect the effluent in a pipe coming out of General Motor's notorious Rimir plant. In 1990, the CFO and AFSC helped the National Toxics Campaign (NTC) collect water samples from key polluted sites for the NTC's report, "Border Trouble: Rivers in Peril." The report revealed that the discharge from General Motors' Rimir plant contained xylene at 2,800,000 parts per billion, which is more than 6,300 times the amount allowed by U.S. drinking water standards. The suspected carcinogen methylene chloride was also detected at levels 215,000 times the U.S. ambient water quality criterion. Although GM continues to dispute the NTC's results, they have begun building a waste treatment facility in the FINSA industrial park.

The canals from the FINSA park run through a number of poor neighborhoods. One of the *promotoras* mentions that people fish and swim in them and I ask her if people understand that the water is dangerous. She explains that some do, but those who fish in the canals do so because they are hungry and have no other choice.

We next turn onto a street nicknamed "Chemical Row," because it runs by several pesticide and chemical plants. These plants are located very near to several poor neighborhoods, and residents dread the long-term health consequences that pollution from the plants pose. One of the most infamous factories along "Chemical Row" is Stepan, which is owned by an Illinois-based family. NTC samples taken from behind the Stepan plant contained, among other things, xylene at 23,200,000 parts per billion—more than 52,700 times in excess of U.S. drinking water standards.

As we head back to the car, I ask one of the promotoras if there's a drug problem in Matamoros. I am shocked when she tells me that the biggest drug problem is addiction to paints, thinners, and glues. She explains that many of the workers become addicted to these substances because of constant exposure at work. She adds that some workers smuggle bags of glue out of the factories at the end of their shifts on Saturdays, so they will have enough glue to make it through Sunday, their day off.

The CFO spends much of its time gathering information about the substances the workers handle in order to determine the risk they pose to the workers and their children. One long-term effort is to convince companies to print warning labels in Spanish. At present, almost all such labels are printed in English only.

Pollution Knows No Borders

A recent and tragic outbreak of anencephaly (children born without brains) has dramatically shown that "the border" cannot shield the U.S. from the effects of the reckless practices of the maquiladora industry.

In recent months, medical authorities in Brownsville, Texas, and Matamoros have reported a dramatic rise in these tragic births. A medical investigation team in Brownsville, Texas believes that these defects are linked to toxic pollution created by the maquiladora industry. Scientific studies have specifically linked xylene to anencephalic birth defects.

The CFO is supporting local efforts to investigate the pollution hypothesis. The CFO has been distributing small air monitors to maquiladora workers in order to gather more information about toxic exposure levels in the plants. Other instruments are being used to test air pollution in the community.

The Struggle Continues

Over the years, CFO has had many successes. Victories include resisting forced overtime, stopping illegal dismissals, stopping abusive supervisors, negotiating *demandas* (claims for severance pay), making government-mandated plant "health-and-safety commissions" real, effective bodies, and insisting on proper safety and health protection. Sometimes these victories are between a worker and her supervisor; sometimes they are factory-wide.

Yet with all the victories, there is much that remains to be done. As I drop my friends off for the day, I wonder with anger and sadness why it's not considered a fundamental violation of human rights for the maquiladora industry to steal the futures from so many generations of young Mexicans, all in the name of "international competition."

I look at the *promotoras*, and wonder how they mange not to become bitter. I am filled with deep respect for their tenacity and courage, and recall one *promotora*'s beautiful summation of the workers' vision: "Our goals will be reached when hundreds of new women workers attend meetings and become skilled in solving work-related problems; when maquiladoras, as a matter of course, install fume extractors, establish safety-and-health commissions; when wages and contracts rise to a better than subsistence wage; and when women maquiladora workers are no longer exploited because they are young, poor, and female."

SIX

NAFTA–
AND BEYOND

More than any other issue, the North American Free Trade Agreement (NAFTA) has galvanized broad public awareness of the importance of international economic policy. At this writing, meanwhile, the focus of the debate is rapidly broadening to a series of initiatives that seek to extend NAFTA-style policies throughout the Americas and, in some cases, the globe.

For groups on both sides of the issue, NAFTA has served a prime example of the promise—or the threat—of global economic integration. While the U.S. government argues that NAFTA has enhanced the U.S. economy and "contributed to the prosperity and stability of our closest neighbors,"[1] others cite evidence that NAFTA has contributed to economic dislocation and environmental degradation.

NAFTA supporters have argued that such ill effects can rarely be traced to the agreement itself with any certainty. Opponents, for their part, respond that NAFTA is part of an overall approach to economic policy, and that it is more meaningful to look at the agreement in its broader context than to attempt to attribute individual phenomena to specific policy measures.

This chapter offers an introductory overview of the issues that have been raised in the debate over NAFTA and similar measures. The directory at the end of this book lists publications and organizations offering more in-depth analysis.

NAFTA and the Maquiladoras

During the campaign to secure the adoption of NAFTA, its proponents frequently predicted that it would decrease the concentration of maquiladoras at the border. Since tariff reductions were to be extended throughout Mexico, according to this view, the border area would be-

come less attractive to the maquiladora industry. A 1993 statement by the Clinton Administration argued that "[M]aquiladora development will tend to be dispersed away from the border area, to other parts of Mexico ... If NAFTA is not implemented, incentives will continue for the maquiladoras to locate facilities in the border areas, thus exacerbating environmental pressures."[2]

Belying such expectations, the maquiladora industry has expanded dramatically since NAFTA went into effect. According to a study by the Economic Policy Institute and other research groups, the maquiladoras employed an estimated 811,000 workers in 1997,[3] up from 689,420 in October 1995.[4] The result has been a continuing intensification of the range of environmental problems discussed in chapter 3, including uncontrolled industrial pollution, inadequate disposal of hazardous wastes, and rapid urban growth without the provision of resources for the development of public services.

Although such effects have not yet been documented in published literature, maquiladora workers report a significant intensification of the labor process through speed-ups and similar measures. Unfortunately, little research has been conducted on the specific impacts of NAFTA on the maquiladora industry. For the first time in 1999, the annual report on the continuing effects of NAFTA issued by the Red Mexicana de Acción Frente al Libre Comercio (RMALC—Mexican Free Trade Action Network) will include a chapter on the maquiladoras, presenting the results of the joint RMALC/CFO/AFSC monitoring project described in chapter 5.

Regionally, according to the UN International Labor Organization (ILO), NAFTA created significant advantages for border-based firms relative to export-processing plants in the Caribbean (which enjoy more limited tariff preferences under the Caribbean Basin Initiative). A 1998 report from the ILO notes that "since the introduction of NAFTA, over 150 companies and 123,000 jobs have been lost in the apparel industry in the Caribbean, and . . . many of those firms have relocated to Mexico." The report went on to project that "Asian apparel-exporting countries may be next to suffer from the residual NAFTA effect," since siting assembly plants at the border permits U.S. textile firms to supply "the bulk of the fabric" for garment manufacture. Notes the ILO, "with the vertically integrated operations some U.S. companies are now establishing in Mexico, we can expect to see the same trend towards competition based on the combined factors of speed, cost, and quality rather than simply on labor costs."[5]

NAFTA and Labor Rights

When introduced, NAFTA made no mention of labor or environmental protections, prompting a major outcry against the agreement by unions and other labor advocates, environmental groups, and human rights organizations. In response, the Clinton Administration proposed the adoption of labor and environmental "side agreements," which accompany NAFTA without actually being included within it. These side agreements were instrumental in muting opposition to the pact and securing its ratification by the U.S. Congress. Advocates, however, have been sharply critical of the implementation of both of these measures.

The North American Agreement on Labor Cooperation (NAALC), as it is formally known, includes measures to ensure the enforcement of national labor codes by each NAFTA country.* NAALC established a Ministerial Council made up of National Administrative Offices (NAOs) from each country. Each NAO is mandated to investigate charges of "failure to enforce" industrial relations laws—the right to freedom of association, collective bargaining, and the right to strike, in addition to laws relating to health and safety, child labor, and the minimum wages set by each nation.

Sanctions, however, cannot be levied against those governments that fail to enforce freedom of association. The most fundamental of all labor rights is thus protected only by the threat of public exposure. As one analysis comments, "NAALC, then, was an agreement based upon a hope and a prayer in a situation where there was . . . a demonstrable record of labor abuses."[6]

Several complaints have been filed under the NAALC since the signing of NAFTA. One of the first major cases involved Mexican workers from a maquiladora in Nuevo Laredo owned by Sony Electronics Corp. This complaint was filed by the International Labor Rights Research and Education Fund, the Coalition for Justice in the Maquiladoras, and Mexico's Association of Democratic Lawyers, along with AFSC and other groups. The workers accused Sony and the Mexican government of thwarting their attempts to form an independent union. The NAO ruled in favor of the workers and recommended formal cabinet-level consultations between then-U.S. Secretary of Labor Robert Reich and his Mexican counterpart at that time, Santiago Oñate.

Although workers have yet to see a significant change in abusive practices, the participants in the ground-breaking Sony hearings feel they were able to demonstrate the institutional strengths and limitations inherent to NAFTA's labor side agreement. According to Pharis Harvey of the International Labor Rights Research and Education Fund, "we continue to file these complaints because they demonstrate two things: one, what the problems are, and two, why we need a stronger agreement."[7]

The Economic Impact of NAFTA

NAFTA's economic impact on the United States has been controversial and difficult to gauge. A study by the U.S. Trade Representative, issued during the 1997 congressional debate over renewing "fast track"§ negotiating authority for the executive branch, stresses the creation of U.S. jobs supported by exports.[8] On the other side, Public Citizen, a Washington-based group inspired by consumer advocate Ralph Nader, argues that NAFTA has already caused the loss of more than 600,000 U.S. jobs.[9]

Economists on both sides of the debate have criticized the methods used to compute these figures as overly facile,[10] and some analysts have questioned the usefulness of emphasizing the creation or loss of U.S. jobs. Border activist Tom Barry, writing in an on-line journal, *The Progressive Response*, argues that progressives need to "leave behind many of the usual measures of impact, such as job loss and trade balance, and construct a new framework to evaluate globalization" that "recognizes the fundamental

---

* Chapter 3 includes a discussion of the experience with the environmental side accord. Experiences with other NAALC complaints are discussed in chapters 2 and 4.

§ For an explanation of "fast-track" authorization, see the following section, "From NAFTA to the MAI."

asymmetries between the United States and other econo-mies."[11] In arguing for a more internationalist approach, Barry states that successful opposition to the "corporate agenda of economic globalization . . . will require enlight-ened cooperation across borders. Ultranationalist positions that demand that the U.S. government protect all sectors of the economy against foreign competition undermine such alliances."[12]

Some more narrowly focused studies have docu-mented NAFTA's negative impact on particular groups in the United States, such as unionized workers, women, or people of color. In 1996, the trinational Labor Secretariat established under NAALC commissioned a study to evalu-ate the merits of charges by the Communications Workers of America and their Mexican counterpart that U.S. em-ployers were undermining freedom of association and col-lective bargaining rights by selectively closing plants that were undergoing organizing drives. The study found that 50 percent of private sector employers have threatened to close down or move in response to union organizing cam-paigns, and, when the unions win the election, a "substan-tial minority" have followed through on their threats. Such threats, in addition, "were found to be unrelated to the fi-nancial condition of the company" and were frequently accompanied by other, largely illegal, attempts to suppress union activity.[13]

The "Latino Review of NAFTA," another of the stud-ies produced to influence the "fast-track" debate in 1997, found that Latinos, women, and African Americans "are overrepresented in jobs lost due to NAFTA."[14] At a news conference announcing the study, thirteen members of the congressional Hispanic Caucus, including several who had voted for NAFTA, also released a letter to President Clinton charging that Latino and other low-wage workers were not receiving a proportionate share of trade adjustment assis-tance and that promised pollution abatement and economic development programs for the border region had also failed to materialize.[15]

In Mexico, meanwhile, the debate over the impact of NAFTA has taken place in the context of a devastating eco-nomic crisis. In 1996, estimated real hourly wages for Mexi-can workers were 27 percent lower than in 1994 and 37 percent below 1980 levels.[16] At the same time, many work-ers reported a significant erosion of working conditions, including speed-ups, an increase in arbitrary and illegal dismissals, and major cutbacks in workplace-related health services.

The U.S. government and other NAFTA supporters are quick to point out that NAFTA had nothing to do with Mexico's economic crisis. In fact, they say, NAFTA "helped to ensure a speedy recovery from the 1995 recession and position Mexico for strong growth in the years ahead."[17]

According to critics, however, a series of disastrous economic decisions made by the government of Carlos Sali-nas de Gortari between 1991 and 1994 were geared towards ensuring the passage and success of NAFTA. For example, the "maintenance of an overvalued peso, in essence subsi-dizing U.S. exporters and helping bolster the image of a huge Mexican market for U.S. goods, was a key component of the Salinas economic strategy. Ensuring extremely high interest rates to attract large amounts of short-term for-eign capital was also essential to convincing foreigners of the value of doing business with Mexico."[18]

In addition, as RMALC points out, when the finan-cial crisis of December 1994 began, NAFTA made it im-possible for the government to cushion its impact. Faced with an investor panic resulting in the outflow of billions in foreign capital, the Mexican government found its hands tied by NAFTA's prohibition of government regulation of speculative capital flows.

RMALC and other critics argue that Mexico's current crisis has been fueled over the long term by a string of poli-cies imposed by international financial elites since 1982, of which NAFTA was only the culmination. For workers on the border who still cannot afford to feed their families, meanwhile, Mexico's "speedy recovery" is little more than a mirage.

From NAFTA to the MAI

In 1997, in order to facilitate the expansion of NAFTA to Chile, the Clinton Administration sought a renewal of its "fast track" negotiating authority. Under "fast track" Con-gress can only accept or reject economic agreements nego-tiated by the executive branch, but cannot amend them. The granting of such authority has become routine in recent decades, and it is often defended as necessary to ensure the integrity of the international negotiating process. The 1997 version, however, placed unprecedented blanket re-strictions on the inclusion of labor and environmental safe-guards in trade agreements, limiting them to redressing negative impacts on the market for U.S.-made goods. Fac-ing concerted opposition to this version of "fast track" from labor unions, consumer advocates, and congressional Democrats, the Administration withdrew the measure, in what many observers saw as a major defeat for advocates of trade and investment liberalization.

Such issues, however, will not long be absent from the U.S. government's legislative and policy agenda, whether they come to the fore as a renewed version of "fast track" or through other measures. As noted in chapter 1, NAFTA represents a codification of "neoliberal" economic policies. Throughout the 1980s, such policies were aggressively promoted by international financial institutions such as the International Monetary Fund (IMF). Wracked by the international debt crisis, developing countries relied on IMF loans to maintain their fiscal and economic stability. The IMF used this leverage to institute economic reforms through to "structural adjustment" programs, which reduced the discretion of national governments to set economic policy and made economies in the developing world increasingly integrated with global markets and subordinated to the transnational corporations that dominate them.[19]

Although the debate in the United States over "free trade" commonly assumes that NAFTA and similar agreements are dedicated to the promotion of commerce, they might better be described as attempts to rewrite the framework for international economic relations, in the process placing severe restrictions on the right of governments to regulate the activities of transnational corporations in order to protect the environment, safeguard labor rights, protect the standard of living or food security of their populations, or promote the development of their own economies. By some readings, even the ability of state governments in the United States to promote industrial redevelopment is seriously constrained by NAFTA and similar agreements.[20]

In the wake of NAFTA, a series of measures have been introduced to further consolidate this framework for economic policy. At the "Summit of the Americas" in December 1994, the Clinton Administration proposed the establishment of a Free Trade Area of the Americas (FTAA), projected to go into effect in 2005. In the global scene, that same month saw the institution of the World Trade Organization (WTO), an outgrowth of the General Agreement on Trades and Tariffs. When a U.S. move to extend the WTO's authority to international investment was defeated, meanwhile, the Organization for Economic Cooperation and Development, which groups together the advanced industrial economies, began negotiations for the Multilateral Agreement on Investment (MAI), which would require governments to treat international investors identically with national firms, thereby hamstringing attempts to protect local industries from transnational competition. At this writing, unfavorable publicity has stalled the OECD negotiations on the MAI; some observers are predicting that a similar initiative may resurface in the WTO.

A thorough discussion of these agreements and institutions is beyond the scope of this book. All of them, however, have been criticized on the same grounds as NAFTA: that they accelerate the deepening gulf between rich and poor on an international scale; that they abandon working people and communities to the vagaries of transnational capital; and that they prohibit social and economic policies that could mitigate the effects of impoverishment and economic dislocation. At this writing, moreover, persistent turmoil in global financial markets, sparked by the so-called "Asian flu," has raised new questions about the wisdom of such policies, giving rise to calls from many quarters for some type of re-regulation of the international financial system. Certain voices within the international financial institutions (IFIs) themselves (that is, the World Bank and the IMF) have called for measures to cushion the social impact of global economic integration. At the same time, new channels have opened up in the IFIs for input from civil society into both policy making and project development.

Although the outcome of such trends remains uncertain, they signal the existence of significant new opportunities to gain a hearing for alternative approaches. Currently, social movements throughout the world are seeking to strengthen their own international ties in order to develop common strategies and initiatives geared toward increasing popular input into policy making. In the Americas, an emergent network known as the Hemispheric Social Alliance is building on the experience of the fight against NAFTA in an attempt to promote a new agenda for international economic relationships, based on social equity, environmental sustainability, community stability, and labor and other human rights. The coming years will be crucial ones in determining the outcome of such initiatives — and with them, the framework within which the global economy will develop.

Notes

1 U.S. Trade Representative, "Study on the Operation and Effect of the North American Free Trade Agreement (NAFTA), GPO No. 42788, U.S. Government Printing Office, Washington, DC, 1997.

2 Sarah Anderson, et al., *NAFTA's First Two Years: The Myths and the Realities,* Institute for Policy Studies, Washington DC, 1996, p. 21.

3 Economic Policy Institute, et al. *The Failed Experiment: NAFTA at Three Years,* EPI, Washington, DC, June 1997, p.12.

4 Anderson, op. cit., p.21.

5 "Labour and social issues relating to export processing zones," International Labor Organization, Geneva, 1998, p. 16

6 Jerome Levinson, "NAFTA's Labor Side Agreement," November 21, 1996, p.12.

7 Interview with Anya Hoffman, July 1997.

8 U.S. Trade Representative, op. cit., p.18.

9 *NAFTA's Broken Promises: Failure to Create U.S. Jobs*, Public Citizen, Washington, DC, February 1997, p. 2.

10 See, for example, David Ranney and Robert Naiman, "Does 'Free Trade' Create Good Jobs?," Institute for Policy Studies, Washington, DC, Jan. 1997; on the pro-NAFTA side of the debate, see Sidney Weintraub, "NAFTA at Three: A Progress Report," Center for Strategic and International Studies, Washington, DC, 1997.

11 Tom Barry, "Issues of Debate: Assessing the Impact of NAFTA," *The Progressive Response,* Vol. 1, No. 4, July 1997.

12 Ibid.

13 Kate Bronfenbrenner, "The Effects of Plant Closing or Threat of Plant Closing on the Right of Workers to Organize," Report to the Labor Secretariat of the North American Commission for Labor Cooperation, Cornell University, Ithaca, NY, Sept. 1996.

14 "Latino Review of NAFTA," William C. Velasquez Institute, Montebello, CA, Aug. 1997.

15 Paul Blustein, "Hispanic Lawmakers Fault NAFTA's Effects," *Washington Post,* July 16, 1997, p. C13.

16 Economic Policy Institute, op. cit., p. 14.

17 U.S. Trade Representative, op. cit., p. 25.

18 Sarah Anderson, et al., *No Laughter in NAFTA: Mexico and the United States Two Years After,* joint report by The Development GAP, Institute for Policy Studies, and Equipo Pueblo, December 1995, p.1.

19 Report on Strategy Session on Trade and Investment, American Friends Service Committee, Philadelphia, 1998.

20 Ibid.

READINGS

The first selection in this chapter, "NAFTA: Trinational Fiasco," summarizes the criticisms of NAFTA made by labor, human rights, and environmental advocates.

The next piece, "Falling Peso, Falling Lifestyle," details the grim circumstances faced by maquiladora workers in the wake of the 1994 peso crash, while simultaneously illustrating how Mexico's crisis reverberated on the U.S. side of the border in the region's highly interdependent economy.

Our two concluding readings emerge from the attempt to forge a truly multinational coalition to press for people-oriented alternatives in the Americas. "Building a Hemispheric Social Alliance to Confront Free Trade" presents a declaration issued at a 1997 meeting in Belo Horizonte, Brazil, when, for the first time, international trade union bodies joined with nongovernmental organizations and social movements to issue a broad critique of corporate-dominated

globalization. The Belo Horizonte meeting also approved a proposal from the Mexican coalition RMALC to form a Hemispheric Social Alliance (HSA), incorporating civil society organizations from throughout the Americas.

The HSA met formally for the first time in April 1998 in Santiago, Chile, in a parallel meeting to the intergovernmental summit negotiating the terms of the FTAA. A major document stemming from that meeting, "Alternatives for the Americas: Building a People's Hemispheric Agreement," contains the first detailed policy recommendations for an alternative, people-oriented approach to economic integration. Included here is the introduction to "Alternatives for the Americas"; the complete document is available in the United States from the Alliance for Responsible Trade, which may be reached through the Development Group for Alternative Policies (see directory listing, page 123).

NAFTA: Trinational Fiasco

By Sarah Anderson, John Cavanagh and David Ranney

One issue you can be sure that Bob Dole and Bill Clinton will not disagree on is free trade. Both men were strong advocates of the North American Free Trade Agreement, which went into effect in January 1994. The peoples of North America have now lived with the agreement for 900 days and contrary to the promises of Dole, Clinton and their advisers, NAFTA has turned out to be a losing proposition for all but the Fortune 500.

Rather than increasing by the hundred of thousands, as promised, jobs have been disappearing in all three countries: those jobs that remain pay less with fewer benefits. The U.S-Mexico border, already a development debacle when NAFTA was signed, is mired even deeper in health and environmental nightmares. Mexico's highly touted middle class has been slammed back into poverty. In Canada, one of the world's finest social welfare systems is under siege. . . . Many more promises on funding, immigration, agriculture and other issues did materialize. The leaders of the three NAFTA countries rarely mention the trade pact, fearing, perhaps, that they will remind voters of their exaggerated claims for it and how much needless misery it has produced.

Several dozen researchers and activists from all three countries have recently completed a series of comprehensive studies on NAFTA that debunk the prevailing myths. We focus here on five of the most prevalent ones. But first a caveat: We do not argue that NAFTA caused Mexico's latest economic collapse, nor did it create the growing inequality in all three nations, nor most of the other problems outlined below. NAFTA did, however, make them worse. In economic terms, NAFTA eased the movement of goods and investment among the three countries; it sped up the free-trade model that large corporations have been pushing for decades. NAFTA codifies an economic ideology that glorifies the market, that demonizes and defunds government, and that regards human being as little more than customers in a continental shopping mall.

Reprinted with permission from *The Nation* magazine, July 15/22, 1996.

Myth #1: NAFTA Had Nothing to Do With the Recent Mexican Crisis

The evidence of Mexico's economic failure, which burst into public view on the eve of Christmas in 1994, is so overwhelming that even the Clinton Administration doesn't deny it. What it says is that the fault lies with poor economic management by the Mexican government. Although NAFTA proponents claim that the crisis has postponed many of the benefits they predicted would emerge from the agreement, they argue that Mexico is continuing on the right free-trade track and that things would be much worse in the absence of NAFTA. In fact, NAFTA merely formalized and extended policies that were first imposed upon the country by the International Monetary Fund in 1982 in response to Mexico's massive foreign debt. These policies, popularly known as structural adjustment, represent an approach to economic development that requires slashing government expenditures and opening the country to foreign goods, services, and capital without government regulation; in four words: Trade more, spend less.

In Mexico's case and for many other countries suffering structural adjustment, the effect of everyone exporting more drives prices down and makes servicing the debt even harder. Meanwhile, during NAFTA negotiations, the International Monetary Fund and World Bank pressured the Mexican government to ease trade and investment barriers even further. As a result, foreign capital is increasingly coming in the form of speculative portfolio investment, or "hot money," which requires high interest rates that discourage productive investment.

In previous crises, Mexico saved scarce foreign exchange by using controls to exclude non-essential imports. But under NAFTA, this is no longer allowed, even during emergencies. The agreement also prohibits restrictions on foreign-exchange transactions without special permission. Finally, under NAFTA's "rules of origin" provisions, Mexico cannot impose requirements that could channel foreign investment into productive endeavors and away from speculation.

Myth #2: Increased Exports Will Lead to More Jobs

President Clinton boasted that NAFTA had created some 340,000 U.S jobs. But the President's claim is based on an erroneous formula that asserts that every $1 billion in new exports creates another 15,000 to 20,000 jobs. The formula is flawed in part because it considers only exports and doesn't subtract jobs lost when the United States imports goods that used to be produced here. Although U.S. exports to Mexico have grown some since NAFTA went into effect, the Administration's own numbers show that imports from Mexico have gone through the roof: U.S trade surplus of $1.7 billion in 1993 spiraled downward into a deficit of $15.4 billion by 1995. Hence, by the Administration's formula, many more U.S. jobs have been destroyed by NAFTA than have been created.

The Administration admits that 75,000 U.S. workers have been thrown out on the street as a result of the free-trade agreement. These figures are from NAFTA Transitional Adjustment Assistance program, which provides retraining and other aid to U.S workers who lose their jobs as a result of a shift in production to Mexico or Canada, or of increased imports from those nations.

The surge in Mexico's exports to the United States should in theory, have created many new jobs in Mexico. Indeed, Mexico's plummeting peso has drastically lowered labor costs for global companies operating there and several hundred thousand new maquiladora jobs have been spawned on the border. However, this increase has been dwarfed by the 1.4 million to 2 million jobs that vanished during NAFTA's first two years, as record numbers of small and medium-sized businesses lost the battle with high interest rates and filed for bankruptcy. NAFTA proponents had claimed that the agreement would so improve the Mexican economy that pressures to migrate to the United States would greatly subside. In fact, displaced workers and peasants swelled the number of Mexicans apprehended in attempted border crossings by a dramatic 43 percent from 1994 to 1995.

And there is an even deeper flaw in the NAFTA jobs argument. Even if a country does have a trade surplus, it is faulty to assume that corporations always use profits generated by exports to create new jobs. Many successful exporting companies have instead chosen to use these profits to finance mergers or invest in labor-saving machinery, which can lead to job cuts. Firms like Zenith, Xerox, Caterpillar, and Allied Signal are major exporters from the United

States, yet all of them have eliminated thousands of U.S. jobs. A study of Illinois's top export industries showed they were laying off workers at a higher rate than other industries.

In Canada, an equally alarming job hemorrhage dates back to the Canada-U.S. Free Trade Agreement, which was signed in 1988. Between 1988 and 1994, Canada lost 17 percent of its manufacturing jobs, and unemployment rose from 7.5 percent in 1989 to just under 10 percent in 1995. A study by the Canadian Center for Policy Alternatives shows that companies that lobbied hard for the free-trade pacts have been the biggest job slashers. Thirty-seven firms belonging to a pro-NAFTA business association have cut more than 215,000 jobs since 1998.

Myth #3: Increases in Productivity Will Be Spread to Workers

In lobbying for the free-trade agreement, the corporate group USA*NAFTA claimed that "NAFTA itself will improve working conditions by generating economic growth, which will enable all three countries to provide more jobs with higher pay in a better working environment." . . . To the contrary, NAFTA has given corporations increased power to drive down wages and working conditions.

The most direct method is through "whipsaw bargaining," or threatening to shift production to Mexico unless workers agree to concessions. Xerox used this technique effectively in Webster, New York, where workers agreed to reduce the base pay rate by 50 percent for new employees and cut workers' compensation in exchange for job guarantees through the year 2001. The Webster workers had reason to take the company's relocation threats seriously since Xerox had recently moved jobs south of the border from plants in Illinois and Massachusetts.

Another common corporate tactic is to use the argument that increased international competition under NAFTA requires greater "flexibility" through hiring more workers on a part time or temporary basis. Corporate-backed lawmakers are using the same argument to push antiworker legislation, such as the efforts to strip away the government's power to enforce health-and-safety regulations, outlaw union shops and unions' use of corporate campaigns, legalize company unions, and abolish overtime pay.

Thus while corporations experience productivity growth, workers are not sharing in the benefits. In all three NAFTA countries, increases in real wages are lagging far behind increases in productivity. In Mexico, real wages as of May 1996 were 35 percent below their pre-1994-crisis levels. In Canada, as in the United States, real wages are stagnating and the proportion of full-time workers living in poverty continues to grow.

In response to NAFTA's critics, the Clinton Administration negotiated a labor side agreement, but it contains a narrow definition of worker rights and is weighted down with an enormously complex, time-consuming, and bureaucratic dispute resolution mechanism. Not surprisingly, to date, complaints about violations of worker rights have been filed at only four plants (three in Mexico and one in the United States). Not a single worker involved in these complaints has benefited so far from the process. However, through tremendous persistence, unions and other groups have been able to use the agreement to draw more attention to the general problem of worker rights violations.

Myth #4: Increased International Competitiveness Will Benefit All

"We must be internationally competitive." This is the mantra now parroted by heads of state throughout the world, including Clinton, Ernesto Zedillo in Mexico, and Jean Chrétien in Canada. The benefits of such enhanced competitiveness, however, have turned out more often than not to be a mirage, as the evidence presented above indicates. But the tragedy of NAFTA and free trade runs deeper than lost jobs and falling wages. A key element of the drive for international competitiveness has been an assault on government.

Nation readers are familiar with the attack on social programs and federal regulations in the United States. In Canada, cuts in unemployment insurance reduced the number of unemployed Canadians who qualify for benefits from 87 percent in 1989 to 49 percent in 1994; this will fall to 33 percent when the latest round of cuts is fully implemented.

In Mexico, NAFTA has worsened conditions engendered by twelve previous years of austerity. These measures have been particularly devastating for rural Mexicans. A requirement for entry into the agreement was the removal of subsidies for family farmers, who also face drastic cut in available credit and public services in areas such as veterinary medicine, agricultural extension and public health. In December 1995, Mexico's Institute of Social Security, which oversees health care and social security for salaried workers, shifted from public to private administration and funding.

Myth #5: Growth From Trade Will Help Clean Up the Environment

NAFTA supporters promised that the trade agreement would mean increased investment in environmental cleanup and a decline in the concentration of maquiladoras along the already heavily polluted U.S.-Mexico border. But as Public Citizen has documented, the increase in industrial activity in the border zone has not been met by any appreciable improvement in the disposal of industrial wastes or expansion of health care facilities. Many communities still lack access to both water and sewage systems. Today, only 10 percent of Mexico's yearly output of seven million tons of hazardous waste receives adequate treatment, with the rest poured into clandestine waste dumps or municipal sewers.

Nor are NAFTA's environmental threats confined to the U.S.-Mexico border. Standards established through the struggle of environmental groups throughout each of the countries can now be challenged as "nontariff trade barriers." Groups trying to protect these standards will have to justify them according to the principles of "risk assessment"—the notion that health risks incurred because of lower standards must be great enough to justify the cost of restrictions on trade. Rather than the highest possible standards for a healthy environment, risk assessment leads to standards that pose the lowest restrictions on businesses.

As with labor, the Clinton Administration used the handy device of a side agreement to gain support of some environmental groups during the NAFTA fight. A number of them—dubbed "the shameful seven"—acquiesced. Yet the institutions set up under NAFTA have made little progress in addressing environmental concerns. The North American Development Bank has yet to fund a single cleanup project. Widely perceived as ineffectual, the North American Commission for Environmental Cooperation was supposed to insure high levels of environmental protection and foster public discussion. Yet the C.E.C. has received only four petitions, three of which it has rejected. It has also been asked to investigate the mysterious mass death of birds in a reservoir in Guanajuato, Mexico.

NAFTA has not, however, been a total failure. Its most salutary effect was to catalyze new coalitions that crossed borders and political party lines, and embraced constituencies as diverse as workers, farmers, environmentalists, consumers, and religious groups. Unfortunately, one would scarcely know this from press accounts. With its blinkered focus on officialdom, the press gave credence only to critics on the right. Hence, coverage of NAFTA opposition focused on Pat Buchanan, who, although correctly critiquing the agreement, presented a racist, "America First" solution that called for sealing U.S. borders to goods, capital, and people from other countries.

The progressive opposition to NAFTA, on the other hand, has rejected the process, politics, and policies of the pro-NAFTA forces. Opponents attacked the process because NAFTA was negotiated secretly, without a hearing from ordinary citizens; opponents advocated a transparent process that would bring all parties to the table. They condemned the politics because NAFTA's passage revealed how legislators' votes are often sold to the highest bidder in a system corrupted by corporate money. And on the policy level, they rejected the deregulatory framework of NAFTA and the new protections for corporations.

The main progressive citizen networks in NAFTA countries proposed alternative policies that would protect worker rights, advance environmental standards and food security, and promote sustainable energy and agriculture. This approach was summed up in a document titled "A Just and Sustainable Trade and Development Initiative for the Western Hemisphere"* by the key networks in all three countries that fought NAFTA.

These groups continue to fight for better economic alternatives. The Action Canada Network, which includes a broad array of social forces from the Canadian Labor Congress to cultural and indigenous movements, has helped forge an "Alternative Federal Budget" aimed at creating jobs through public investment and halting the dismantling of social programs.

In the United States, the Alliance for Responsible Trade, the Citizens Trade Campaign, and many other groups from the economic and environmental justice movements continue to monitor NAFTA's impact and promote bi- and trinational alternatives.

In Mexico, a similar array of citizen groups, represented by the Mexican Action Network on Free Trade, has worked with others to draft a twelve-point "Liberty Referendum," which outlines a national alternative to the government's neoliberal policies. At polling places around the country, half a million Mexicans signed their approval by November 1995.

NAFTA has unleashed a major war in all three countries over our economic future. While the pro-NAFTA forces won the opening battle, evidence continues to build that the agreement is not in the interest of the vast majority of people in any of the three countries. And in their silence over trade issues, candidates Clinton and Dole are acknowledging that they face even more difficult battles in new areas: the trade deficit with China, NAFTA expansion to other countries, and proposals to enhance the powers of the World Trade Organization.

---

* This document was a precursor to the two readings from the Hemispheric Social Alliance presented in this chapter.

Falling peso, falling lifestyle
By Carlos Guerra

Thousands living along the U.S.-Mexico border watched helplessly as their lives crumbled.

The falling peso had focused attention on political figures and financial institutions, but between Matamoros and Ciudad Acuña falling exchange rates and skyrocketing prices claimed more than half of the purchasing power of Mexicans.

Many are like Vicki Barajas Durán, 28, a Matamoros maquiladora worker whose weekly check shrank from $54 to $26.

In Del Rio, the H.E.B. parking lot now is half-full and out-of-state plates often outnumber those from Mexico.

In Eagle Pass, Monica Lee's store has no customers and is stocked with winter fashions. On the river's southern edge, young men such as Eduardo Rodríguez prepare for illegal crossings many would rather not make but feel it is their only out.

A week-long bus trek along the border revealed the peso crisis is having a harsh impact on both sides of the Rio Grande.

Domingo Gonzalez of Brownsville worries the environmental cleanup of the Rio Grande will be scaled back or forgotten, but Alicia Ybarra of Ciudad Acuña has a more immediate concern.

"Could you feed your family with 70 pesos ($10) a week?" she asks.

"Devaluations are like earthquakes," explains Jorge Bustamante, president of the Colegio de la Frontera Norte in Tijuana. "And the border is the epicenter."

When the peso began its slide in December, Christmas spending softened the impact.

In January, however, higher costs for foreign products and rising fuel prices sent Mexican prices soaring.

As exchange rates plummeted, Mexicans cut back on Mexican purchases—and stopped buying most American goods altogether.

"People were expecting this," Larry Norton said, as eight clerks were idle at his family's Los Dos Laredos clothing store. "For the last two years, we'd hardly gotten any pesos, and most of our customers are Mexican."

They are "trying not to let any (employees) go, but hours have been cut dramatically," he says.

Texas Employment Commission offices were deluged.

"On Jan. 17, I arrived at the office at 7:30 a.m. and there was a line of people three blocks long," recalls Gerardo H. Peña, TEC area manager in Laredo, "more than 450 claimants in one day."

Additional layoffs, like the one at the warehouse built in Laredo to service the new Wal-Mart and Sam's Clubs stores, are feared.

"I took 320 (unemployment insurance) claims at the Wal-Mart warehouse in one day," recalls Robert C. Cavasos of TEC. "They have about 20 people left there now."

This devaluation could affect many more people. When maquiladoras—factories that produce American products for Mexican wages—began sprouting here two decades ago, a migration began to both sides of the border, and the flow was encouraged by Mexico's elimination of import restrictions. More recently, NAFTA lured another major wave to the region.

Laredo, McAllen, and Brownsville became hot transshipping and retail centers, and real-estate markets sizzled as housing and commercial rents skyrocketed.

High poverty and unemployment levels were maintained, however, and the "gray labor market" of short-term undocumented Mexican workers flourished and grew. Hundreds of colonias sprouted around the cities to accommodate the growth.

Growth on the Mexican side was even more skewed.

As tens of thousands fled the poverty of the interior for maquiladora jobs, they ran into higher costs for housing.

Vast plywood-and-cardboard shanty towns mushroomed, many with neither electricity nor running water and none with sewerage systems. Now, signs on colonia walls tell of the toll: "Combate el cólera (fight cholera)."

"People don't know that a disaster has been building up here," says Domingo Gonzalez, staffer for the Texas Center for Policy Studies. "And if there wasn't enough money to clean it up before, now there will be less—or none at all."

Colonias, however, still represented hope for Vicki Barajas Durán of Matamoros.

Originally published in the *San Antonio Express-News*, Mar. 26, 1995. Reprinted by permission of the *San Antonio Express-News*.

The family's principal wage earner, she makes 185 pesos a week. Since her husband, Martin Alvarez, lost his plant-guard job, he has been selling hardware at a weekend flea market. Sales have all but vanished, he says, "because people buy food before buying hardware."

Vicki's purchasing power has dropped from $54 to $26, ending the weekly trips to Brownsville to buy milk, chicken, other staples and, occasionally, a pair of discount-store shoes. Now she struggles to pay rising utility bills and bus fare, which has doubled to $4.28 a week, to the plant.

"Everything, especially the indispensable things, is rising," she says, "We hardly eat chicken or meat anymore. We are barely making it, but next year my son will need books and uniforms when he goes to middle school."

A second job isn't likely, she says, "since I am 28 and the maquiladora only wants younger women."

Most maquiladora workers, however, make 120 pesos a week—$17—or less each week.

In Ciudad Acuña's plaza, a long line waited to buy fish left after the co-op that fishes Lake Amistad delivered its wholesale contract. At eight pesos per kilo—51 cents a pound—it was a bargain, but even with a 2-kilo limit, many left empty-handed.

Around the plaza, young men toting duffel bags plotted river crossings. Maquiladoras hire few males, so many are jobless.

"I would rather stay," Eduardo Rodriguez said, "but I have to go."

On previous trips, this roofer in his mid-twenties had earned $50 a day working for employers who knew he was undocumented but hired him anyway.

"Fifty dollars is what I made here in a week before," he says, "now, it is what I would make in two weeks—but there is no work."

Far more brazen is an undocumented eighteen-year-old from a village in southern Mexico.

Enrolled in a Laredo high school, "Paco" makes high grades, speaks good English and works restaurant jobs for less money than the Americans.

He lives with family in Laredo who are "legal" and was twice "sent back" to Nuevo Laredo. He walked back across the bridge, telling inspectors he is American.

"About 60 or 70 people" from his village work in Laredo now, and the dollars they've sent back have made his village dollar-wise, he says.

"I was there during the devaluation," he muses, "and peso prices went up about 25 percent as soon as we heard."

Alicia Ybarra, a Sunbeam-Oster plant worker in Ciudad Acuña, doesn't think of crossing, but she does worry.

A 25-peso raise increased her check to 143 pesos for a 48-hour week. This was $42 before but only $20 now, about 42 cents an hour.

She, her husband and two children don't cross to Del Rio because food prices there have doubled, she says, and the gallon of milk she purchased each week would cost her almost a day's pay.

If U.S. manufacturers plan to rush to the border for the significantly lower Mexican labor costs, it isn't evident at her plant, which recently shut down for a week.

"There were no American components," she says stoically, "so they paid us only half a paycheck."

Carlos Lozano, who sells staples in Matamoros out of a stall in front of a new—and still half-empty—housing project, has suspended credit. Customers ran weekly tabs, paying him Fridays, but "now, I sell (products) for one price, and they cost me more to replace them," he explains.

And the chicken quarters that he used to buy in Brownsville have become unaffordable now.

More families have moved into the project, but sales still are down.

Now, he tracks the exchange rates, like many others. Some do it for security and other for added profits. U.S. businesses take pesos at rates higher than banks, and Mexican businesses accept dollars at deep discounts.

Growth in trade has made currency trading a huge business over last decade.

For several years, Mexico's central bank bought pesos in currency markets to keep the value high, a strategy that postponed inflation but also overvalued the peso, making American products cheaper for Mexicans and creating an illusion of prosperity.

The percentage of Mexicans living below Mexico's poverty line, however, continued to grow.

But along the border Mexicans maintained an ability to purchase U.S. products made cheap with overvalued pesos. Now, the impact of a more realistically priced peso and skyrocketing inflation is quite evident in Eagle Pass. Near the international bridge, one of two Golden Fried Chicken restaurants and half dozen clothing and electronic retailers are closed, and more are shutting down.

"About 95 percent of my customers are Mexican, and in 1992 my business was great," says Monica Lee, who opened a fashion outlet here during the boom. "But I stocked what they (Mexicans) like, and now they've stopped buying; so I'm stuck."

Bus service between the cross-border towns of Eagle Pass and Piedras Negras has been cut by 20 percent, driver Daniel Hernandez says, "because 75 percent fewer people are riding."

"This devaluation is much worse than the ones before," he says, and the handful of riders agree.

"Mira," said one woman, hoisting a bag with a loaf of bread, some cans and little else. "It is all I can afford."

Not all are hurting equally, however. Closest to the bridge, the UETA Duty-Free Store's parking lot is full of late-model cars with Mexican plates.

A few UETA customers buy tax-free American cigarettes and resell them in Piedras Negras to Americans. Most, however, are wealthier Mexicans browsing over stocks of American cigarettes and fine liquors, perfumes, and expensive watches.

"Sure, it has affected us" says Robert Amado, regional vice president of UETA. "Sales are down some, and we've cut some people back to 35 or 32 hours. But so long as people drink and smoke they'll buy."

Belo Horizonte Declaration:
Building a Hemispheric Social Alliance to Confront Free Trade

Representatives of labor and social movements from throughout the hemisphere met in Brazil in May of 1997. They gathered in Belo Horizonte at the time of another round of ministerial meetings to establish the FTAA, a 34-country Free Trade Area of the Americas. The four days of discussions, debates, and cultural events culminated with a massive street demonstration and a declaration. The joint declaration sets out their vision of what issues need to be addressed if the FTAA is to go forward.

The meeting that was held in Belo Horizonte, Brazil and this declaration mark a historical moment in continental movement building. It was the first time the continental labor organization known as the ORIT [the Latin American affiliate of the International Confederation of Free Trade Unions, or ICFTU], its affiliates, and many social sector groups (community groups, coalitions, and nongovernmental organizations) from different countries in the Americas came together. The ORIT-sponsored "Labor Forum" was the first of what we hope will be many steps taken together by both labor and social sector groups in the years to come.

At the Brazil meeting the Mexican trade coalition (RMALC) launched the idea of building a "Hemispheric Social Alliance." This would be not one particular act or the signing of any particular document, and certainly not the building of any new organization. It would demand a commitment by all of us and each of our organizations, in each of our countries to an ongoing process to work together to confront the model embodied by agreements like NAFTA, APEC, MAI, and the FTAA.

There were many labor and social organizations in Belo Horizonte but even more were absent. The groups that were in attendance and signed the declaration are committed to an open process that will enable more groups to sign on, help organize and participate in upcoming events like the FTAA Summit in Santiago, Chile in April of 1998 and joint actions, campaigns, and events in the years to come.

Now as we embark on the road to the Santiago Summit we are undoubtedly stronger— and better prepared to fight, to have our voices, our demands, and our alternatives heard. The challenge is here for all of us to keep working together and to build a Hemispheric Social Alliance.

Declaration

On the occasion of the Third Trade Union Summit, held parallel to the Trade Ministers' Meeting on the Free Trade Area of the Americas (FTAA) in Belo Horizonte, Brazil from 12 to 13 May 1997, representatives of the trade union organizations of the Americas, affiliated and fraternal organizations of the ORIT/ICFTU, and a number of important social organizations have had the opportunity to share our respective work on the social dimension of economic integration.

As part of this meeting, the trade union movement has reviewed the joint statement prepared by citizens' networks from Mexico, the United States, Canada, Chile, and El Salvador and presented it to U.S. President Clinton during his recent tour of Mexico, Central America, and the Caribbean.

As an example of the intention to achieve effective complementarity between the perspectives and action strategies of the trade union movement and those of other social movements, we have approved this declaration, based on the aforementioned document and on the trade union experience gained in various subregional integration processes. Therefore, this declaration should be seen as complementary to that issued by the Third Trade Union Summit.

1. There should be no FTAA agreement if it is to be created along the lines of other existing agreements such as NAFTA. We need an agreement that promotes genuine development for all of the peoples of the hemisphere, one that recognizes and attempts to reduce the differences in levels of development, one that allows for integration of our economies based on democratically determined national development models, and one that is based on consensus. Strong national economies must be the basis for a strong hemisphere. We are proposing an agreement designed for sustainable development rather than for trade liberalization. Any trade agreement should not be an end in itself, but rather a means toward combating poverty and social exclusion and for achieving just and sustainable development. We do not

support isolationism or traditional protectionism. We are not nostalgic for the past. We are looking forward, and we have viable proposals. We know that our economies cannot be isolated from the dynamics of the world economy, but we do not think that free trade is the solution. The problem is that free trade involves more than the opening of borders; it involves the abandonment of national development models and poses a serious threat to democracy. Any national development model, to be viable, must take trade and world economic conditions into account. It must also build on each nation's potential and develop a strategy to establish its unique position in the world. It has never been demonstrated that the market achieves an optimal distribution of resources or the benefits of development. So-called free trade is actually trade regulation that increases the advantages of international capital, speculative or not, over productive investment and over the rights and well-being of workers.

2. There should be no FTAA if it does not include a social agenda that contains at least the following fundamental elements:

    i.   There must be broad-based citizen participation in the negotiation of any agreement, and its ratification must occur in each country through genuinely democratic means.

    ii. Any agreement must include respect for and improvement of the social and economic rights of workers, women (who have suffered the greatest impacts of the restructuring of production), campesinos, indigenous peoples, and migrant workers.

3. Our countries' competitiveness must not be based on the exploitation of workers or social dumping. The current tendency toward downward harmonization of working conditions and wages must be stopped, promoting instead an upward harmonization of working conditions over the medium term, as well as recovery of wage levels. The starting point should be ILO conventions that guarantee freedom of association and collective bargaining, that prohibit child labor and forced labor, as well as discrimination based on sex, race, or religion. Moreover, we demand a Charter of Social and Economic Rights for the Citizens of the Americas, accompanied by democratic and transparent enforcement mechanisms.

4. There should be no FTAA if it does not include protection and improvement of the environment, ensure respect for the rights of migrant workers, and devote special attention to food security, and therefore on protection and support for *campesinos*, small-scale farmers, and the social sector, without subsidizing large agribusiness corporations. It should also protect and promote micro and small urban enterprises because of their capacity for generating employment.

5. There should be no FTAA if it does not protect people from the vulnerability and instability caused by speculative capital and fly-by-night investments. Chile, despite the fact that it is the Latin American pioneer in free trade, has protections on portfolio investment: authorization is required; a percentage must be deposited in the Central Bank; and it must be held in the country for a minimum period. Performance requirements on foreign investment must be negotiated, along with regulations to protect labor rights. Intellectual property, which is primarily held by large corporations, should be protected, but not at the expense of global progress toward a social dimension in trade or of national sovereignty. The subject of foreign debt must also be taken up again, as it continues to reduce the ability of governments to act in such key areas of development as housing, health care, education, and the environment.

6. On trade issues, the problem of nontariff barriers must be resolved. The elimination of nontariff barriers to legitimate trade should not be confused with lowering sanitary and phytosanitary barriers that protect the environment. Interactions among our economies must support national integration of linkages among productive sectors, for which we demand rules of origin with national content requirements. This Summit was a first step toward complementary work between trade unions and other social organizations, which could be made more concrete at the time of the Second Summit of Heads of State of the Americas next March in Santiago, Chile, with the convening of a Peoples' Summit of the Americas in order to achieve a hemispheric social alliance. Toward that end, in the coming months we must establish mechanisms of communications and coordination, draw new organizations into the initiative, exchange joint proposals, and participate together in activities linked to these goals.

We will work in our respective countries to defeat any agreement that is not consistent with these demands. This Declaration remains open to endorsements by other trade union and social organizations.

Signed by:
— *Interamerican Regional Organization of Workers (ORIT)/International Confederation of Free Trade Unions (ICFTU)*
— *Mexican Action Network on Free Trade (RMALC)*
— *Alliance for Responsible Trade (ART-U.S.)*

— *Common Frontiers (Canada)*
— *Action Canada Network*
— *Chilean Network for a Peoples Initiative (RECHIP)*
— *Brazilian Association of NGOs (ABONG)*
— *Coalition for Justice in the Maquiladoras (U.S.)*
— *National Indigenous Council of Mexico*
— *Union Nacional El Barzón (Mexico)*
— *Reseau Québécois sur l'intégration continental*
— *Conféderacion des syndicats nationaux (CSN – Quebec)*
— *Canadian Association of Labour Lawyers (CALL)*

Alternatives for the Americas:
Building a Peoples' Hemispheric Agreement
Discussion Draft 2 – November 1998

Alliance for Responsible Trade (United States)
Common Frontiers (Canada)
Red Chile por una Iniciativa de los Pueblos (Chilean Network for a People's Initiative)
Red Mexicana de Acción Frente al Libre Comercio (Mexican Free Trade Action Network)
Réseau québécois sur l'intégration continentale (Quebec Network on Continental Integration)

Introduction and Summary

This document reflects an ongoing, collaborative process to establish concrete and viable alternatives, based on the interests of the peoples of our hemisphere, to the Free Trade Area of the Americas (FTAA). It is the second draft of a document initially prepared for the April 1998 Peoples Summit of the Americas—a historic gathering of activists determined to change the prevailing approach to trade and investment policy in the Western Hemisphere.

This is a working document, designed to stimulate further debate and education on an alternative vision. The paper focuses on positive proposals, while dealing only implicitly with the impact of "neoliberalism" and free trade agreements on our countries. At this stage of the struggle, it is not enough to oppose, to resist, and to criticize. We must build a proposal of our own and fight for it.

The document addresses the major topics on the official agenda of the FTAA negotiators (investment, finance, intellectual property rights, agriculture, market access, and dispute resolution), as well as topics that are of extreme social importance but which governments have ignored (human rights, environment, labor, immigration, the role of the state, and energy). Issues concerning two other important groups—women and indigenous peoples—have been incorporated throughout the document. The paper begins with a chapter on the general principles underlying an alternative vision, followed by chapters that lay out more concrete proposals. The topics and chapters are complementary. Therefore, the paper is to be viewed and discussed as a whole.

Summary

General Principles: Trade and investment should not be ends in themselves, but rather the instruments for achieving just and sustainable development. Citizens must have the right to participate in the formulation, implementation, and evaluation of hemispheric social and economic policies. Central goals of these policies should be to promote economic sovereignty, social welfare, and reduced inequality at all levels.

Human Rights: Countries of the Americas should build a common human rights agenda to be included in every hemispheric agreement, along with mechanisms and institutions to ensure full implementation and enforcement. This agenda should promote the broadest definition of human rights, covering civil, political, economic, social, cultural, and environmental rights, gender equity, and rights relating to indigenous peoples and communities.

Environment: Hemispheric agreements should allow governments to channel investment towards environmentally sustainable economic activities, while establishing plans for the gradual "internalization" (taking into account) of the social and environmental costs of unsustainable production and consumption.

Labor: Hemispheric agreements should include provisions that guarantee the basic rights of working men and women, ensure proper assistance for adjustment as markets are opened up, and promote the improvement of working and living standards of workers and their families.

Immigration: Economic and financial agreements should include agreements regarding migrant workers. These agreements should recognize the diversity in immigration-related situations in different countries by allowing for variation in immigration policies but also facilitating funding for programs designed to improve employment opportunities in areas that are major net exporters of labor. At the same time, governments should ensure uniform application of their national labor rights for all workers—regardless of immigration status—and severely penalize employers that violate these rights.

Role of the State: Hemispheric agreements should not undermine the ability of the nation state to meet its citizens' social and economic needs. At the same time, the goal of national economic regulations should not be traditional protectionism, but ensuring that private sector economic activities promote fair and sustainable development. Likewise, agreements should allow nation states to maintain public sector corporations and procurement policies that support national development goals while fighting government corruption.

Investment: Hemispheric rules should encourage foreign investment that generates high-quality jobs, sustainable production, and economic stability, while allowing governments to screen out investments that make no net contribution to development, especially speculative capital flows. Citizens groups and all levels of government should have the right to sue investors that violate investment rules.

Finance: To promote economic stability, agreements should establish a tax on foreign exchange transactions that would also generate development funds, while allowing governments to institute taxes on speculative profits, require that portfolio investments remain in the country for a specified period, and provide incentives for direct and productive investments. To help level the playing field, low-income nations should be allowed to renegotiate foreign debts to reduce principal owed, lower interest rates, and lengthen repayment terms.

Intellectual Property: Agreements should protect the rights and livelihoods of farmers, fishing folk, and communities that act as guardians of biodiversity and not allow corporate interests to undermine these rights. Rules should exclude all life forms from patentability and protect the collective intellectual property of local communities and peoples, especially with regard to medicinal plants. Rules should also ensure that copyright laws protect artists, musicians and other cultural workers, and not just the publishing and entertainment industries.

Sustainable Energy Development: A hemispheric agreement should allow members to file complaints against countries that try to achieve commercial advantage at the expense of sustainability. International agencies should cooperate to create regulatory incentives for energy efficiency and renewable energy and promote related technologies, while eliminating policies that subsidize or encourage fossil fuel sales, consumption and use.

Agriculture: To ensure food security, countries should have the right to protect or exclude staple foods from trade agreements. Hemispheric measures should also support upward harmonization of financial assistance for agriculture (as a percentage of GDP [gross domestic product]), strengthened protections for agricultural laborers, and traditional rights of indigenous peoples to live off ancestral lands.

Market Access: Access for foreign products and investments should be evaluated and defined within the framework of national development plans. Timetables for tariff reduction should be accompanied by programs to ensure that domestic industries become competitive during the transition. With regard to nontariff barriers, measures are necessary to ensure that they reflect legitimate social interests rather than protections for specific companies.

Enforcement and Dispute Resolution: If the proposed rules and standards are to be meaningful, they must be accompanied by strong mechanisms for dispute resolution and enforcement that are focused on reducing inequalities and based on fair and democratic processes. Agreements may also include special safeguards for countries suffering as the result of surges in imports.

Resource Directory

Listed below are key groups directly engaged in maquiladora activism in the United States and in Mexico, as well as organizations whose work focuses on global trade issues. For a more comprehensive listing, consult the directories published by the Interhemispheric Resource Center. Many organizational publications are noted in this listing; a bibliography of additional readings on maquiladora issues is provided following this directory.

U.S.-Based Organizations

Coalition for Justice in the Maquiladoras (CJM)

530 Bandera
San Antonio, TX 78228
Tel: (210) 732-8957
Fax: (210) 732-8324
Email: cjm@ipc.apc.org
Contact: Susan Mika, Marta Ojeda, Jennifer Collin

A trinational coalition of religious, environmental, labor, Latino, and women's organizations that seek to pressure U.S.-based transnational corporations to adopt socially responsible practices within the maquiladora industry to ensure a safe environment along the U.S.-Mexico border, safe working conditions inside the maquila plants, and a fair standard of living for the industry's workers.

A central vehicle for achieving these goals is the establishment of the Maquiladora Standards of Conduct. This document provides a code through which CJM demands that corporations alleviate critical problems created by the industry. CJM's efforts are grounded in supporting worker and community struggles for social, economic, and environmental justice in the maquiladora industry.

Publications

Annual Report and periodic newsletter which describe ongoing worker and community struggles in the border region.

The Human Face of Work: Human Rights, Democracy, and Working Conditions in Mexico. This booklet exposes worker wages, safety concerns, and abuses of democracy in and around the maquiladora factories of Mexico. 88 pp.

The Issue Is Health. Offers newspaper accounts, toxic substances summaries, and selected readings on health issues affecting the U.S.-Mexico border region, as well as an in-depth presentation on the high incidences of anencephaly in the area.

Maquiladora Standards of Conduct. Provides a code through which CJM is demanding that corporations address the environmental, health and safety, and community infrastructure concerns, as well as wage levels. (Included in chapter 4.)

Border Trouble: Rivers in Peril. Report on water pollution due to the industrial development along the U.S.-Mexico border; published by the National Toxics Campaign in May 1991.

Maquiladoras: A Broken Promise. A collection of newspaper articles about accidents, fires, and problems in plants in the Matamoros area.

Stepan Chemical: The Poisoning of a Mexican Community. Video which outlines the combined efforts of colonia

American Friends Service Committee

1501 Cherry Street
Philadelphia, PA 19102
Tel: (215) 241-7132
Fax: (215) 241-7119
E-mail: RHernand@afsc.org
Contact: Ricardo Hernández, director, Mexico-U.S.
    Border Program

AFSC's Mexico-U.S. Border Program addresses the multiple and complex questions of human rights and economic and development policy that emerge along the world's longest border between a developing nation and an advanced industrial nation. The program includes the Maquiladora Project, which focuses on increasing public awareness of and addressing the negative impact of the maquiladora industry on labor rights, health and safety, and community environmental health, as well as the exploitation of women as a cheap and vulnerable labor force. AFSC works in close partnership with the Comité Fronterizo de Obreras (Border Committee of Women Workers).

Comité Fronterizo de Obreras

Ocampo 509B
Centro Piedras Negras, Coahuila
C.P. 26000, México
U.S. mailing address: 2305 El Indio Hwy., Box 115,
Eagle Pass, TX 78852.
Tel/fax: 52 (878) 2-38-45
E-mail: CFO@comuni-k.com
Contact: Julia Quiñonez, coordinator

A grassroots organization of maquiladora workers. The CFO supports worker efforts to learn about their rights under Mexican labor law, identify health concerns, and develop strategies for improving working conditions.

residents in Matamoros and the CJM to pressure Stepan Chemical Company to clean up the site of its chemical plant adjacent to Colonia Privada Uniones. A National Toxics Campaign report indicates discharges from this plant contained xylene at nearly 53,000 times the U.S. standard for receiving waters.

The Market Basket Survey. Compares purchasing power of UAW Assembly Workers in the United States and the purchasing power of maquiladora assembly workers in Mexico using a given set of consumable items. Researched and written by Ruth Rosenbaum.

Report on Sony Workers and the NAO Process. Tells the story of the Sony workers in Nuevo Laredo and their struggle to establish an independent union.

Sustainable Wage Campaign. Chronicles the events along the border on May Day 1995. CJM is advocating that corporations pay a sustainable wage to the maquiladora workers.

Environmental Health Coalition

1717 Kettner Blvd. Suite 100
San Diego, CA 92101
Tel: (619) 235-0281
Fax: (619) 232-3670
Email: ehcoalition@igc.org
Contact: Cesar Luna, Border Environmental Justice
    Campaign

A proactive environmental rights organization. Works in community-based education and advocacy focused on restricting toxic dumping by maquiladoras and other industries in Tijuana/San Diego. EHC seeks to strengthen and expand the toxics movement in this area and to advocate for pollution prevention and protection of air, water, and public health. Member of the Southwest Network for Economic and Environmental Justice *(see)*.

Interfaith Center on Corporate Responsibility (ICCR)

475 Riverside Drive, Room 566
New York, NY 10115
Tel: (212) 870-2295
Fax: (212) 870-2023
Contact: David Schilling

This coalition of diverse religious institutional investors works to promote change in unjust or harmful corporate policies and practices by utilizing the stock holdings of religious organizations to raise issues of corporate responsibility at strategically selected corporate meetings.

Publications

The Corporate Examiner. ICCR newsletter reports "Corporate Action News," tracks shareholder resolutions, analyzes trends in issue briefs, reviews publications and media, and presents the opinions of leaders in the corporate responsibility movement. $35 individual subscription.

The Proxy Resolutions Book 1997. Contains texts of social responsibility shareholder resolutions submitted for 1997 annual shareholder meetings. $30.

A Step Toward Ending Sweatshops: The Report and Recommendations of the White House Apparel Industry Partnership on Sweatshops, by Rev. David Schilling and Dr. Ruth Rosenbaum. (*Corporate Examiner* XXV:9, 9 May 1997). Text and critique of the report and recommendations by a member of the White House panel. $2.

Maquiladora Workers Deserve a Sustainable Living Wage, by Rev. David Schilling. (*Corporate Examiner* XXIII: 10, 1995). Analyzes wages of maquiladora workers in light of the 1995 cost-of-living increases following the 1994 peso devaluation. $2.

Interhemispheric Resource Center (IRC)

PO Box 2178
Silver City, NM 88062
Tel: (505) 388-0208
Fax: (505) 388-0619
Email: irc1@zianet.com
Web site: www.zianet.com/irc1
Contact: Debra Preusch

A nonprofit research and policy institute founded in 1979. Produces books, reports, and periodicals about U.S. foreign relations with Third World countries and citizen efforts to forge alternative directions for international integration. U.S.-Mexico Borderlands project follows and encourages citizen diplomacy and cross-border organizing.

The INCITRA project (Information for Citizen Transboundary Action) is a clearinghouse for information and resources on sustainable development issues. The project has a Mexican counterpart (Información Ciudadana Transfronteriza) that is carried out by the Red Fronteriza de Salud y Ambiente (Border Health and Environment Network), a grassroots organization in Hermosillo, Sonora. INCITRA distributes information through an action kit, an informational database, a database of contacts, and a website (www.zianet.com/irc1/incitra).

Publications

Cross-Border Links Directories. Annotated listings of fair-trade networks, labor, and environmental groups. Published annually. $5.95 each, postpaid.

borderlines. Monthly newsletter providing information and analysis for border and cross-border activists and others. $12 per year (11 issues).

Border Briefing Papers. Occasional in-depth reports on issues relevant to border and cross-border activists. Existing papers titled "NAFTA-Related Border Funding: Separating Hype from Help" (November 1993) and "Switching Tracks: Using NAFTA's Labor Agreement to Move Toward the High Road" (May 1996, copublished with International Labor Rights Fund). $3.00 each, postpaid.

Border Updater, listserv with additional news and analysis. To receive send an e-mail to irc_jorge@zianet.com.

The Challenge of Cross-Border Environmentalism. 1994. 121 pages. $9.95 plus shipping.

Crossing the Line: Immigrants, Economic Integration, and Drug Enforcement on the U.S.-Mexico Border. By Tom Barry, Harry Browne, and Beth Sims. 1994. 146 pages. $9.95 plus shipping.

For Richer, For Poorer: Shaping U.S.-Mexican Integration. By Harry Browne, Beth Sims, and Tom Barry. 1994. 128 pages. $9.95.

Maquiladora Health and Safety Support Network

P.O. Box 124
Berkeley, CA 94701
Tel: (510) 568-8602
e-mail: gbrown@igc.apc.org
website: www.igc.org/mhssn
Contact: Garrett Brown

This network includes professional health workers from Mexico, the United States, and Canada. Through the network, industrial hygienists, occupational physicians and nurses, epidemiologists, health educators, and other public health workers collaborate on maquiladora-related health issues. The network has organized Spanish-language health-and- safety trainings with community-based groups of maquiladora workers in various sites along the border and with physicians in Tijuana, to provide basic information on hazard recognition, toxicology, control of hazards, workers' rights, and action planning. The network has also published a directory of occupational health professionals volunteering their services to border organizations (January 1998).

Publications
Border/Line Health & Safety, quarterly print newsletter. A quarterly electronic newsletter is also available.

Reading and Resource List. Includes technical information, background, and other resources; posted on the MHSSN website.

Southwest Network for Economic and Environmental Justice (SNEEJ)

P.O. Box 7399
Albuquerque, NM 87194
Tel: (505) 242-0416
Fax: (505) 242-5609
Email: sneej@igc.org
Contact: Richard Moore, Coordinator

A Border Justice Campaign is one of SNEEJ's five areas of activism. It seeks to bring together nongovernmental organizations working on community environmental justice and workplace justice in five natural corridors: the Baja-California Pacific corridor, the Sonora-Arizona desert corridor, the Chiuhuahua desert corridor, the Coahuila-Texas corridor, and the Gulf Coast. The Border Justice Campaign works with grassroots organizations of maquiladora workers to expand outreach, networks, and training.

Support Committee for Maquiladora Workers

Craftsmen Hall
3909 Centre Street, Suite 210
San Diego, CA 92103
Tel: (619) 542-0826
Fax: (619) 297-9858
Email: mtong@igc.apc.org
Web: www.pctvi.com/laamn/maquiladora.html
Contact: Mary Tong

San Diego–based volunteer effort of unionists, community activists, and others dedicated to supporting maquiladora workers in the Tijuana/Tecate region of northwestern Mexico. The Support Committee was formed in the belief that working people and communities must form cross-border ties to challenge corporate impunity. It works to facilitate community-based organizations of workers maquiladora- wide while responding to requests for assistance from workers in individual plants. The Support Committee is also an active participant in coalition efforts along the length of the border, throughout the U.S., Canada, and Mexico, and in endeavors to provide ongoing coordination between Mexican maquiladora worker organizing and organization of workers in Central America and Asia.

United Electrical, Radio and Machine Workers of America (UE)

One Gateway Center Suite 1400
420 Ft. Duquesne Blvd.
Pittsburgh, PA 15222-1416
Tel: (412) 471-8919
Fax: (412) 471-8999
Email: ueintl@igc.apc.org
Web: www.igc.apc.org/unitedelect
Contact: Robin Alexander, Director of International Affairs

A union representing industrial and public sector workers founded in 1936. Includes assembly workers, machinists, clerical workers, custodians, truck drivers, and public employees. The UE has had a large impact on U.S.-Mexico labor relations due to its internationalist perspective and its willingness to work closely with independent labor groups in Mexico, particularly the Frente Auténtico del Trabajo (FAT).

Publications

UE News. Monthly newspaper.

Mexico-Based Organizations

Casa de la Mujer/Grupo Factor X

Junípero Serra #14634-1
Fracc. Reynoso, La Mesa
Tijuana, BC 22460
Mexico
U.S. mailing address: PO Box 1490, 710 San Ysidro Blvd.,
San Ysidro, CA 92173.
Tel: 52 (66) 22-42-17
Fax: 52 (66) 22-42-17
E-Mail: factorx@tij.cetys.mx
Contact: Carmen Valadez

A women's organization focused on issues of labor rights, reproductive health, workplace safety, and gender issues. Women associated with Casa de la Mujer/Grupo Factor X create their own agenda: they have asserted their right to work while pregnant in maquiladoras that discriminate against pregnant women and have demanded the creation of an interdisciplinary group to investigate health problems on the border, especially those relating to women's or reproductive health. The group works in conjunction with women's organizations along the western part of the border.

Centro de Estudios y Taller Laboral A.C. (CETLAC)

V. Guerrero 5038-1
Col. 2da. Burócrata
Ciudad Juárez, Chihuahua 32040
Mexico
Tel: 52 (16) 16-20-73
Fax: 52 (16) 16-20-73
E-mail: CETLAC@infolnk.net
Contact: Beatriz Luján

CETLAC is a workers' education center established by the Frente Auténtico del Trabajo (FAT; see separate directory listing) to offer labor education and leadership development for maquiladora workers in Ciudad Juárez. CETLAC opened in 1996 with support from the United Electrical Workers union (UE), as one of the projects established under the Strategic Alliance between FAT and UE to support the development of independent unions in the maquiladora industry.

Centro de Información para Trabajadores y Trabajadoras (CITTAC)

Av. Central #12931 antes #137
Col. Hipódromo No. 2
Tijuana, BC 22420
Mexico
Tel: 52 (66) 81-55-82
Contact: Jaime Cota

This worker service organization provides maquiladora workers with information and other resources such as: representation in labor arbitration hearings, labor rights training, counseling on unionization issues, and strike support.

Frente Auténtico del Trabajo (FAT)

Godard #20
Col. Guadalupe Victoria
Mexico DF 07790
Mexico
Tel: 52 (5) 556-9314, 556-9375, or 556-0642
Fax: 52 (5) 556-9316
Contact: Antonio Villalba, Bertha Luján, or Benedicto
    Martínez, National Coordinators; Matilde Arteaga,
    Women's Program
e-mail: fat@laneta.apc.org

An independent federation of labor unions, worker-owned
cooperatives, farm workers, and community organizations.
The FAT was founded in 1960 and now represents workers
in over half the states of Mexico in manufacturing industries including textiles, garment, shoemaking, rubber, and
auto parts, as well as agriculture and construction. The FAT
works to create independent, democratic unions. In 1992
the FAT joined with United Electrical, Radio and Machine
Workers of America (UE) in the Strategic Organizing Alliance in an effort to organize and improve standards on both
sides of the border.

Servicio, Desarrollo y Paz (SEDEPAC)

Huatusco No. 39
Col. Roma Sur Apd. 27-054
Mexico DF 06760
Tel: 52 (5) 574-0892 or 574-6397
Fax: 52 (5) 584-3895
Contact: Gloria Tello
e-mail: sedepac@laneta.apc.org

This nongovernmental organization has been working with
maquiladora workers in the state of Coahuila since 1989.
SEDEPAC strives to promote and defend worker rights in
the face of the maquiladora industry. Connects workers
with labor, environmental, community, and human rights
organizations. Coordinates regional workshops with
women workers that address their specific social condition
and health issues.

Resources on Trade/Global Economy Issues

Development Alternatives for Women in a New Era (DAWN)

c/o Extramural Department
University of West Indies
Pinelands, St. Michael
Barbados
Tel: 1809 426 9288
E-mail: pegandawn@gn.apc.org
Contact: Peggy Antrobus

Analyzes development processes and strategies through a
framework that foregrounds the lives of Third World
women. DAWN's goal is to understand the economic, social, cultural, and political processes which cause and perpetuate inequalities of gender, class, and race, and to work
toward building alternative visions and strategies. Attempts
to fulfill these objectives through research/analysis, training, advocacy, international relations, and communications
activities.

Publications

Women and Development: An Alternative Analysis. By
Peggy Antrobus in *Development,* 1989:1. pp. 26–56.

*Disarmament, Peace and Solidarity in the Changing World
Order: A Woman's Vision.* By Peggy Antrobus in *Development,* 1991:1. p. 79.

*Women and the Informal Sector: Priorities for Socially
Sustainable Development.* By Peggy Antrobus in *Development,* 192:3. pp. 54–56.

*Environment and Development: Grassroots Women's
Perspectives.* By Rosina Wiltshire. St. Michaels, Barbados:
DAWN, 1992.

Challenging the Given. By DAWN in *Development,* 1995:1.
Oxford, GB: Blackwell.

The Development Group for Alternative Policies (Development GAP)

927 Fifteenth Street NW
4th Floor
Washington, DC 20005
Tel: (202) 898-1566
Fax: (202) 898-1612
Email: dgap@igc.apc.org
Web site: www.igc.org/dgap
Contact: Karen Hanson-Kuhn

A center for analysis, advocacy, and action. The Development GAP publicizes perspectives from peoples and nations of the global South to inform Northern policy makers, particularly around issues of structural adjustment and international trade liberalization.

Publications

Structural Adjustment and the Spreading Crisis in Latin America. Structural adjustment policies imposed by the World Bank and the IMF are causing economic and social unrest throughout Latin America. This document examines the situations in Mexico, Nicaragua, Costa Rica, Bolivia, and El Salvador. June 1997.

In Focus: Free Trade Agreement of the Americas. Volume 1, Number 27, March 1997.

Mexican Government Payback Bad News for Mexicans. Mexico has paid back its short-term debt to the United States by incurring more debt and squeezing the Mexican economy to the point of repression. January 15, 1997.

Alternatives to Structural Adjustment in the Americas Forum. Over the past decade there has been a rising chorus of voices in the Americas challenging the uniform application of structural adjustment programs (SAPs) and demanding that new sets of policies designed to achieve equitable and sustainable development be considered. May 21, 1996.

Mexico's House of Cards. It is impossible to find anyone who believes the claims of the Mexican and U.S. governments that things are getting better here. April 4, 1996.

No Laughter in NAFTA: Mexico and the United States Two Years After. December 1995.

Equipo Pueblo

Apartado 27-467
Mexico, D.F. 06760
Mexico
Phone: 52 (5) 539-0015 or 539-0055
Fax: 52 (5) 672-7453
Email: pueblodip@laneta.apc.org
Contact: Luis Reygadas

Equipo Pueblo (the People's Team) is a nongovernmental development organization dedicated to democratic change in Mexico. It provides a wide array of support services to grassroots organizations, including project formulation and funding-proposal guidance, popular education programs, coalition building across diverse sectors of popular organizations, and international networking between Mexican social organizations and their foreign counterparts.

Publications

The Polarization of Mexican Society: A Grassroots View of World Bank Economic Adjustment Policies. By Carlos Heredia. Mexico, DF, 1995, $7.

NAFTA and Democratization in Mexico. By Carlos Heredia. Mexico, DF, 1995.

The Other Side of Mexico. Bimonthly bulletin.

Institute for Policy Studies (IPS)

733 15th St. NW #1020
Washington, DC 20005
Tel: (202) 234-9382
Fax: (202) 387-7915
Web site: www.igc.org/ips
Contact: John Cavanagh

The mission of IPS is to provide the country's most important social movements—such as those promoting fair trade and sustainable communities—with strong intellectual ammunition. IPS's work is divided among five principal program areas: global economic justice, sustainable communities, economic and social rights, real security, and culture. Within each program area IPS scholars conduct research, stimulate debates, and propose policies that can help related social movements to succeed.

The Global Economic Justice program area analyzes the impact of the world economy on the United States in areas such as immigration flows, jobs, and community. It designs economic policies that aim to protect workers, consumers, communities, and ecosystems. This program offers vital criticism of the growing power of multinational corporations and laissez-faire trade. It develops new strategies for expanding jobs at home and abroad and suggests alternative structures to manage global flows of finance, trade, and money.

Publications
Reports
NAFTA's Corporate Camouflage. By Sarah Anderson, John Cavanagh, and Nicole Clark, April 24, 1997.

Top 200: A Profile of Global Corporate Power. By Sarah Anderson and John Cavanagh, September 25, 1996, 16 pp. Uncovers alarming trends in corporate concentration, corporate dominance of the world's economic activity, and new data on job slashing by the Top 200 firms. $5.

NAFTA's First Two Years: The Myths and the Realities. Edited by Sarah Anderson and John Cavanagh. March 26, 1996, 50 pp. (also available in Spanish). With contributions from twenty citizen groups, this report presents a comprehensive analysis of the impact of NAFTA on workers, communities, and the environment. $7.50.

Consultative Group to Assist the Poorest: Opportunity or Liability for the World's Poorest Women? By Nan Dawkins Scully and Daphne Wysham. September 23, 1996, 31 pp. Examines the World Bank's latest foray into microcredit and questions whether this approach will benefit or harm the world's poorest, two-thirds of whom are women. $3.

Workers Lose, CEOs Win 1995: The widening wage gap between U.S. executives and their U.S. and Mexican workers. By Sarah Anderson and John Cavanagh. April 1995, 10 pp. A year- and-a-half into NAFTA, this report looks at how the U.S. companies with the most employees in Mexico are treating their executives and workers. $5.

Books
Beyond Bretton Woods: Alternatives to the Global Economic Order. John Cavanagh, Daphne Wysham, and Marcos Arruda, eds., 1994, 229 pp. A collection of twenty essays by leading progressive researchers and activists presents alternatives to the World Bank, the International Monetary Fund, and the General Agreement on Tariffs and Trade. $12.95.

Global Dreams: Imperial Corporations and the New World Order. By Richard J. Barnet and John Cavanagh, 1994, 512 pp. An authoritative portrait of how global corporations have evolved into gigantic institutions that replace national power, dominate the fate of the world's economy and people, and control the world's money, assets, goods, and information. $25.

Toward a Global Village: International Communities Development Initiatives. By Michael Shuman, 1994, 189 pp. Documents a growing worldwide movement of communities promoting a progressive vision of North-South, people-centered development cooperation and local initiatives. $18.95.

International Labor Rights Fund (ILRF)
733 15th Street, NW, Suite 920
Washington, DC 20005
Tel: (202) 347-4100
Fax: (202) 347-4885
Email: laborrights@igc.apc.org
Web site: www.laborrights.com
Contact: Pharis Harvey

Nonprofit organization representing human rights, labor, religious, consumer, academic, and business groups dedicated to assuring that all workers labor under reasonable conditions and are free to exercise their right to associate, organize, and bargain collectively. Founded in 1986, ILRF has monitored practices such as child labor, forced labor, attacks on and imprisonment of union leaders, and other violations of international labor standards. ILRF is committed to environmentally sound development that promotes broad-based economic growth and equitable distribution of wealth.

ILRF works to advance U.S. and international trade, investment, and aid policies that promote workers' rights in countries around the world. Rather than simply criticizing trade liberalization, ILRF focuses on linking trade expansion to enhancement of labor standards in order to more broadly distribute the benefits of increased global trade and economic integration.

Publications

Reports

The Failed Experiment: NAFTA at Three Years. June 26, 1997, 34 pp.

NAFTA's First Two Years: The Myths and the Realities. March 1996, 49 pp.

The North American Agreement on Labor Cooperation, a Non Governmental View. 1996, 18 pp.

Chile's Accession to NAFTA. Testimony before USTR, April 1995, 11 pp.

Chilean Labor and NAFTA. Testimony before U.S. House of Representatives, Ways and Means July 1995, 10 pp.

A Missed Opportunity: The World Bank's World Development Report 1995: Workers in an Integrating World. By Jerome I. Levinson, 1995, 18 pp.

Country Labor Practice Reports (submitted under U.S. GSP program.) Mexico, June 1993, 43 pp.

Books

Pinochet's Shadow over NAFTA: Chile's Workers and Free Trade, by Rachel German and Mark Hager. Washington, DC: ILRF, 42 pp.

North American Trade As If Democracy Mattered: What's Wrong with NAFTA and What Are the Alternatives? By Ian Robinson. Ottawa: Canadian Centre for Policy Alternatives and ILRF, 1993.

Global Village vs. Global Pillage: A One-World Strategy for Labor. Revised edition of 1991 classic. By Jeremy Brecher and Tim Costello. Boston: South End Press, 1998.

National Labor Committee

275 Seventh Avenue
New York, NY 10001
Tel: (212) 242-3002
Fax: (212) 242-3821
Contact: Maggie Poe, Network Coordinator

The mission of NLC is to promote greater public awareness of human rights abuses and labor injustices confronted by workers producing goods for the U.S. market and to promote international worker and human rights principles as a means of giving people greater opportunity to improve their living standards. To this end, the NLC organizes public education campaigns and U.S./international support networks and researches the links between internationally recognized labor rights and foreign and trade policies. Work has been focused on Central America and the Caribbean, and is in the process of expanding to Mexico.

Publications

Paying To Lose Our Jobs. A special report prepared by the National Labor Committee Education Fund in Support of Worker and Human Rights in Central America, 1992, 100 pp.

Red Mexicana de Acción Frente al Libre Comercio (RMALC)

Godard 20
Col. Guadalupe Victoria
Mexico, D.F. 07790
Mexico
Tel: 52 (5) 355-1177, 356-4724
Fax: 52 (5) 556-9316
Email: rmalc@laneta.apc.org
Contact: Bertha Luján

This network of organizations made up of labor, women's, peasant, and environmental activists seeks to publish information and stimulate debate regarding the economic integration of North America, its social costs, and suggested responses. RMALC believes in national sovereignty and the social agenda of the common people and works to develop cross-border links with similar social organizations in the United States and Canada.

Publications

Espejismo y Realidad: El TLCAN Tres Años Después. Analisis y Propuestas desde la Sociedad Civil. RMALC, Mexico, April 1997. (Spanish only.)

We Have an Alternative! Mexico, DF: RMALC, March 1995.

Third World Network (TWN)

228 Macalister Road
10400 Penang, Malaysia
Tel: (60) 4-226-6728/ 226-6159
Fax: (60) 4-226-4505
Email: twn@igc.apc.org

An independent nonprofit international network of organizations and individuals involved in issues relating to development, the Third World, and North-South issues. Conducts research on economic, social, and environmental issues pertaining to the South, publishes books and magazines, organizes and participates in seminars, and provides a platform representing broad Southern interests and perspectives at international fora such as the UN conferences and processes.

Publications

Third World Resurgence. Monthly magazine on development, ecology, economics, health, alternatives, and South-North relations.

Third World Economics. A bimonthly economics magazine focusing on the GATT/WTO, the World Bank/IMF, etc.

BIBLIOGRAPHY

Bacon, David. "Laboring to Cross the NAFTA Divide," *The Nation,* Volume 261, November 13, 1995, pp. 572–74.

Barry, Tom and Beth Sims. *The Challenges of Cross-Border Environmentalism.* Silver City, NM: Interhemispheric Resource Center, 1994.

Blecker, Robert A. "NAFTA and the Peso Collapse: Not Just a Coincidence." Briefing paper. Washington, DC: Economic Policy Institute, 1997.

Blumenfield, Rebecca and Dianne Solis. "GM's Mexican Houses on Shaky Ground," *The Wall Street Journal,* June 20, 1997, p. A15.

Brannon, J. T., and G. W. Lucker. "The Impact of Mexico's Economic Crisis on the Demographic Composition of the Maquiladora Labor Force," *Journal of Borderland Studies,* 4(1), 1989: 39–70.

Brecher, Jeremy. "After NAFTA: Global Village or Global Pillage?" *The Nation,* December 6, 1993, pp. 685–688.

Bronfenbrenner, Kate. "We'll Close! Plant Closings, Plant-Closing Threats, Union Organizing and NAFTA," *Multinational Monitor,* March 1997, pp. 8–13.

Buvinic, Mayra. *Women and poverty in Latin America and the Caribbean: a primer for policy makers.* Washington, DC: International Center for Research on Women, 1990. 64 pp.

CEC (Commission for Environmental Cooperation). "New Directions in North American Environmental Reform," *Proceedings of a Dialogue on Environmental Law,* December 4-5, 1996.

Collier, Robert. "Cleanup Along Border Still a Dream," *San Francisco Chronicle,* September 26, 1995.

Compa, Lance and Stephen F. Diamond. *Human Rights, Labor Rights, and International Trade.* Pennsylvania Press, 1996.

Coppinger, Philip F. "Mexico's Maquiladoras: Economic Boon and Social Crisis," *New Solutions,* Spring 1993.

DePalma, Anthony. "For Mexico, NAFTA's Promise of Jobs Is Still Just a Promise," *The New York Times,* October 10, 1995, p. 1A.

DePalma, Anthony. "NAFTA Environmental Lags May Delay Free Trade Expansion," *The New York Times,* May 21, 1997.

Dillon, Sam. "At U.S. Door, Huddled Masses Yearn for Better Pay," *The New York Times,* December 4, 1995.

Eskenazi, Brenda, Sylvia Guendelman, and Eric P. Elkin, "A Preliminary Study of Reproductive Outcomes of Female Maquiladora Workers in Tijuana, México," *American Journal of Industrial Medicine,* Volume 24, Number 6, December 1993, pp. 667–676.

Fernández Kelly, P. "Technology and Employment along the U.S.-Mexican Border." In *The United States and Mexico: Face to Face With New Technology.* Ed. C. L. Thorup et al. Washington, DC: Overseas Development Council, 1989, pp. 149–167.

Fernández Kelly, P. *For We Are Sold, I and My People: Women and Industry in Mexico's Frontier.* Albany: State University of New York Press, 1983.

Fischer, Kurt (ed.). *Environmental Strategies for Industry: International Perspectives on Research Needs and Policy Implications.* Washington, DC: Island Press, 1993.

Global Trade Watch. *NAFTA's Broken Promises: Failure to Create U.S. Jobs,* Public Citizen, Washington, DC, February 1997.

González, Soledad, Olivia Ruiz, Laura Velasco, and Ofelia Woo (eds.). *Mujeres, Migración y Maquila en la Frontera Norte.* Mexico City: El Colegio de la Frontera Norte (COLEF), 1995. (Spanish)

Grinspun, Ricardo and Maxwell Cameron. "Mexico: The Wages of Trade," *NACLA Report on the Americas,* February 1993.

Hall, Kevin G. "Environment Rule Change Draws Fire in Mexico," *The Journal of Commerce,* October 26, 1995.

Hays, Rachel. "Los Dos Laredos Grapple with Environmental Cleanup," *borderlines* 35, Volume 5, Number 5, May 1997.

Heredia, Carlos. "Downward Mobility: Mexican Workers After NAFTA," *NACLA Report on the Americas,* November/December 1996.

Holmes, Stanley. "When jobs go south," *Seattle Post Intelligencer,* November 12, 1995.

Imaz, Jose Maria. "NAFTA Damages Small Businesses," *El Barzón,* Mexico City, January 1997 (in Spanish).

Jasis, M. and Sylvia Guendelman. "Maquiladoras and women on the U.S.- México border: A benefit or a detriment to occupational health?" *Salud Pública de México,* Volume 35, Number 6, November-December 1993, pp. 620–629. (in Spanish)

Johnson, Pierre Marc and Neaulieu Andr. *The Environment and NAFTA: Understanding and Implementing the New Continental Law.* Washington, DC: Island Press, 1996.

Kamel, Rachael. *The Global Factory.* Philadelphia: American Friends Service Committee, 1990.

Kamel, Rachael. " 'This is How It Starts:' Women Maquila Workers in Mexico," *Feminizing Unions: Labor Research Review No. 11,* 1988.

Kopinak, Kathryn. *Desert Capitalism: Maquiladoras in North America's Western Industrial Corridor.* Tucson: University of Arizona Press, 1996.

Kopinak, Kathryn. "Maquiladorization of the Mexican Economy." In *The Political Economy of North American Free Trade.* Ed. R. Grinspun and M. Cameron. New York: St. Martin's Press, 1993, pp. 141–161.

Kopinak, Kathryn. "Household, Gender, and Migration in Mexican Maquiladoras: The Case of Nogales." In *International Migration, Refugee Flows, and Human Rights in North America.* Ed. Alan B. Simmons. New York: Center for Migration Studies, 1996, pp. 214–228.

Knott, Elizabeth B. "Hostages of Greed," *Horizons,* September/October 1992.

La Botz, Dan. *Mask of Democracy. Labor Supression in Mexico Today.* Boston: South End Press/ILRF, 1992.

La Botz, Dan. *Mexican Labor News and Analysis.* Bi-monthly journal. Available at the web site of the United Electrical, Radio and Machine Workers of America (UE): www.igc.apc.org/unitedelect/ or contact Dan La Botz at 103144.2651@compuserve.com for a subscription.

Laurell, Asa Cristina. "The Role of Union Democracy in the Struggle for Workers' Health in Mexico," *International Journal of Health Services,* Volume 19, Number 2, 1989, pp. 279–293.

Levinson, Jerome. *NAFTA's Labor Side Agreement.* Joint report by Institute for Policy Studies and International Labor Rights Fund, November 21, 1996.

McGinn, Chris. "NAFTA Numbers: Three Years of NAFTA Facts," *Multinational Monitor,* January/February 1997, p. 31.

McGinn, Mary and Kim Moody. "Labor Goes Global," *The Progressive,* March 1993, p. 24.

McKinney, Phoebe and Leslie Gates. "Zenith's Maquiladora Factories," *Z Magazine,* July/August 1994.

Moberg, David. "Labor Unites to Fight the Multinationals," *Newsday,* June 6, 1989, p.71.

Montes, Eduardo. "Workers sue to recover damages for birth defects," *The Monitor,* McAllen, TX, October 7, 1991, p. 9A.

Moure-Eraso, Rafael, Meg Wilcox, Laura Punnett, Leslie Copeland, and Charles Levenstein. "Back to the Future: Sweatshop Conditions on the Mexico-US Border. I. Community Health Impact of Maquiladora Industrial Activity." *American Journal of Industrial Medicine,* Volume 25, 1994, pp. 311–324.

Myers, Eric. "Maquiladora: survival on the Mexican border," *Christianity and Crisis,* Volume 52, March 16, 1992, pp. 79–81.

Nathan, Debbie. *Women and Other Aliens: Essays from the U.S.-Mexico Border.* El Paso: Cinco Puntos, 1991.

Orme, William A. Jr. *Understanding NAFTA: Mexico, Free Trade, and the New North America.* Austin, TX: University of Texas Press, 1996.

Perry, Tony. "After 50 Years, New Hope for Detoxifying New River," *The Los Angeles Times,* November 4, 1995.

Ramos Escandón, Carmen. "Mujeres y género en México: A mitad del camino y de la década," *Mexican Studies/ Estudios Mexicanos,* Volume 11, Number 1, Winter 1995, pp. 113–130.

Sariego Rodríguez, J. "Trabajo y Maquiladoras en Chihuahua," *El Cotidiano,* 33:15–25, January-February 1990.

Schidheiny, Stephan. *Changing Course: A Global Business Perspective on Development and the Environment.* Cambridge, MA: MIT Press, 1992.

Scott, David Clark. "US Unions Step Over Rio Grande," *The Christian Science Monitor,* July 1, 1991, p. 6.

Seligson, M. A., and E. J. Williams. *Maquiladoras and Migration. Workers in the Mexico-United States Border Industrialization Program.* Austin, TX: Mexico-United States Research Program, 1981.

Shaiken, H. *Mexico in the Global Economy: High Technology and Work Organization in Export Industries.* Monograph Series No. 33. San Diego: Center for U.S.-Mexican Studies, University of California at San Diego, 1990.

Shields, Janice. "'Social Dumping' in Mexico Under NAFTA," *Multinational Monitor,* Volume 16, Number 4, April 1995.

Sklair, Leslie. "Transnationals Across the Border: Mobilizing US Support for the Mexican Maquila Industry," Great Britain: *Journal of American Studies,* Volume 24, Number 2, 1990, pp. 167–185.

Skolnick, Andrew. "Along the U.S. Southern Border, Pollution, Poverty, Ignorance and Greed Threaten Nation's Health," *JAMA Medical News & Perspectives,* May 17, 1995, p.1478.

Stoddard, E. *Maquila.* El Paso: Texas Western Press, 1987.

Tiano, Susan. *Patriarchy on the Line.* Philadelphia: Temple University Press, 1994.

Tolan, Sandy. "The Border Boom: Hope and Heartbreak," *The New York Times Magazine,* July 1, 1990, p. 16.

Tooher, Nora Lockwood. "Mexico: Where the jobs go," *The Providence Journal Bulletin,* September 27, 1992.

Unterberger, Alayne, and Ken Sturrock, "Health Status of Maquiladora Workers: What They Don't Know CAN Hurt Them," unpublished report, AFSC, Philadelphia, 1998.

Varady, Robert, and Maura Mack. "Transboundary Water Resources and Public Health in the U.S. Mexico Border Region," *Journal of Environmental Health,* Volume 57, Number 8, April 1995, p. 11.

Wallach, Lori. "Impact of NAFTA on the U.S. Economy: NAFTA's Failure at 41 months," Testimony by Public Citizen/Global Trade Watch before the International Trade Commission, May 15, 1997.

Weston, Ann. *The NAFTA papers: Implications for Canada, Mexico and developing countries.* Ottawa: The North-South Institute, 1994. 123 p.

Wise, Cavel (ed.). *The Post-NAFTA Political Economy: Mexico and the Western Hemisphere.* Baltimore: Johns Hopkins University, JAIS School of Advanced International Studies, 1997. Published bimonthly by the Labor Project of the Resource Center of the Americas. 317 Seventeenth Avenue Southeast, Minneapolis, MN 55414, Tel: (612) 627-9445, Fax: (612) 627-9450, rctamn@tc.umn.edu.

Grateful acknowledgement is made for permission to reprint the following previously published material:

Robin Alexander and Peter Gilmore, "The Emergence of Cross-Border Labor Solidarity," *NACLA Report on the Americas,* July/Aug. 1994, Vol. 28:1, pp. 42–48. Copyright © 1994 by the North American Congress on Latin America, 475 Riverside Dr., No. 4, New York, NY 10115.

Sarah Anderson, John Cavanagh, and David Ranney, "NAFTA: Trinational Fiasco." Reprinted with permission from *The Nation* magazine, July 15/22, 1996.

David Bacon, "May Day on the Border" (excerpts). Reprinted with permission from *The Nation* magazine, Nov. 13, 1995.

Arturo Cano, "In the Maquila Kingdom," originally published as "En el reino de maquilotitlan" in *Reforma,* Dec. 1, 1996, "Enfoque," pp. 11–14.

Arturo Cano, "The Cardboard Door," originally published as "La puerta de cartón," in *Reforma,* Dec. 15, 1996, "Enfoque," pp. 11–14.

Carlos Guerra, "Falling peso, falling lifestyle," *San Antonio Express-News,* Mar. 26, 1995. Reprinted with permission *San Antonio Express News.*

Ricardo Hernández, "Taking Flight," originally published in slightly different form as "Con alas propias," *La Jornada,* "Masiosare" No. 32, July 5, 1998.

Human Rights Watch, "No Guarantees: Sex Discrimination in Mexico's Maquiladora Sector," summary and recommendations, Washington, DC, April 1996.

Mary E. Kelly, "Free Trade: The Politics of Toxic Waste," *NACLA Report on the Americas*, Vol. 26, No. 2, Sept. 1992. Copyright © 1992 by the North American Congress on Latin America, 475 Riverside Dr., No. 4, New York, NY 10115.

George Kourous, "Workers' Health Is on the Line: Occupational Health and Safety in the Maquiladoras," *borderlines* 47, Vol. 6, No. 6, Aug. 1998. Reprinted by permission of the Interhemispheric Resource Center, PO Box 2178, Silver City, NM 88062.

"Maquiladora Standards of Conduct," Coalition for Justice in the Maquiladoras, San Antonio, TX.

"NAO Findings on Working Conditions at Han Young Plant," reprinted by permission from *Border/Line,* the newsletter of the Maquila Health and Safety Support Network, Vol. 2, No. 3, Sept. 1998.

Debbie Nathan, "Death Comes to the Maquilas: A Border Story." Reprinted with permission from *The Nation* magazine, Jan. 13/20, 1997.

Debbie Nathan, "Double Standards: Notes for a Border Screenplay" (excerpts), *Texas Observer,* June 6, 1997.

Cyrus Reed, "Hazardous Waste Management on the Border: Problems with Practices and Oversight Continue," *borderlines* 46, Vol. 6, No. 5, July 1998. Reprinted by permission of the Interhemispheric Resource Center, PO Box 2178, Silver City, NM 88062.

"Someone Has to Stop This": Testimony of an Autotrim Worker in Matamoros, Coalition for Justice in the Maquiladoras, San Antonio, TX.

Mary E. Tong, "Reaching Across the Rio," *Beyond Borders,* Spring 1993.

Nora Lockwood Tooher, "For Mexican Women, Sexism Is a Daily Battle," *Providence* (RI) *Journal-Bulletin,* Sept. 29, 1992.

María Guadalupe Torres, "We Are Not Machines," reprinted with permission from *The Other Side* magazine, Jan.-Feb. 1997.

Rick Ufford-Chase, "Glimpsing the Future," reprinted with permission from *The Other Side* magazine, Jan.-Feb. 1997.

"Women on the Border: Needs and Opportunities," *borderlines,* Vol. 5, No. 4, April 1997. Reprinted by permission of the Interhemispheric Resource Center, PO Box 2178, Silver City, NM 88062.

DATE DUE